Focus on Literacy

Effective Content Teachers
for the Middle Grades

Edited by
Jan Lacina
Patricia A. Watson

Association for Childhood Education International
17904 Georgia Ave., Ste. 215, Olney, MD 20832
800-423-3563 • www.acei.org

Views expressed do not necessarily agree with positions taken by the Association for Childhood Education International.

Bruce Herzig, ACEI Editor
Anne Bauer, ACEI Editor
Deborah Jordan Kravitz, Production

Copyright (c) 2008, Association for Childhood Education International
17904 Georgia Ave., Ste. 215, Olney MD 20832

Focus on literacy : effective content teachers for the middle grades / edited by Jan Lacina, Patricia A. Watson.
    p. cm.
  ISBN 978-0-87173-172-2 (pbk.)
 1. Content area reading--United States. 2. Language arts (Middle school)--Correlation with content subjects--United States. 3. First year teachers--Training of--United States. I. Lacina, Jan. II. Watson, Patricia A.

 LB1050.455.F63 2008
 428.0071'2--dc22

                    2007035167

Table of Contents

Preface

I never thought I would use reading strategies, but honestly, being in the classroom and school, comprehension is the number one thing students have got to learn. It doesn't matter what course subject they are in. If they can't comprehend, understand, what they are reading, if they don't understand it, they aren't going to get it. I think reading strategies help them say, "Oh, this is what happened!" It breaks it down so they can understand the process and the chronological order of things happening. (Interview Transcripts, April 2007)

As Brooke's (a pseudonym) comments above indicate, many future content area teachers often question the requirements to enroll in a college content literacy course (Lesley, 2005; Nourie & Lenski, 1998). Unfortunately, not all states in the United States require teacher candidates to complete a content literacy course (Barry, 1994, 2002; Mangieri & Kemper, 1979). In Brooke's case, she was fortunate to be placed in an exemplary 8th-grade social studies teacher's classroom for student teaching. Throughout the semester, Brooke observed her mentor teacher integrate literacy strategies as the 8th-graders completed an in-depth examination of U.S. history. Their class studied the American Revolution, while the teacher found innovative and engaging ways to connect social studies content to content literacy. Brooke modeled the strategies she learned as she began to teach social studies lessons, and then wrote her own lesson plans integrating content literacy strategies to ensure that students comprehended the content texts they read. Unfortunately, not all teacher candidates have the same experiences when student teaching as Brooke did. The purpose of this edited book is to provide examples of exemplary, child-centered content area literacy teaching practices to better prepare teacher candidates and new teachers. Throughout the book, we showcase exemplary content area teachers who are masters of content literacy strategy instruction.

Why is such a book needed? For more than a decade, researchers have documented content area teacher candidates' resistance to learning about literacy strategies while enrolled in content area reading courses (Bean, 1997; Fox, 1993; Hollingsworth & Teal, 1991; Lesley, 2005; Nourie & Lenski, 1998; Wilson, Konopak, & Readence, 1993). We define *content literacy* as the ability to read, write, and communicate

Jan Lacina

effectively within each content area (Brozo & Simpson, 2007; Draper, Smith, Hall, & Siebert, 2005; Sturtevant & Linek, 2004). Resistance to content literacy remains an issue, and finding teachers who have the expertise to integrate literacy within their content area is a challenge (Barry, 2002; Fisher & Ivey, 2005; Zimpherer, Worley, Sission, & Said, 2002). Most teachers have trouble with content literacy, since few have observed content literacy within the classroom. Many teachers report that they do not view literacy to be a high priority for content area teaching, since they view it as the responsibility of the English teachers (Lester, 2000). Despite the U.S. Department of Education making reading instruction a priority, content area teachers have made very few changes in the ways they provide instruction (Fisher & Ivey, 2005; Lesley, 2005; O'Brien, Stewart, & Moje, 1995).

Teacher candidates need to see and experience active literacy engagement strategies when working with adolescent students in the content areas (Fisher & Ivey, 2005; L'Allier & El-ish-Piper, 2007). This book provides myriad examples of ways to integrate content literacy throughout many content areas and middle grade levels.

Book Organization and Features

We began the process of writing this book by seeking the help of exemplary content area literacy teachers from throughout the United States to demonstrate the various ways teachers blend literacy with their content area subject matter. We purposefully recruited teachers from 4th through 8th grades to support the many ways that teachers connect reading, writing, and speaking with content learning. ACEI's position paper on child-centered middle schools defines middle school students, or young adolescents, as students ranging in age from 10 to 15 years old (Manning, 2000). Across the United States, these students are schooled in both elementary and middle schools, and the type of campus—elementary or middle school—tends to vary depending on the school district. For example, some of the schools featured in the book house 6th-graders on the middle school campus, whereas others include 6th-graders on an elementary campus. For that reason, we sought a variety of settings, both middle schools and elementary schools, to describe the practices of content area teachers and the young adolescent students they teach.

The book's introductory chapter explains the importance of content area literacy and characteristics of effective middle grade teachers. Chapter 1 also describes how ACEI and the National Middle School Association define effective middle level teachers, while connecting research to the practices of a middle school principal and middle school association leader. The characteristics of effective middle grade teachers in this chapter present a framework for the remaining chapters, and the teachers described in the chapters that follow also skillfully model and demonstrate effective strategies to use in content area disciplines.

The remaining chapters are organized based on discipline, type of classroom, strategies for all classrooms, and professional development resources. Part II, which includes Chapters 2-3, examines the content area methods implemented in self-contained middle grade classrooms. Chapter 2 describes the ways in which a 4th-grade teacher integrates the arts into her curriculum, finding unique ways to teach students about Australia while connecting drama, visual arts, and the content areas. Chapter 3 highlights the strategies used by a 5th-grade teacher to implement a reading and writing workshop in order to scaffold content area learning. The chapter author brings the 5th-grade class to life by including vivid descriptions of classroom instruction and conversations with the students as they reflect on the reading and writing workshop.

Part III, covering Chapters 4-7, looks at specific content disciplines that integrate content literacy into instruction. Chapter 4 notes ways that a middle school social studies teacher uses an inquiry curriculum to enable students to utilize literacy strategies as they learn social studies content. The chapter thoroughly describes a unit on discrimination undertaken during Black History Month. The students became avid participants and consumers of literacy strategies as the teacher encouraged them to think more deeply about complex issues of discrimination. Chapter 5 investigates methods for content literacy integration within math instruction at the middle school level. The teacher featured in this chapter incorporates a variety of literacy strategies into math instruction to assist students in better understanding math concepts, solve word problems, and compute basic number equations. The chapter is supported with a strong research base, while showing practical examples of content literacy teaching in math. Chapter 6 describes learning cycles and arts integration in a 5th-grade science classroom. The chapter explains a long-term NASA unit, in which teams of science teachers work together to integrate the science classroom with content literacy. Chapter 7 describes the ways in which a physical education teacher integrates movement, language instruction, and literacy.

Part IV includes Chapters 8-9, which describe literacies for all content areas. Chapter 8 details the ways in which an English teacher uses the sheltered instruction observation protocol (SIOP) model to teach ESL students who are enrolled in a mainstream English class. The author provides practical ideas for using SIOP in any content area. Chapter 9 illustrates ways to use media literacy to encourage critical thinking across all content areas. The author brings classroom media literacy to life for readers, providing detailed classroom examples.

Finally, the chapters in Part V address professional development in content literacy. Chapter 10 portrays a literature study group among 6th- and 7th-grade content teachers. The teachers in the study group discuss *Do I Really Have To Teach Reading?*, by Cris Tovani; as the teachers participated in this study group, they made commitments to apply their learning to classroom instruction. Chapter 11 includes various research-based content literacy techniques that teachers in this book use while presenting step-by-step instructions on how to use the teaching techniques.

Acknowledgments

Last but not least, with heartfelt thanks, we want to thank our reviewers and the teachers who worked with us on this project. To our ACEI reviewers—thank you for the thoughtful and useful suggestions you gave us. Also, thank you, Anne Bauer at ACEI Headquarters, for the encouragement and support you gave throughout the review process. Thank you to our graduate assistants, who continuously helped us with research: Susan Horton, Texas Christian University, and Chiu-yin Wong, Texas Tech University. Finally, we want to recognize the numerous teachers from Kansas, Missouri, Ohio, Pennsylvania, West Virginia, and Texas who made this book possible. Thank you for the time you allowed us to observe you teach, and for the many hours of answering our questions. Most importantly, thank you for the tremendous job you do to integrate literacy within your specific content area.

References

Barry, A. L. (1994). The staffing of high school remedial reading programs in the United States since 1920. *Journal of Reading, 38*, 14-22.

Barry, A. L. (2002). Reading strategies teachers say they use. *Journal of Adolescent & Adult Literacy, 46* (2), 132-141.

Bean, T. W. (1997). Preservice teachers' selection and use of content area literacy strategies. *The Journal of Educational Research, 90*(3), 154-163.

Brozo, W. G., & Simpson, M. L. (2007). *Content literacy for today's adolescents: Honoring diversity and building competence* (5th ed.). Upper Saddle River, NJ: Merrill Prentice Hall.

Draper, R. J., Smith, L. K., Hall, K. M., & Siebert, D. (2005). What's more important—literacy or content? Confronting the literacy-content dualism. *Action in Teacher Education, 27*(2), 12-21.

Fisher, D., & Ivey, G. (2005). Literacy and language as learning in content-area classes: A departure from "Every teacher a teacher of reading." *Action in Teacher Education, 27*(2), 3-11.

Fox, D. L. (1993). The influence of context, community, and culture: Contrasting cases of teacher knowledge development. In D. J. Leu & C. K. Kinzer (Eds.), *Examining central issues in literacy research, theory, and practice* (pp. 345-366). Forty-second Yearbook of the National Reading Conference. Chicago: National Reading Conference.

Hollingsworth, S., & Teal, K. (1991). Learning to teach reading in secondary math and science. *Journal of Reading, 35*, 190-194.

L'Allier, S. K., & Elish-Piper, L. (2007). "Walking the walk" with teacher education candidates: Strategies for promoting active engagement with assigned readings. *Journal of Adolescent & Adult Literacy, 50*(5), 338-353.

Lesley, M. (2005). Looking for critical literacy with postbaccalaureate content area literacy students. *Journal of Adolescent and Adult Literacy, 48*(4), 320-334.

Lester, J. H. (2000). Secondary instruction: Does literacy fit in? *The High School Journal, 83*, 10-16.

Mangieri, J. N., & Kemper, R. E. (1979). Reading: Another challenge for teacher education. *Journal of Teacher Education, 30*(6), 11-12.

Manning, M. L. (2000). Child-centered middle schools: A position paper. *Childhood Education, 76*(3), 154-159.

Nourie, B., & Lenski, S. (1998). The (in) effectiveness of content literacy instruction for secondary preservice teachers. *The Clearing House, 71*, 372-374.

O'Brien, D. G., Stewart, R. A. , & Moje, E. B. (1990). Why content literacy is difficult to infuse into the secndary school: Complexities of curriculum, pedagogy, and school culture. *Reading Research Quarterly, 30*, 442-463.

Sturtevant, E., & Linek, W. M. (2004). *Content literacy: An inquiry-based case approach.* Upper Saddle River, NJ: Pearson.

Wilson, E. K., Konopak, B. C., & Readence, J. E. (1993). A case study of preservice secondary social studies teachers' beliefs and practices about content area reading. In D. J. Leu & C. K. Kinzer (Eds.), *Examining central issues in literacy research, theory, and practice* (pp. 335-343). Forty-second Yearbook of the National Reading Conference. Chicago: National Reading Conference.

Zimpherer, F., Worley, M., Sission, M., & Said, R. (2002). Literacy education and reading programs in the secondary school: Status, problems, and solutions. *NASSP Bulletin, 86*, 3-17.

Meet the Author

Jan Lacina has focused her research and teaching on English language learners (ELLs) and on reading and writing instruction. She teaches undergraduate and graduate literacy courses in both the middle/secondary and early childhood programs at Texas Christian University. She is co-author of the book Helping English Language Learners Succeed in Pre-K-Elementary Schools *(TESOL, 2006), and she has published in numerous journals. Jan also writes the "Technology in the Classroom" column that is published in the journal* Childhood Education. *Prior to teaching at the college level, Jan taught ESL in Texas and Kansas.*

Part I

Introduction

Chapter 1

Teaching and Learning Through Content Area Literacy:

Characteristics of Effective Instruction and Successful Teachers

Our knowledge-based society and information-driven economy increasingly demand a more highly literate population. In the 21st century United States, it is not enough to be able to read and write—the literacy demands of the global marketplace have grown more complicated. The U.S. economy depends upon developing new generations of workers who are competent and confident practitioners of complex and varied forms of literacy. (NCTE Principles of Adolescent Literacy Reform, April 2006)

In order to function effectively in today's information-rich global community, students must exit our schools with the ability to access information across all content areas; to use sophisticated comprehension and critical reasoning abilities; and to be able to read, write, listen, speak, and think effectively. For a number of years, much emphasis has been given to ensuring that our youngest students acquire foundational literacy skills during the first three years of school. While ensuring that 3rd-graders are reading effectively is a worthwhile and demanding goal, the needs of older readers have been largely ignored until recently. Finally, educators and policymakers have begun to focus their attention on ensuring that adolescents receive the continuing instruction in reading and other literacy skills demanded by higher education, employment in today's complex world, and the responsibilities that come with living in a democracy.

Literacy acquisition is a developmental process continuing well into the middle school years and beyond. According to the National Middle School Association (NMSA), schools serving young adolescents should provide continuous reading instruction throughout the middle grades, and all middle school teachers should know how to help students develop the competence to read complex materials across the curriculum (NMSA, 2001). Middle school students bring many literacy-related abilities with them as they move into the middle grades, but they also face many challenges as they confront the literacy demands and disciplinary concepts of the content fields. Middle school students need teachers who can guide them through the literacies of the academic disciplines (National Council of Teachers of English [NCTE], 2006).

Content area literacy has been defined as "the ability to use reading and writing for the acquisition of new content in a given discipline" (McKenna & Robinson, 1990). Research repeatedly demonstrates that using instructional strategies incorporating reading and writing are effective in acquiring content knowledge

Patricia A. Watson

11

and understanding (Alvermann & Moore, 1991; Alvermann & Swafford, 1989). However, research also points to content teachers' reluctance to incorporate these instructional strategies into their daily classroom routines (Irvin & Connors, 1989; Lesley, 2005; O'Brien, Stewart, & Moje, 1995). Most teachers are introduced to content area literacy strategies through either preservice or inservice education courses or professional development workshops. Even though these instructional methods are widely disseminated, school districts are spending large amounts of money each year on staff development, and the federal government is promoting wider implementation of these methods through such initiatives as the Striving Readers grants, preservice and inservice teachers remain skeptical about implementing these methods in content area instruction (Moje, 2006). In fact, many teachers end up planning instruction so that the reading and writing done by students is minimal and instruction in these skills is almost non-existent (Allen, 2000; Cziko, 1998). By eliminating the need for reading and writing, teachers can deny the need for content area literacy instruction.

When questioned about this resistance to emphasizing literacy in content classes, teachers respond with a number of reasons (McKenna & Robinson, 2002; Stewart & O'Brien, 1989). Teachers sometimes feel they are not capable of delivering the kind of literacy instruction that struggling readers need. Resistance is also sometimes seated in the belief that incorporating literacy-based instruction takes up valuable time that should be devoted to teaching the content of the discipline (McKenna & Robinson, 2002). Teachers are especially concerned about time, given the current mandates for content knowledge and the pressures of high-stakes accountability systems, whereby teachers and students alike are judged by their performance on tests based on content-related standards. These teachers often support what has been called a "pedagogy of telling," through which teachers can maximize content "coverage" in the shortest amount of time (Moje, 2006; O'Brien, Stewart, & Moje, 1995).

Perhaps the most convincing reason teachers give for resisting literacy instruction in content classes is that the "strategies do not match the realities of classroom contexts" (O'Brien et al., 1995, p. 450). Preservice and inservice teachers alike often perceive content area instruction to be at odds with the curriculum, the accepted pedagogical approaches, and the culture of their particular institutions (O'Brien, Stewart, & Moje, 1995). While most teachers are introduced to the goals, tenets, and strategies of content area literacy instruction through coursework and professional development opportunities, few have had the opportunity to observe, firsthand, expert teachers skillfully combining the learning of literacy processes with the teaching of discipline-specific content. It is our hope that this volume can provide a bridge between the methods of teaching content area literacy and the realities of classroom practice. This chapter presents the characteristics of these effective middle level teachers. Then, each succeeding chapter provides a rich narrative view of one teacher's classroom, while supporting the vignettes with theoretical perspectives. These characteristics of effective instruction and expert teaching should be kept in mind while reading the narratives presented in the chapters that follow.

Characteristics of Effective Middle Level Teachers

Although teaching with an emphasis on literacy while delivering instruction in a content discipline requires a complex set of instructional strategies, teaching the young adolescents who inhabit middle level classrooms also places complex demands on teachers. Teachers of young adolescents ages 10 to 15 must understand the developmental characteristics unique to this age group. For instruction to be developmentally appropriate and effective, teachers must recognize and understand the physical, psychosocial, and cognitive developmental characteristics of the young adolescent (Manning, 2002). Effective teachers of young adolescents must consider the physical changes and diversity in development observed in middle level classrooms. They also must consider the importance of social interactions with peers and the preoccupation with self that is characteristic of middle school students. Planning effective instruction also requires consideration of cognitive differences. While some young adolescents are engaging in abstract thought by 4th grade, others do not begin to reason abstractly until much later (Manning & Bucher, 2005).

Effective middle school teachers who are aware of these developmental characteristics will address student needs by planning instruction that engages students in active participation. Students in these classrooms will learn through collaborative and social opportunities. Knowledge of adolescent development will lead teachers to design experiences that boost self-esteem and build trust. Effective teachers will adapt instruction to consider students' varied learning styles and intelligences (Manning, 2002).

According to the National Middle School Association (NMSA, 2006), effective middle level teachers understand the interdependence of content and learning. Effective content area teachers realize that content can be learned through literacy-related processes, such as reading, writing, speaking, and listening. According to the NMSA, effective teachers address students' learning needs through the use of a variety of teaching and assessment strategies. These teachers realize that no one instructional method will meet the needs of all students. Effective teachers also develop close relationships with students. Students are partners in the learning process, and so opportunities for student voice and choice facilitate the acquisition of new knowledge (NMSA, 2006).

These characteristics of an effective middle school teacher were echoed by Chris Huber, a middle school principal in Lubbock, Texas. Chris also serves as Vice President of the Texas Middle School Association and exhibits a passion for effective middle level instruction. In discussing the hiring of effective teachers, Chris described his ideal teacher as having vision, passion, and confidence. He also emphasized that the effective teacher must develop positive and supportive relationships with students and possess an "instructional toolbox that is full" (personal communication, 2006).

Vision, Passion, and Confidence. In his view of an effective middle level teacher, Chris emphasized high expectations. Quoting the motto of Southwest Airlines, he said that administrators need to "hire for attitude, then train for skills" through effective, ongoing professional development. Chris believes that "a teacher must be convinced that she or he is the determinant of success for the students in the classroom. That attitude, that passion, is what hooks students to the idea that they can be successful." In addition to a passion for success, Chris also asserted that effective teachers must have a passion for their content and a vision of success for all learners. A teacher who has this vision will set high expectations for students, and these expectations will lead teachers to seek the instructional skills and practices necessary to meet the needs of these learners. "Frankly," stated Chris, "passion for content and kids is the key to achieving high expectations."

This We Believe: Successful Schools for Young Adolescents (NMSA, 2003), the landmark position paper of the National Middle School Association, emphasizes this same point. According to NMSA, educators and students should hold themselves and each other to high expectations. This vision and confidence can motivate students to tackle challenging learning activities.

Respectful, Positive Relationships. "R-E-S-P-E-C-T. Find out what it means to me." This refrain from the Aretha Franklin R&B standard could be the motto for middle school student/teacher relationships. Chris Huber would agree. "In addition to the vision and passion," Chris stated, "effective middle level teachers must be willing to develop positive relationships with their students."

The position statement on adolescent literacy drafted by the International Reading Association echoes Chris' words: "Adolescents deserve teachers who understand the complexities of individual adolescent readers, respect their differences, and respond to their characteristics" (Moore, Bean, Birdyshaw, & Rycik, 1999, p. 8). Powell (2005) described the effective teacher as having achieved a balance between sensibility and sensitivity. Such teachers can facilitate cognitive growth and learning while also meeting the developmental needs of young adolescents for close relationships within a learning community. Manning (2000) described child-centered middle schools as those where teachers provide adolescents with "educational experiences that demonstrate caring, concern, and nurturing" (p. 159). Chris Huber discussed these nurturing interactions by saying, "These relationships are vital. If middle level students do not feel safe and emotionally comfortable in the learning environment, then their learning is severely limited."

An Instructional Toolbox That Is Full. While passionate attitudes and caring relationships are crucial to the creation of middle level learning environments, Chris emphasized that skilled teaching is also an essential factor. "A knowledge of diverse instructional practices, or a toolbox that is full, is a characteristic of the truly effective teacher. Classroom organizational strategies are important as well. These practices are what enable the teacher to bring students to the level of those high expectations." Studies of effective instruction agree that the key to achievement in literacy is instruction from a knowledgeable teacher (Braunger & Lewis, 2006). Topping and McManus (2002) suggest answering three questions that can guide teachers in the selection of instructional "tools" that will focus teaching on education for life.

- Are we guiding our students to know how to read, listen to, and view information that is presented to them?
- Are we guiding our students to write and speak appropriately for the tasks at hand?
- Are we guiding our students to learn for a lifetime? (p. 18)

Through the use of these critical questions, teachers can select appropriate "tools," based on student need, not on the current trend of the day.

Characteristics of Effective Content-Area Instruction

Through the narratives found in this volume, you will visit the classrooms of effective middle level teachers. Four elements of effective instruction can be identified through the descriptions of their teaching. In these classrooms, students are engaged in reading and writing not just for the purpose of producing products, but as a means for acquiring content knowledge in many disciplines. Each of these classrooms is a unique environment where social interactions and access to a rich array of resources extend learning beyond the traditional course text. And in each of these classrooms, expert teachers model and demonstrate the strategies learners need for engaging in the work and acquiring the knowledge of specific disciplines.

Reading and Writing To Learn. For many years, the phrase "every teacher a teacher of read-ing" has been applied to the teaching of literacy (specifically, reading) in the content areas (Gray, 1925). However, this phrase has often been misunderstood and just doesn't work for many content area teachers. A better model for the use of literacy in content classes might be that every teacher should be an enabler, one who enables students to think and learn through text. Vacca (2002) proposed that literacy should be both visible and invisible in all content class. Teachers should explicitly teach students how to read the texts of their disciplines (NCTE, 2004). At the same time, literacy instruction should be invisible, as teachers seamlessly combine subject matter learning with reading and writing. In this way, literacy becomes a scaffold for students' learning.

Fisher and Ivey (2005) asserted that today's students can, and must, use reading, writing, speak-ing, listening, and viewing as part of the meaning-making process in their content area classes. In their words, teachers should "capitalize" on the use of reading and writing, rather than try to attempt to teach reading and writing in content classes. Literacy should be used as a way to engage students in the content through such activities as writing-to-learn prompts, the Cornell method of note-taking, reading aloud, reciprocal teaching, and exit slips. Through these activities, teachers can help students learn to read and write from the perspective of the discipline. Students might approach reading from the stance of a historian, identifying bias and examining how historical events are linked to the present. Or students might be engaged in writing as a scientist would as they complete data records and lab reports. Langer (2000), in her study of middle and high schools that were "beating the odds" for achievement, found that teachers in successful schools make these kinds of connections across subject matter, connecting lessons across content areas and throughout the year. Moje (2006) stated that content area literacy should move away from a focus on accessing texts to an emphasis on understanding how these texts are written in particular ways and how they represent different ways of knowing and doing in the different disciplines.

Effective instruction in content area classes makes use of reading and writing as often as pos-sible. The use of literacy processes in content disciplines can lead to improved understanding and retention of content area knowledge. Through literacy strategies and instruction, students can come to know that knowledge is something that is created, not just passively received (Buehl, 2001).

Opportunities for Learning As a Social Experience. Knowledge of the disciplines related to academic content areas is constructed through human interaction (Moje, 2006). The most com-mon way that humans communicate with each other is by telling stories or narratives about their experiences. Through the telling of stories, people make connections to prior knowledge that support the acquisition of new knowledge. It is through the telling of stories that we "bridge the gaps between what we know and what we might learn" (Johnson & Freedman, 2005). People are social beings, and these stories are a basic function of human communication. This social inter-action is a necessary element of effective content area classrooms. Allington (2002), in reporting research that characterized effective reading instruction in elementary classrooms, asserted that the classroom talk observed in these classrooms was "purposeful talk, not simply chatter. It was problem-posing, problem-solving talk related to curriculuar topics" (p. 744). Similarly, Langer (2000) found that effective middle and high school classrooms "foster cognitive collaboration" (p. 14). She found that in higher performing schools, students participate in the kinds of social interactions engaged in by teams in the business world. Students in these classrooms worked in groups, and teachers facilitated the use of thoughtful dialogue to deepen the students' understanding of content. Students in these successful classrooms brought their personal and cultural background knowledge—their stories—to these discussions. She found that these students were given opportunities to question and challenge each other, as well as opportunities to share their ideas and responses to texts. Students in lower performing classrooms tended to focus more on individual work and thinking. Applebee, Langer, Nystrand, and Gamoran (2003) also found that discussion played an important role in content area achievement. They found that increased achievement through discussion-based approaches occurred across a range of settings and among students with very different abilities and backgrounds, even in lower track classes.

Reading and writing are acts of communication. In order to make meaning through text, students must have opportunities to work together and collaborate through talk. Focused discussions about academic texts can help students acquire literacy-related skills as they learn more about a specific field (NCTE, 2004, 2006).

Modeling of Strategies for Learning New Words and Comprehending Complex Texts. Effective readers use a range of strategies to make meaning from text. Being an effective reader does not mean that the reader never struggles to comprehend, but rather that the reader has internalized ways of approaching difficulties and working through complex text. In effective content classrooms, teachers model reading, writing, and thinking strategies that allow students to access subject matter knowledge through text. In these classrooms, students not only learn the content, but also learn how to approach the work of that discipline.

In many ways, instruction in effective content area classrooms resembles coaching. Coaches know that verbal explanations (the pedagogy of telling) are not sufficient. They model the skills and strategies necessary for success, acting as knowledgeable experts, with students as their apprentices (Schoenbach, Greenleaf, Cziko, & Hurwitz, 1999). Current research shows that student learning is affected by teachers who explicitly model and guide students in the use of strategies for coping with complex materials (Allington & Johnston, 2002; Langer, 2002). These teachers are aware of their own reading habits and behaviors and can make the use of these strategies visible to students. After thorough modeling and thinking-aloud, they then gradually release responsibility for the use of the strategies to the students, supplying prompts to scaffold thinking as needed. Teaching students the strategies for monitoring their own literacy practices and for drawing on their own prior knowledge has been found to increase student motivation towards literacy and help them to think deeply about content (NCTE, 2006).

Reading and writing are different tasks in different disciplines. Reading a scientific report is not the same as reading historical documents or novels. While similar literacy skills are needed across disciplines, significant variability also exists. Therefore, it is important for teachers in all content areas to teach students how to navigate the complexities of texts commonly found in their specific discipline.

Access to a Wide Variety of Print and Non-print Resources. Historically, content area reading instruction has focused on textbook reading and providing students with strategies for accessing difficult content area texts (Fisher & Ivey, 2005; Moje, 2006). However, many teachers (and students) find content area texts difficult and boring. This leads teachers to view textbooks as obstacles to learning in their classrooms, rather than as rich resources. They tend to avoid assigning textbook reading, rather than endure the often painful process of requiring students to read (Fisher & Ivey, 2005). In fact, findings from the 1996 National Assessment of Educational

Progress (NAEP) indicate that a significant proportion of adolescents report reading five or fewer pages of school-related material each day, including both classwork and homework (Moore, Bean, Birdyshaw, & Rycik, 1999).

Expert content area teachers realize that students will not be motivated to read or learn much from materials that are too hard for them (Allington, 2002). Even the best instructional strategies will not help students access texts that are too difficult. Effective content area classrooms are rich with multi-level instructional resources that go beyond the traditional textbook (NCTE, 2006; NMSA, 2001). Trade books, primary source materials, videos, Web-based resources, journals, magazines, and even student-generated materials all serve to link concepts and expand the curriculum (Wade & Moje, 2000). When students are seeking content knowledge, the text needs to be easy enough to allow the reader to focus on the information. Effective teachers do not rely on a one-size-fits-all textbook. In effective classrooms, lower achieving students often benefited most from the wide range of texts available. But higher achieving students benefited as well from having access to texts they could read and comprehend easily. In these classrooms, motivation to read was influenced by student success with readable texts found in the multi-source, multi-level classroom collections (Allington, 2002).

Learning From the Stories of Middle Level Teachers

We have found that many teacher education textbooks document content area reading strategies and methods of instruction, while few include detailed descriptions of content area teachers who include literacy strategies in their daily instruction. In this text, we seek to document and describe effective middle school teachers and how they incorporate literacy learning strategies in their content areas. In the pages that follow, you will enter the classrooms of teachers who have vision, passion, and confidence. You will read descriptions of classrooms where reading and writing are embedded seamlessly into the fabric of classroom routines. The teachers in these chapters use a wide range of resources, skillfully model and demonstrate the strategies used by efficient readers, and engage students in thoughtful discussions as they learn the content of disciplines. We invite you to turn the pages, enter the classrooms, and learn from these teachers.

References

Allen, R. (2000). *Before it's too late: Giving reading a last chance.* Alexandria, VA: Association for Supervision and Curriculum Development.

Allington, R. L. (2002). What I've learned about effective reading instruction from a decade of studying exemplary elementary classroom teachers. *Phi Delta Kappan, 83*(10), 740-747.

Allington, R. L., & Johnston, P. H. (2002). *Reading to learn: Lessons from exemplary fourth-grade classrooms.* New York: Guilford.

Alvermann, D. E., & Moore, D. W. (1991). Secondary school reading. In R. Barr, M. L. Kamil, P. B. Mosenthal, & P. D. Pearson (Eds.), *Handbook of reading research* (Vol. 2, pp. 951-983). White Plains, NY: Longman.

Alvermann, D. E., & Swafford, J. (1989). Do content area strategies have a research base? *Journal of Reading, 32,* 388-394.

Applebee, A. N., Langer, J. A., Nystrand, M., & Gamoran, A. (2003). Discussion-based approaches to developing understanding: Classroom instruction and student performance in middle and high school English. *American Educational Research Journal, 40*(3), 685-730.

Braunger, J., & Lewis, J. P. (2006). *Building a knowledge base in reading* (2nd ed.). Newark, DE: International Reading Association.

Buehl, D. (2001). *Classroom strategies for interactive learning* (2nd ed.). Newark, DE: International Reading Association.

Cziko, C. (1998). *Reading happens in your mind, not in your mouth: Teaching & learning academic literacy urban high school.* Retrieved March 24, 2006, from www.wested.org/cs/sli/view/lib/2378?x-t=sli.html.view

Fisher, D., & Ivey, G. (2005). Literacy and language as learning in content-area classes: A departure from "every teacher a teacher of reading." *Action in Teacher Education, 27*(2), 3-11.

Gray, W. S. (1925). *Summary of investigations related to reading* (Supplementary Educational Monographs, No. 28). Chicago: University of Chicago Press.

Irvin, J. L., & Connors, N. A. (1989). Reading instruction in middle level schools: Results of a U.S. survey. *Journal of Reading, 32*, 306-311.

Johnson, H., & Freedman, L. (2005). *Content area literature circles: Using discussion for learning across the curriculum.* Norwood, MA: Christopher-Gordon.

Langer, J. A. (2000). *Guidelines for teaching middle and high school students to read and write well: Six features of effective instruction.* Albany, NY: Center on English Learning and Achievement. Retrieved March 23, 2006, from http://cela.albany.edu/publication/brochure/guidelines.pdf

Langer, J. A. (2002). *Effective literacy instruction: Building successful reading and writing programs.* Urbana, IL: National Council of Teachers of English.

Lesley, M. (2005). Looking for critical literacy with postbaccalaureate content area literacy students. *Journal of Adolescent and Adult Literacy, 48*(4), 320-334.

Manning, M. L. (2000). Child-centered middle schools: A position paper. *Childhood Education, 76*, 154-159.

Manning, M. L. (2002). Revisiting developmentally appropriate middle level schools. *Childhood Education, 78*, 225-227.

Manning, M. L., & Bucher, K. T. (2005). *Teaching in the middle school.* Upper Saddle River, NJ: Merrill/Prentice Hall.

McKenna, M. C., & Robinson, R. D. (1990). Content literacy: A definition and implications. *Journal of Reading, 34*, 184-186.

McKenna, M. C., & Robinson, R. D. (2002). *Teaching through text: Reading and writing in the content areas* (3rd ed.). Boston: Allyn and Bacon.

Moje, E. B. (2006, March). *Integrating literacy into the secondary school content areas: An enduring problem in enduring institutions.* Paper presented at the University of Michigan School of Education Adolescent Literacy Symposium, Ann Arbor, MI. Retrieved June 1, 2006, from www.soe.umich.edu/events/als/downloads/mojep.html

Moore, D. W., Bean, T. W., Birdyshaw, D., & Rycik, J. A. (1999). *Adolescent literacy: A position statement.* Newark, DE: International Reading Association.

National Council of Teachers of English. (2004). *A call to action: What we know about adolescent literacy and ways to support teachers in meeting students' needs.* Urbana, IL: Author. Retrieved March 14, 2007, from www.ncte.org/about/over/positions/category/literacy/118622.htm

National Council of Teachers of English. (2006). *NCTE principles of adolescent literacy reform: A policy research brief.* Urbana, IL: Author. Retrieved March 14, 2007, from www.ncte.org/library/files/About_NCTE/Overview/Adol-Lit-Brief.pdf

National Middle School Association. (2001). *Supporting young adolescents' literacy learning: A position paper jointly adopted by the International Reading Association and the National Middle School Association.* Westerville, OH: Author. Retrieved March 14, 2007, from www.reading.org/downloads/positions/ps1052_supporting.pdf

National Middle School Association. (2003). *This we believe: Successful schools for young adolescents.* Westerville, OH: Author.

National Middle School Association. (2006). *Middle grades education: Fundamentals and research.* Westerville, OH: Author. Retrieved March 31, 2007, from www.nmsa.org/Advocacy/AdvocacyToolstoUse/MiddleGradesEducation/tabid/1300/Default.aspx

O'Brien, D. G., Stewart, R. A., & Moje, E. B. (1995). Why content area literacy is difficult to infuse into the secondary school: Complexities of curriculum, pedagogy, and school culture. *Reading Research Quarterly, 3*, 442-463.

Powell, S. D. (2005). *Introduction to middle school.* Upper Saddle River, NJ: Pearson.

Schoenbach, R., Greenleaf, C., Cziko, C., & Hurwitz, L. (1999). *Reading for understanding:*

A guide to improving reading in middle and high school classrooms. San Francisco: Jossey-Bass.

Stewart, R. A., & O'Brien, D. G. (1989). Resistance to content area reading: A focus on preservice teachers. *Journal of Reading, 32,* 396-401.

Topping, D., & McManus, R. (2002). *Real reading, real writing.* Portsmouth, NH: Heinemann.

Vacca, R. (2002). Making a difference in adolescents' school lives: Visible and invisible aspects of content area reading. In A. Fartstrup & J. Samuels, J. (Eds.), *What research has to say about reading instruction* (3rd ed.). Newark, DE: International Reading Association.

Wade, S. E., & Moje, E. B. (2000). The role of text in classroom learning. In M. L. Kamil, P. B. Mosenthal, P. D. Pearson, & R. Barr (Eds.), *Handbook of reading research* (Vol. 3, pp. 609-627). Mahwah, NJ: Erlbaum.

Meet the Author

Patricia Watson is an Assistant Professor of Language and Literacy at Texas Tech University. Before completing her doctoral studies at the University of Missouri, Pat taught reading and language arts in middle grade classrooms for 18 years. She enjoys collaborating with practicing and preservice teachers in university/public school partnerships. Her most recent work explores teachers' knowledge, attitudes, and beliefs towards literacy in the content areas.

Part II

Content Literacy in a Self-contained Middle Grades Classroom

Chapter 2

Studying the Arts in
Leah's 4th-Grade Classroom

Leah Anderson was having a frustrating year. She and her 4th-grade class in Topeka, Kansas, were struggling. The new textbooks were uninspiring and the focus on high-stakes testing at the state and federal levels seemed to preclude opportunities for creative, in-depth study. It was going to be a very long year. Fortunately, under the guidance of a new building principal, everything was about to change. Working together, the principal and faculty developed a project whereby 4th- and 5th-grade classes were paired with 1st- and 2nd-grade classes to conduct in-depth studies of the continents. Creativity was strongly encouraged.

Leah and her students joined a 2nd-grade class for a month-long study of Australia. The older children first read stories about Australia to the younger children and learned to do Internet searches; soon, however, the project took on a life of its own as Leah began to incorporate information about Australia into all aspects of instruction. She had her students do choral readings; thus, those who were shy or less skilled would not suffer the embarrassment that reading aloud often prompts. Vocabulary words came from the readings, including words specific to Australian cultures. The class, in small groups, performed plays about the history and varied cultures of Australia, and individual and group projects reinforced history lessons. In addition, geography, math, map skills, writing, teamwork, and critical and creative thinking were taught and reinforced through visual, musical, and performing arts.

The project culminated in a presentation for the entire school. Leah's class chose to create a "wax museum." As students, teachers, and parents entered Leah's classroom, they were greeted by the 4th- and 2nd-grade students arranged in various tableaux. In front of each scene, a brightly colored circular sticker prompted visitors to push it to "activate the scene." Then, the students would give a rehearsed performance. One group sang Australian songs. Another gave the history of the boomerang and displayed the ones they had made. Yet another group showed how to calculate the distance between Kansas and Australia and the amount of time it would take to fly from one place to the other. The "wax museum" provided a comprehensive and detailed look at the country under study, and the students' depth of learning was obvious. Students were active, engaged, and proud of their accomplishments.

Literacy and the Arts

Utilizing the arts to teach and reinforce literacy skills is as natural as breathing. Early humans left behind drawings and sculpture they created to explain and celebrate their world. Today, we

Connie Corbett-Whittier and Leah Anderson

struggle to understand and learn from their symbolic representations in the same way that we sometimes struggle with the vast amount of information constantly bombarding us from textbooks, traditional media, and the Internet. Other arts, like creative dramatics and storytelling, reflect the oral tradition upon which our modern world is based. To assert that education is only valid if it is based on reading, writing, and arithmetic, and evaluated through high-stakes testing, denies the very essence of learning.

One needs only to observe small children to understand the importance of activity and imagination in the learning process. Current brain research confirms that movement and creativity are essential to effective learning (Hannaford, 1995). Still, defining the arts and the part they play in learning can be problematic. The arts may include theater, music, dance, drawing, and painting, but they encompass much more. Teachers rely upon the arts every day without even realizing it.

Many teachers feel that they cannot effectively use the arts in their classes because they believe that their use requires innate artistic talent and/or specialized training. As Zull (2005) points out:

> *One facet that is common in all these arts is the sense of mystery. We say that a person has mastered an art when they succeed but can't say how. Wonderful things happen but no one is able to dissect the steps or write out the formula for success. It is just an art!* (p. 1)

The concept of art as a mystery that cannot be adequately explained limits our understanding of the arts and the ways they can be used to promote learning; however, limiting the definition of the arts creates an artificial barrier to effective teaching and learning. In reality, teaching is an art, as are all of the tasks we truly master. In fact, "whatever we have mastered in our life can be considered our 'art' " (Zull, 2005, p. 1).

Perhaps the most important reason to incorporate the arts in education is the proven connection between emotion and learning. The arts trigger emotion, and emotion causes physical changes in the brain that can result in learning (Hannaford, 1995; Zull, 2005). We have all experienced the effects that negative experiences can have on learning, but we often downplay the effects of positive emotional experiences, instead attributing success to that "mystery" Zull (2005) discusses. We might say, "I'm just not a math person" or "English is just something I am good at" without thinking about why. Brain research indicates that the emotions associated with learning experiences in particular disciplines dictate both success and beliefs about our ability (Hannaford, 1995; Zull, 2005).

Teaching with the arts also encourages students to understand rather than simply know subject matter. In their book *Understanding by Design*, Wiggins and McTighe (2005) state, "Without lessons designed to bring ideas to life, concepts such as honor, manifest destiny, or the water cycle remain empty phrases to be memorized, depriving learners of the realization that ideas have power" (p. 43). Therefore, it is the teacher's responsibility to deliberately develop educational experiences that ensure student understanding. Wiggins and McTighe also assert the critical importance of providing students with a "real problem of thought" for understanding to occur: "This is very different from giving students lessons and tests that merely require taking in and recalling from memory, based on highly cued exercises in which learners simply plug in what is unambiguously required" (p. 42).

Students experiencing curricula in which the arts are an integral part score higher on the Scholastic Aptitude Test (SAT) "by an average of 31 to 50 points on the verbal and math sections" (Dickinson, 1997, p. 5). Multiple studies indicate that arts education improves reading comprehension, language development, and writing skills (Catterall, 2002; Dickinson, 1997; Tucker, 2003) as well as spatial temporal reasoning (Dickinson, 1997; Hannaford, 1995). Arts activities also can teach such social skills as teamwork, leadership, interpersonal communication, discipline, work ethic, following directions, respect, and appropriate behavior (Catterall, 2002).

The variety and creativity inherent in arts education accommodate a variety of learning styles and cultural heritages. Teaching through the arts brings diverse groups of students together for a common purpose. Research shows that the arts significantly improve the academic and social achievement of students at all levels of academic achievement and ages, as well as proving effective with students diagnosed with behavior disorder (BD), attention deficit disorder (ADD), and attention deficit hyperactivity disorder (ADHD) (Catterall, 2002; Hannaford, 1995).

The key to successful use of the arts, and learning in general, is a welcoming classroom climate. Students must feel encouraged and emotionally safe for effective learning to occur. Blasingame and Bushman (2005) assert that:

> Establishing a classroom climate in which students feel good about themselves and about what they are doing is very important for students in grades 6 through 8. While this climate must continue through the 12th grade, it is very important for the preadolescents, who are struggling with physical, emotional, and cognitive changes. (p. 19)

Of course, a safe physical and emotional environment is critical at all ages and stages of development, but it is especially necessary for students and teachers who may be asked to step out of their comfort zones to engage in the arts and experience learning at a deeper level than that provided by lecture and simple memorization tasks.

Teaching with the arts provides almost unlimited opportunities for growth and development in every academic and social discipline. Unfortunately, education in the United States has evolved in such a way that the arts are seen as separate disciplines, with little or no relationship to so-called academic concerns. Classes in foreign languages and the arts often are the first to go when budget cuts are required. Many educators and parents now are striving to reverse the detrimental effects of this misguided approach to education.

The arts encompass a variety of skills and activities. In reality, the distinctions that follow are somewhat arbitrary. Most activities involve a combination of arts, rather than focusing on only one at a time. The most effective learning lessons utilize combinations of drama, drawing, painting or computer graphics, music, movement, individual and group work, discussion, reading, and writing. Look back at the unit on Australia that Leah's class experienced. At the end of the unit, Leah said, "They KNOW Australia—AND they KNOW English, math, science, research, and computer skills."

Drama

Drama in the classroom is nothing new. In addition to the daily "dramas" of students' lives, structured dramatic activities are traditional learning opportunities. Years ago, teachers taught elocution, or a dramatic interpretation of significant literary works. Although memorization of the chosen piece was a requirement, the focus was on communication and presentation. More specifically, students analyzed the piece to discern the author's meaning and the meaning for them personally, and then they practiced recitation to share the meaning with their peers. Simply reciting the piece by rote was not acceptable.

However, many adults have unpleasant memories of having to recite a soliloquy from *Hamlet* or a long poem to the teacher. The grade for these activities became based on accuracy of memorization rather than analysis or meaning making or fun; as a result, students approached such requirements with trepidation and teachers viewed the activity as just another way to provide points for the gradebook. As with many educational endeavors, the problem is not so much with the activity as it is with the purpose, which has become distorted with time.

Nevertheless, a number of teachers continue to find creative ways to incorporate drama into the curriculum, regardless of the discipline. In Leah's class, some of the "wax museum" participants acted out scenes representing important aspects of Australian history, such as a prison colony, a pioneer family, and an aboriginal village. Leah's students did choral readings and readers theater in class to prepare and learn the stories and history. Role-play activities also helped students prepare for the final performance. Teachers do not need to be classically trained and students do not have to be Shakespearean actors to engage in these activities. For students who experience extreme discomfort with dramatic performances, alternative activities could be found within the overall project. Ultimately, students created their own versions of the stories they studied. They practiced storytelling and writing as they fine-tuned the scenes they would portray. Using drama, Leah was able to teach and reinforce skills in reading, writing, communication skills, leadership, and teamwork.

Generally, "creative dramatics" is the term used to describe the types of drama useful in the classroom. It is an umbrella term that may include improvisation, role play, readers theater, choral reading, pantomime, or the traditional dramatic representation of a play. The Nebraska Department of Education (1999) defines creative dramatics as "informal dramatization of a story using simple staging and few, if any, sets and costumes" or "creation of an original story idea through dramatic play, usually in an informal setting." Sun (2003) further refines that definition, explaining that " 'Drama' and 'theatre' generally refer to the process and the production respectively; however, in classroom application, the focus should be shifted from learning drama to emphasizing the process of learning through drama" (para. 2). Use of creative dramatics does not preclude production, but the production tends to evolve from a series of activities rather than from a published script. In Leah's class, both scripted plays and improvisational activities provided sources for dramatic production. By its very nature, creative dramatics lends itself to a variety of definitions and forms.

Johnson (1998) identifies the major components associated with creative dramatics. Structure relates to the fact that it is necessary for the teacher to have a clear purpose in mind for the activity, to set boundaries of acceptable and appropriate behavior and language, and to model actions and dialogue. Creative dramatics requires abstract thought, and the role of teacher is not one of director (in the theatrical sense), but rather one of facilitator who aids students in their understanding of the process. Although structure is important, open-endedness and flexibility also are essential. Johnson states, "Provide structure, but encourage improvisation by letting students find their own words to carry the meaning and explore alternate endings" (p. 2).

Classroom climate is an important component of creative dramatics. In a creative endeavor like drama, a certain amount of emotional risk is involved. For drama activities to work effectively, students must feel that the environment is safe and affirming, free from ridicule. In the beginning, it is recommended that only students who volunteer be expected to participate. Related to climate is feedback. It is imperative that immediate positive feedback be given after—and sometimes during—the activity, especially when the students are new to performing drama. Both verbal and nonverbal feedback are appropriate. As students become more comfortable, specific elements, like the volume or tone of a student's voice, may be critiqued. Other acting elements include use of the body through movement, gestures, and facial expressions to express emotion and action; characterization and the imagination used when creating a character that is believable; and the concept of drama as ensemble acting or group work (Johnson, 1998).

The effects of using drama in the classroom have been extensively researched. Sun (2003) stated, "The mental requirements for understanding drama are similar to those for reading" (p. 1). According to Sun, using drama in the classroom results in significant improvements in reading, writing, vocabulary, and understanding literary structure. Cramer (2003) found that using drama significantly improved the reading comprehension and interpretative skills among 4th-graders from low socioeconomic homes. Gaspero and Falletta (1994) studied the effects of dramatizing poetry in English as a second language (ESL) classrooms and concluded that "the dramatization of poetry is a powerful tool in stimulating learning while acquiring a second language because the learners become intellectually, emotionally, and physically involved in the target language within the framework of the new culture" (p. 1). Hertzberg (1998) discovered that drama activities improve reading and writing skills. Finally, Martello (2001) states, "The learning that can be promoted through drama defies curriculum boundaries" (p. 196). She identified advanced achievement in language, spatial awareness, social/cultural skills, creativity, and critical thinking.

Perhaps the Shakespearean character Jaques, from *As You Like It*, was correct:

> *All the world's a stage,*
> *And all the men and women merely players.*
> *They have their exits and their entrances;*
> *And one man in his time plays many parts...*
> (Act II, Scene vii)

Drama can help students learn about the many parts they will play in their lives in a safe and supportive environment while gaining the skills they need to succeed in whatever roles they choose to play.

Visual Arts

> *Paradoxically though it may seem, it is none the less true that life imitates art far more than art imitates life.* (Oscar Wilde)

The visual arts are used commonly in lower grades. Art activities are considered appropriate for students through 5th or 6th grade, depending on the structure of elementary schools and junior high or middle schools in particular districts. Even in the lower grades, however, art is often considered an add-on, without a role to play in teaching and reinforcing literacy.

Marge Shuberg's 1st-grade class is making ducks from bright yellow paper bags stuffed with newspaper. When finished, they will be displayed on the bulletin board at the front of the class-room, to which is attached a blue background and a large umbrella cutout. As Marge unveils the theme of the board, she holds up the words that will surround the ducks and umbrella and asks the students to read the words and guess what the next word might be.

Marge: *"What does this say?"*
Children: *"Lowman!"*
Marge: *"And this?"*
Children: *"Hill!"*
Marge holds up the next word.
Children: *"is"*
She holds up another word.
Children: *"just"*
Marge: *"So, what do we have so far?"*
Children: *"Lowman Hill is just"*
Marge: *"Good! What do you think the next word will be?"*
Children: *"Wonderful?" "Fun?" "School?"*
Marge: *"What are we getting ready to make?"*
Children: *"Ducks."*
Marge: *"Right . . . so, Lowman Hill is just . . . DUCKY."*

The children are thrilled by this revelation and laugh and talk as they set about the task at hand. As the activity unfolds, Marge continues to reinforce prior learning by asking students about the colors they are using and how ducks differ from other animals. Even elementary math concepts are covered as each student counts to 30 as they wait for glue to dry on wings, feet, beaks, and eyes.

This simple activity taught and reinforced a variety of skills in a painless and enjoyable way. Students were required to read, count, and think while also developing fine motor skills by cutting and gluing, thus applying what they know to things they do. This kind of "backdoor" teaching is an effective and efficient way for people of all ages to learn, sometimes in spite of themselves. Of course, making ducks for a bulletin board might not be an appropriate choice for older children, but the idea is that art activities provide a valid alternative to lecture, isolated access to information, and multiple choice tests.

In Leah's class, students have made boomerangs and decorated them with the aboriginal symbols they had researched on the Internet. They created collages of Australian culture; they drew animals indigenous to the continent as well as characters, events, or settings from the stories they read, and they re-created scenes for their "wax museum." Leah often uses art activities to teach and reinforce a variety of skills. For Valentine's Day, a local artist came to class and led students through a project that was part of a unit on self-knowledge. Using heart shapes for the bodies, students created symbolic representations of themselves that identified specific personal characteristics. The colors they chose had meaning, as did the type of eyes, arms, legs, feet, and mouth. The result was a room full of highly individualized craft projects, each of which was deeply meaningful to the student who made it.

Use of the visual arts need not be confined to art projects. Lee (2003) described the use of kamishibai (pronounced kam-ee-shee-bye) storyboards with novels to increase her middle school students' comprehension skills. The storyboards each have a picture on the front and a corresponding part of the story typed on the back. The teacher or student reads the story card by card as the audience views the pictures.

Discouraged that her students, so insightful and competent when reading novels and short stories, seemed unable to comprehend academic textbooks, Lee decided to try kamishibai with that genre also. According to Lee, "In this age of multiple literacies, one literacy critical for all students is the ability to read academic texts" (p. 36). Student groups used computer software to create cluster maps of textbook chapters; they then transferred the information into artistic representations to create storyboards to present to the rest of the class. Lee stated, "I'm not assessing them on their artistry, only on the information and understanding that they convey with it. Stick figures are fine if that is their best work" (p. 38). The activity was an overwhelming success.

Batel (2005) used art prints with her classes to teach reading and writing. First, students learned to "read" a work of art, identifying how the various art elements create meaning. The connection between reading art and reading words evolved over time, and the students became more aware of the elements of writing that create the meaning of the story. Students were encouraged to seek out art that represented characters or meanings in the stories they read, and to create their own pictures. Works of art also were used as writing prompts. Finally, students wrote their own stories, complete with illustrations.

Oring (2000) promotes the use of photography to teach art as a visual language. Photography is a "safer" form of creativity than drawing or painting. When they are required to paint, draw or sculpt, students often feel that their work is not "good enough." Learning to "read" a picture provided the foundation for teaching photography as "the language of vision" (p. 58). Oring asserts, "Visual language creates a doorway to understanding and perception that cannot be experienced through verbal communication" (p. 58). Photography can teach such skills as perception, conceptualization, verbalization, description, self-direction, and decision-making: "The child can be the director of the learning process by deciding what picture to take, setting up the composition, and then actually taking the picture" (p. 58). Finally, the photographs should be shared with an audience. As students explain the meanings they were trying to capture in their photographs, they learn and use verbal skills and writing.

Lin (2005) and Morrison, Bryan, and Chilcoat (2002) support the use of comics in the classroom. Popular culture will always appear more relevant to children than the classics, and helps ensure student interest and motivates students to read, write, and think. Morrison, Bryan, and Chilcoat (2002) state, "Given the opportunity to create and share their own comic books, students engage in greater literacy exploration than they otherwise would, due to comics' popular and easily accessible format" (p. 759). They also support the use of other media, such as film, television, and popular music.

Popular culture is not limited to entertainment. One science class studied the environmental impact of bats. Critical thinking was enhanced by creating life-size paintings of bats, including the Malayan flying fox, which has a wingspan of six feet. The project culminated in a "Save the Bats" brochure that the students distributed throughout the community (McKee & Ogle, 2005). Through these activities, students learned to conduct research, draw to scale (thus utilizing math skills), think critically about an issue, and format a brochure. The students' writing skills were reinforced as they wrote text to explain the drawings and photographs they included in the brochure.

Strong evidence exists showing that, at the very least, the visual arts are effective in teaching students history, reading, and writing; in addition, they positively affect organization and persistence (Catterall, 2002). Additional research shows a strong correlation between the visual arts and scientific reasoning (Catterall, 2002; McKee & Ogle, 2005). The visual arts also contribute to the development of spatial-temporal reasoning (Dickinson, 1997; Hannaford, 1995).

Ohler (2000) believes that a name change is in order; art should be referred to as visual literacy, thus distancing it from the view that it is "tangential, soft, or not entirely relevant to preparing children for work and citizenship" (p. 17). In fact, he makes the compelling case that art should be considered the fourth "R." With the advent of the Internet, multimedia presentation of information is becoming the standard format for sharing information. Ohler contends that "a shift away from text-centric communication and toward pictures, diagrams, sound, movement, and other more universal forms of communication seems inevitable" (p. 118). Further, Ohler asserts that understanding how to organize information in this format is critical to the future success of students: "Those who do not grow up to create art for a living will nevertheless use it, manage it, interpret it, or interact with it in many ways that simply did not exist 10 years ago" (2000, p. 17).

Music

> Musick has Charms to sooth a savage Breast,
> To soften Rocks, or bend a knotted Oak.
> I've read, that things inanimate have mov'd.
> And, as with living Souls, have been inform'd
> By Magick Numbers and persuasive Sound.
> (*The Mourning Bride*, Act I, Scene I, Congreve, 1697)

The ability of music to evoke emotion is well-known. Parents sing to their children, teachers use soft background music to soothe restless students, and students rush to listen to music that reflects their many moods, joys, and frustrations. Research indicates that responses to music can be noted even in the womb. Programs like *Sesame Street* have relied on music to teach basic skills, and what American child has not been encouraged to sing the ABC song?

Recent brain research has much to do with the music renaissance being experienced in many American schools. After decades of cuts related to the so-called "back-to-basics" movement, which continue today in some locations, parents and teachers are beginning to appreciate the role that music can play in learning. As Undercofler (1997) wrote, "Effective arguments have been made that reading, writing, and mathematics are actually tools that allow students access to the real basics of education—those associated with thinking, evaluating, judging, synthesizing, and creating" (p. 15). The passage of *Goals 2000: Educate America Act* and the establishment of national standards for music and other arts validated what many educators already knew—music is an important tool for learning (U.S. Department of Education, 2000).

In 1993, Rauscher and Shaw released a study in which college students listened to Mozart before a test. These students scored higher than those in the control group, thus initiating a flurry of media attention and the birth of the "Mozart Effect." Parents snapped up the compact disks, books, and videos that were subsequently produced. After all, who does not want to make their children smarter? Since that time, a number of follow-up studies indicate several flaws in the initial research. First, the effect was short-lived and probably served more to relax students than to increase brain power. Second, Mozart's music was no more effective than other music selections (Chipongian, 2000; Fischer, 2004). The result, however, was to prompt a number of more controlled studies that began to uncover the true nature of the relationship between music and learning.

Although the connection between listening to music and academic achievement remains unclear, a strong relationship between music activities and learning is much clearer. One important aspect of music instruction is the connection between music and math. According to Gardiner, a leading researcher in music education, children involved in "music training that is sequenced according to a progression in difficulty" experienced significant gains in mathematical skills (Chipongian, 2000; Gardiner, 1999). Specifically, Gardiner has determined that involvement in music studies and performance is related to improved performance in math skills that include patterns and functions, as well as algebra. Less significant gains were reported in the areas of measurement, estimation, and problem-solving strategies (Gardiner, 1999).

Students who learn to play an instrument and/or learn to read music appear to have the most significant gains. In China, Taiwan, and Japan, all students are required to play a musical instrument. Instruction begins at an early age and continues throughout their education (Perrin, 1997). Math and science skills are especially positively affected due to music's proven relationship to the development of spatial-temporal reasoning (Catterall, 2002; Hannaford, 1995). Students involved in music education score higher on standardized tests than those who do not experience music in the curriculum, and those who learn to play an instrument score significantly higher (Hannaford, 1995).

Math and science are not the only disciplines that benefit from music education. Literacy is dependent on mastering sign systems (Ferguson, 2000). Math, language, art, movement, and music all represent interrelated sign systems. Music is an important element in brain development because of its ability to evoke emotion, which is connected to high-level reasoning and memory (Hannaford, 1995). Hannaford reported that students identified as slow learners increased their reading scores by an average of four-and-one-half grade levels after only five months of learning to play a musical instrument. On a basic level, music instruction improves phonemic awareness and vocabulary, while also reinforcing reading skills. As students read the words to songs they learn, the idea that the message is in the words (rather than pictures) becomes integrated into their learning (Fisher & McDonald, 2001).

English teachers often use music and lyrics as writing prompts. Writing and reading poetry become more palatable to a greater number of students when they can approach it as a songwriting assignment, thereby helping to teach for understanding. In Leah's class, students learned Australian songs and a group of singers performed in the "wax museum." Copeland and Goering (2003) use music with their students to stimulate interest in reading. They have found it effective to use blues lyrics and biographies of blues musicians to teach complex literary themes, and they found that students' comprehension improved greatly. Grant and Ammon (2003) used blues and jazz music and biographies of musicians with a class of African American 6th-graders "as a way to help them discover how words and phrases often mimic the sounds of music" (p. 745). Some of the reading was done aloud with a beat to simulate the musical aspects of language. They reported a substantial increase in recreational reading among the students involved.

In addition to learning skills traditionally associated with literacy, students involved in music education learn how to persist in mastering skills and concepts, how to take ownership of their work, and how to use failure as a tool for improvement. The connection between music and emotion allows students to experience passion and to learn about themselves. Music education also helps students develop positive self-concepts, improved communication skills, and a sense of idealism (Perrin, 1997). Exploring and expressing emotion in a controlled environment, such as a classroom, is essential to the development of altruism, compassion, empathy, and other complex positive emotions and values (Hannaford, 1995). Incorporating music into the curriculum provides an enjoyable and painless way to improve every aspect of a student's life.

Movement

Movement never lies. It is a barometer telling the state of the soul's weather. (Martha Graham, 1953)

Hannaford (1995) explains the connection between movement, the brain, and learning, stating: "Research shows that muscular activities, particularly coordinated, balanced movements, appear to stimulate the production of neurotrophins, such as dopamine, natural substances that stimulate the growth of existing nerve cells, and neural connections in the brain" (p. 113). Although we know that movement is critical to learning in young children and it stimulates learning in older children and adults, we spend a good deal of time in school actively trying to suppress movement. Controlled movement, however, helps our students learn.

Creative movement does not refer only to dance, although dancing is an aspect. Dickinson (1997) described the "Dance of the DNA" performed for a number of years at the Northwest School in Seattle. She stated, "The complexity of DNA became clearly understandable as the program unfolded and as participants learned with both mind and body" (p. 2). In Leah's class, students practiced controlled movement in their "wax museum." Not only did they act, sing, and demonstrate, they also had to move only on cue—when visitors pressed round stickers to turn the scene "on." When the scene finished, students had to revert to stillness (as much as possible in their excitement). In this situation, Leah's class covered all of the academic disciplines and they learned the information on a deep level, in part because of the incorporation of movement. Leah's class utilized movement and the other arts for teaching and assessment, both of which are appropriate uses of the arts.

While movement activities may appear chaotic to the outside observer, it is controlled chaos as long as they are planned to meet specified outcomes and objectives. As Witherell (2000) asserts, "Targeted outcomes must be clear. They cannot change because the teaching or assessment is nontraditional" (p. 180). In addition, the teacher needs to discuss the purpose and expectations of movement activities with students prior to implementation. At times, demonstration also may be needed. Witherell describes the use of a combined movement and music activity to teach the concept of mood in literature. Students were asked to create drumbeats to describe the changing moods in a literary work. Prior to the students composing their own renditions of the various moods, the teacher and students discussed the activity and brainstormed the "sounds" of moods. Witherell also discusses in detail the use of movement and other arts activities as assessment tools. Rubrics and checklists are recommended, and the content of the assessment tools must reflect the desired outcomes; "the teacher must look for the traditional answers in the nontraditional assessment" (p. 182).

Current research also shows a positive correlation between movement, both in regular and physical education classes, and academic achievement. Blakemore (2003) reviewed results of a study done by the California Department of Education that showed students who scored high on the state physical fitness tests also scored significantly higher in both reading and math on the SAT9. Arguing both the importance of physical education in schools, and that the role of physical educators must include a commitment to reinforcing academic disciplines, Blakemore stated, "If teachers can get students to think while they are doing physical activity, the movement is especially beneficial" (p. 23).

Minton (2003) described her use of movement activities to teach a variety of academic principles. Designing activities that successfully transform principles and concepts into movement may be difficult at times. Minton suggests that it is first necessary to identify the "dominant trait or characteristic of a concept" (p. 37), which may include quality or type, starts or stops, direction, path, level, size, shape, position, and duration. An example of an activity focusing on quality or type of movement is to have students use hand movements or movement of objects to demonstrate the movement of tectonic plates during an earthquake. Starts and stops are useful when teaching electricity; the way a current is started or stopped by a switch can be reinforced by asking students to move and freeze. The concept of alternating current can be taught by having students walk around the room in appropriate directions, and the zigzag pattern of lightning also can be re-created through movement (Minton, 2003).

In a unit on the rain forest, Minton (2003) suggested having students group themselves to represent the emergent layer, canopy, understory, and the ground layer, reinforcing the dominant trait of levels. Size helped students better understand the Aztec calendar; students physically re-created the stone calendar with their bodies. For shape, students created the dominant profiles of different styles of housing, like igloos or castles, in pairs or groups, using only their bodies. In a study of Japan, students were asked to position themselves in the crescent shape created by the four largest islands, thereby reinforcing geography, and duration was represented by asking students to position themselves in relation to the history of the country (Minton, 2003).

Movement activities do not have to be complex or incorporate traditional dance, although dance may play a part in cultural studies, including popular culture. The important idea is that movement needs to be incorporated into lessons to improve learning, often in combination with other arts. Hong (2000) stated, "Literacy involves the progressive development of our abilities to both interpret and convey meaning through multiple sign and symbol systems, which includes . . . kinesthetic, visual and aural modes of communication" (p. 3).

Concluding Thoughts

The arts contribute a great deal to the quality of life for both children and adults. As such, they should not be separated from so-called "basics," but rather integrated into all aspects of the curriculum. Current research clearly shows that the arts enhance learning and achievement in ways and to degrees far superior to lecture and high-stakes testing. Individual teachers and some enlightened school districts already understand this, although they may focus more on reading about the use of the arts than embodying the concept through modeling and continuous experience. Howard Gardner's (1999) work on multiple intelligences, however, has slowly been incorporated into most teacher education programs, and his explanations and examples make the importance of the arts in education clear. When educators make a commitment to teach to the intelligences that Gardner describes, they also commit to teaching the whole child, and teaching content area literacy through the arts is an important component of this commitment.

Perhaps the following lyrics sum up this chapter best:

Well I'm strugglin' baby
To teach things in a brand new way
Yeah I'm struggling honey
To teach things in a brand new way
But I know one day I'll make it baby
And all this work will finally pay

Gonna make those connections darlin'
If it's the last thing I ever do
Gonna make those connections darlin'
If it's the last thing I ever do
Gotta take my teachin' past where I found it
Now you go on and do it too

(Copeland & Goering, 2003, p. 436)

References

Batel, V. (2005). Merging literacies: A case study. *Childhood Education, 81,* 196-201.

Blakemore, C. L. (2003). Movement is essential to learning. *The Journal of Physical Education, Recreation & Dance, 74*(9), 22-27.

Blasingame, J., & Bushman, J. H. (2005). *Teaching writing in middle and secondary schools.* Upper Saddle River, NJ: Pearson.

Catterall, J. S. (2002). *Critical links: Learning in the arts and student academic and social development.* Washington, DC: Arts Education Partnership.

Chipongian, L. (2000, May). Can music education really enhance brain functioning and academic learning? *Brain Connection.* Available from www.brainconnection.com

Congreve, W. (1697). *The mourning bride.* Retrieved February 6, 2006, from www.farid-hajji.net/books/en/Congreve_William/mb-b1c01.html

Copeland, M., & Goering, C. (2003). Blues you can use: Teaching the Faust theme through music, literature, and film. *Journal of Adolescent and Adult Literacy, 46*(5), 436-441.

Cramer, N. V. (2003). *Literacy as a performing art: A phenomenological study of oral dramatic reading.* Doctoral dissertation. Louisiana State University, Baton Rouge, LA. Retrieved February 10, 2006, from http://etd.lsu.edu/docs/available/etd-0127103-211254/unrestricted/Cramer_dis/pdf

Dickinson, D. (1997). Learning through the arts. *New Horizons for Learning Online Journal.* Available from www.newhorizons.org

Ferguson, D. B. (2000). Book shows how art and music can help teach literacy [Review]. *Curriculum Administrator, 36*(7), 19.

Fisher, D., & McDonald, N. (2001). The intersection between music and early literacy instruction: Listening to literacy! *Reading Improvement, 38*(3), 106-116.

Fischer, K. (2004, Spring). The myths and promises of the learning brain. *Ed. Magazine: The Magazine of the Harvard Graduate School of Education.* Retrieved September 12, 2006, from www.gse.harvard.edu/news/features/fischer12012004.html

Gardiner, M. F. (1999). *The relationship of two WEB project activities to math learning: An analysis.* Available from www.webproject.org/pdf/derby.pdf

Gardner, H. (1999). *Intelligence reframed: Multiple intelligences for the 21st century.* New York: Basic Books.

Gaspero, M., & Falletta, B. (1994, April). Creating drama with poetry: Teaching English as a second language through dramatization and improvisation. *ERIC Digests.* Washington, DC: ERIC Clearinghouse on Languages and Linguistics. (ERIC Document

Reproduction Service No. ED 368214)

Grant, R. A., & Ammon, R. (2003). Jazzy possibilities in urban education. *The Reading Teacher, 56*(8), 745-747.

Hannaford, C. (1995). *Smart moves.* Salt Lake City, UT: Great River Books.

Hertzberg, M. (1998). Theory into practice: Using drama to enhance literacy development. *The Australian Journal of Language and Literacy, 21*(2), 159-175.

Hong, T. (2000, July). *Developing dance literacy in the postmodern: An approach to curriculum.* Lecture presented for Dancing in the Millennium: An International Conference, Washington, DC.

Johnson, A. P. (1998). How to use creative dramatics in the classroom. *Childhood Education, 75,* 224-228.

Lee, G. (2003). Kamishibai: A vehicle to multiple literacies. *Voices From the Middle, 10*(3), 36-43.

Lin, C. (2005). Instruction through communicative and visual arts. *Teacher Librarian, 32*(5), 25-28.

Martello, I. (2001, October). Drama: Ways into critical literacy in the early childhood years. *Australian Journal of Language and Literacy, 24*(3), 195-209.

McKee, J., & Ogle, D. (2005). *Integrating instruction: Literacy and science.* New York: Guilford Press.

Minton, S. (2003). Using movement to teach academics: An outline for success. *The Journal of Physical Education, Recreation & Dance, 74*(2), 36-40.

Morrison, T. G., Bryan, G., & Chilcoat, G. W. (2002). Using student-generated comic books in the classroom. *Journal of Adolescent & Adult Literacy, 45*(8), 758-768.

Nebraska Department of Education. (1999). Title 92, Nebraska Administrative Code, Chapter 10. *Regulations and procedures for the accreditation of schools.* Available from www.nde.state.ne.us/LEGAL/documents/Rule10HearingDraft-Mar3.pdf

Ohler, J. (2000). Art becomes the fourth R. *Educational Leadership, 58*(2), 16-19.

Oring, S. A. (2000). A call for visual literacy. *School Arts, 99*(8), 58.

Perrin, S. B. (1997). Education through the arts in secondary schools. *New Horizons for Learning Online Journal.* Retrieved December 17, 2005, from www.newhorizons.org

Rauscher, F. H., Shaw, G. L., & Ky, K. N. (1993). Music and spatial task performance. *Nature, 365,* 611.

Sun, P. Y. (2003). Using drama and theatre to promote literacy development: Some basic classroom applications. *ERIC Educational Reports.* Retrieved December 14, 2005, from LookSmart database.

Tucker, K. (2003, Winter). Arts are basic education. *Washington State Arts Commission.* Retrieved December 15, 2005, from www.arts.wa.gov

Undercofler, J. F. (1997). Music in America's schools: A plan for action. *Arts Education Policy Review, 98*(6), 15-19.

United States Department of Education. (2000). Summary statement: Education reform, standards, and the arts. *National standards for arts education.* Available from www.ed.gov/pubs/ArtsStandards.html

Wiggins, G., & McTighe, J. (2005). *Understanding by design.* Alexandria, VA: Association for Supervision and Curriculum Development.

Witherell, N. (2000, Summer). Promoting understanding: Teaching literacy through the arts. *Educational HORIZONS, 78*(4), 179-183.

Zull, J. E. (2005, March). Arts, neuroscience, and learning. *New Horizons for Learning Online Journal.* Retrieved December 17, 2005, from www.newhorizons.org

Meet the Authors

Connie Corbett-Whittier teaches undergraduate courses in English composition and literature, as well as graduate courses in classroom assessment and evaluation at Friends University. Her research focuses on Kansas literature, writing apprehension, the adult learner, and self-study as a tool for teachers and students. In addition to her university commitments, she is often called upon to speak to groups about Kansas history and literature, teaching writing, and adult learners.

Leah Anderson is a 4th-grade teacher in the Topeka Public School District (USD 501). She also works for the Topeka & Shawnee County Public Library as a homework coach in the library's homework center. Leah collaborates with Amy Ketterman, a 2nd-grade teacher, on activities for 4th-grade and 2nd-grade "Study Buddies." Currently, Leah is working on her M.A. in education.

Chapter 3

Reading and Writing Workshop as Scaffold for Content Area Learning

in Rachel's 5th-grade Classroom

Act One, Scene One— An Opening Vignette

I am reading aloud to a group of 5th-graders in Rachel Mazzocco's classroom as an observer/ participant during this daily routine. They are seated at their tables, and we are continuing the reading of *The City of Ember* by Jeanne DuPrau (2003). As I begin reading, a buzz of conversation subsides, a few chairs scrape to new positions, and papers shuffle to a resting place. As we progress through the pages, silence penetrates the classroom. Every face is turned in my direction. The students are intent on the story and their engagement with the text subsumes all else.

One boy, seated a few feet to my left, focuses his eyes on my face. He almost seems to be reading my lips. It's a bit unnerving. Because I have observed in this classroom several times, I know that this boy will have many questions and connections that he will share with the entire class at the close of our reading. As we conclude our short discussion, my eyes survey the class. There are seven girls and 11 boys. They are predominantly African American; some are of mixed race, and a few are of white, non-Hispanic, heritage. Many live near the school, which is situated in an economically depressed neighborhood. Despite the reports of minorities being "silenced" in our public schools (Fine, 1987), *these* students are anything but silenced. They are invited to speak and their ideas cover the walls and hang from lines strung across the room. The students may be of different abilities, but none are strangers to the acts of reading and writing, talking and listening. These activities go on in this classroom throughout the day, and they are the focus of attention during reading and writing workshop (hereafter often referred to as just "workshop").

Workshop is the structure that scaffolds language arts instruction in this classroom and in this school, but there is more to workshop than a period of time on classroom schedules. Workshop contributes to the environment of the room and supports the work throughout the day. As I observed in this classroom, interviewed the teacher, and examined classroom artifacts, I discovered the attributes of workshop support the students' learning in other content areas.

The most evident themes that emerged from our collected data were the attributes of reading and writing workshop itself, the teacher's background and developing pedagogy, the kinds of text exhibited in and around the room, and the connections between reading/writing workshop structure and teaching/learning in a content area.

Terre Folger and Rachel Mazzocco

Some Background, Just in Case—"How Does Workshop Work?"

The purpose of workshop is to align reading and writing with the concrete concept that becoming literate is part of life's work. In reading workshop, as in an artist's workshop, the process and the product are both to be discovered, reflected upon, and revised. Reading workshop in the middle grades, as conceived by Nancie Atwell (1987), involves three important concepts: time to read, engagement with chosen text, and opportunity to respond to the text and to other readers. Committing to the use of an uninterrupted block of time for reading and writing is committing to the centrality of reading in the learning process and in life. The exact structure of the workshop is dependent on the class schedule, and engagement with text varies throughout the workshop time. Read-aloud, shared reading, guided reading, strategy lessons, literature groups/pairs, and conferencing are all ways that readers deepen engagement with text.

Varied opportunities to respond to text and to readers are part of workshop. Talk is central to this response (Gilles, 1991). In any of the settings described above, readers share, question, and mull over the critical aspects of fiction or nonfiction pieces. Writing in response to reading makes the connection between reading and writing clear, whether it is on sticky notes during reading (Harvey & Goudvis, 2000), in the form of a letter to the teacher or another reader, or in a self-reflective journal. Writing holds the reader's thinking "still" and invites revision of thought.

The workshop structure also includes opportunities for cognition and metacognition. Strategy lessons include reflection on the *process* of reading. Formal responses to reading, as noted in this chapter, give readers a chance to present while inviting closure and transmediation. For instance, in the Revolutionary War unit of study, students presented what they thought was most important about their chosen topics. They wrote about these ideas in their own words in their nonfiction book.

Middle grade students need the aspect of inquiry or reading to learn "to pursue answers to questions or as part of a class inquiry" (Five & Egawa, 1998, p. 3). Workshop practice makes perfect sense for promoting engaged and effective learning in content areas where inquiry is an effective methodology. For example, developing inquiry questions relates to asking questions while reading. Note-taking while reading for information on the topic follows from the use of sticky notes during fiction reading to keep track of important characters, plot developments, or critical text themes. Rachel introduced both of these strategies and encouraged and assessed their use during reading and writing workshop. They were then applied specifically to the Revolutionary War inquiry projects during social studies.

The mini-lesson segment of reading and writing workshop has been enriched by the recent development of strategy lessons that are explicitly taught within the context of literacy learning. Harvey and Goudvis (2000) provide the seminal text for teachers in this regard. They relegate strategies to six categories: making connections, questioning, visualizing, inferring, determining importance, and synthesizing. They encourage teachers to begin by modeling the strategies, thinking aloud as they do so. The students are given the opportunity to use such strategies as note-taking, first practicing as a group, then in scaffolded situations, until gradually the reader retains full responsibility for applying the strategy to a "new genre" or a "more difficult text" (p. 13). The goal is for the developing readers to become "strategic"; that is, they use the strategies to meet their own reading goals and needs.

While reading and writing workshop is student-centered, it is the teacher who is the architect, the designer of the curricular day. In this chapter, I introduce you to Rachel Mazzocco and help you see inside her classroom, visualizing the walls, the shelves, the bulletin boards, and the 5th-graders' voices in conversation with each other, their teacher, and, as we draw conclusions, with me. I hope to make explicit the connections between what literacy educators call reading and writing workshop and the learning in workshop that extends to and supports students' learning in other content areas. Finally, I hope that you, the reader, are able to draw conclusions and understand the strategies that Rachel and her students employ as they practice being strategic readers and writers.

Meet Ms. Mazzocco, The Queen of Room 202

Rachel and her class have a running joke of sorts. It stems back to the beginning of the year, when she needed the class' attention and a student remarked, with a note of defiance that sometimes marks the beginning of a new school year and new relationships, "And why should we listen to you?" She promptly replied, "Because I am the queen of Room 202. My voice is the most important voice in this room! When I talk, you need to listen!" This made these disengaged learners laugh. No one got in trouble or was sent to the office, and Rachel had their attention, which was her ultimate goal. Now, when attention strays, Rachel stops, looks at the students and asks,

> "Whose voice is the most important in this room?"
> The answer is chorused, "Yours!"
> She continues, "And why is that?"
> With smiles, "Because you're the queen of Room 202!"

It's a routine that seems to empower and entertain them all. The students recognize that Rachel is the instructional leader in the classroom, but they know, too, that *their* voices are *really* the most important ones to their *teacher*. Maybe that's why they smile. This teacher obviously knows, after nine years in middle school, how to engage her students and think on her feet. She has learned that the best way to respond to confrontation is to take the questioner seriously, even if her answer to the question isn't.

During a videotaped "tour" of her classroom, Rachel shared not only her classroom, but also the background for her beliefs about reading and writing, as well as her pedagogy. She became reflective as she talked, and we both seemed to have reached new understandings by the close of our time together that day. Shared reflection often has that effect. Rachel discovered more about why she held certain beliefs as she talked to me, and I began to appreciate her journey to that point of discovery more fully.

One of the most striking observations is that Rachel is a voracious reader of the books that her students are reading or may want to read. She gives book talks at least once a week on the four to five novels, picture books, or nonfiction works she has read at home. She reads books *with* the students, in the same time frame, so that she can talk *with* them in their literature groups. She wants her students to see her as a reader, and shares with them how she selects the books she reads, especially nonfiction. "I don't want it to sound textbooky. I want it to be entertaining but have facts, you know what I mean?" she says.

Rachel remembers being a student, and confesses, "I can't believe I'm telling you this, but in high school, I never read a textbook. Never. I didn't have to, because I was a good listener." Interestingly, the first textbook that Rachel remembers reading was on young children's language acquisition. "It got me very excited about learning, and I still remember that it had a lot to do with Helen Keller and learning language and how people learn language, and I remember desperately wanting to talk about it. No one else had read it, and my teacher and I had a really good discussion, but it was like we were the only ones who were talking. What college students can't do a lot of the times is talk about textbooks. . . . No one reads textbooks, because you don't have to. And I think that's why that summer I spent time reading from the library on my own, only biographies. I was challenging myself to read more nonfiction text, because it's not easy reading."

This point connects to one of Rachel's strongly held beliefs about her purposes in reading workshop. "My whole goal really is to teach them conversation in reading workshop. First, I teach them how to talk about fiction, because that's what they're familiar with, and then I want to get them to talk about nonfiction, which is what you do in classrooms for the rest of your life."

Rachel also shares her thinking with the students by leaving her own Post-it notes in her copies of the books the students are reading. These notes have the questions she asked and the connections she made when reading the books. On a shelf next to the classroom library, she points to these books and elaborates, "These are all the books that I've read so far with kids. I leave my Post-it notes in them. Students like to read the books with my Post-it notes in them, even if they aren't in that lit group. I've found that they respond to what I've written, which is kind of cool."

Another of Rachel's closely held tenets is that she must convey to the students that workshop is serious time, and that she values their work. The students have opportunities to make decisions about the work they are doing—how and if they want to do a project at the conclusion of a book, which "Mark Twain" books to read next, choosing books and people with whom they wish to read. They also know they can choose to abandon a book. Rachel explained, "We talk about abandoning books. That it's okay to abandon books. It's okay to put it down. I had several people this week abandon books. Sierra dropped a book this week, but she picked something else up . . . she's very into that romance teenage thing."

Rachel knows her students as readers, and workshop helps her do so. Conferencing is a key part of reading and writing workshop for her. While many teachers choose to sit with students on the floor or wherever the students are reading for a conference, Rachel makes it a point to have conferences at the front of the room at her reading and writing conference table. It preserves the conference as "sacred time" (Calkins, 1994) in an appointed place. When she is conferencing with an individual during workshop, the other students know and accept responsibility for their actions. They go to and from the restroom and the book storage room across the hall when necessary without having to ask permission. They solve their own problems. Primarily, they take on the responsibility of reading and writing with each other and on their own.

To this end, they have questions to answer with their literature groups, general ones like, "Did you make any connections to this book? Did it make you laugh or cry? Tell me about it." The students must make vocabulary lists on their own—words that they didn't understand or that they want to remember. Rachel admits that she wonders, sometimes, if these students will complete these questions and make the lists on their own, but notes, with a tone of surprise, that she has no such concern about vocabulary sheets, for example. "They have to have one per book and most of them, I mean, like Tyler, have two going. They like it. It's all very serious."

To facilitate self-sufficiency, each student has a "bookbox" that contains his or her reading journal, Post-it notes, the literature group book, and an independent reading book. Rachel pulls one out at random and identifies the owner by the books inside, one of which is *The Last Dog on Earth* (Ehrenhaft, 2003). She shares that "it's one of his all-time favorites. It's a new book." She opens his reader's notebook at random and finds her own handwriting—some circles with names in them. She explains, "We just drew these circles to lump characters together and try to figure out who the characters went with because there were two story lines going on, and he was confused by that, so we talked about it" during the reading conference.

To summarize, Rachel is a reader and writer, herself, and she displays this identity to her students. She "thinks aloud" often with her students, sharing her own model of literacy and her strategies. She models for them another strategy that is used over and over—making thinking visible in different genres of writing. As a result, her students write on Post-it notes and in their reading journals; more formally, they write poems, letters, and skits. When they complete a project, they present it to the class, which is important, "because they'll have to do a lot of that in middle school, talk about *why* they create things." Roe (2004) notes that many middle level teachers are trained as English teachers or as elementary teachers. Rachel's training exclusively in middle school education is a constant backdrop for her decision-making.

Talk—both presentational, as described above, and exploratory (Barnes, 1992)—is another important part of Rachel's background and pedagogy. The exploratory talk takes place in large groups after read-aloud and during shared reading, in small groups and pairs when students are engaged in literature groups or reading with partners, and in reading and writing conferences with their teacher. Inner speech (Vygotsky, 1986) is the third kind of expression evident during workshop. It is self-talk written down on Post-it notes and in reading journals, encouraging metacognition.

Finally, the availability of text on different levels, in different genres, and on different topics is part of Rachel's strategic plan for teaching language arts, and is crucial to the reading and writing workshop environment. Experience with different kinds of text builds vocabulary and expands readers' models of what reading is.

Text, Text, Everywhere; You Cannot Help But Read

The students write much of the text on the walls of this room and just outside of it. You can spot student-made posters, puppet plays, card games, and a bulletin board of word strips filled with words students have found in their reading. The "word warrior" is one of the classroom jobs for which students can apply, along with librarian, line leader, etc. The job description for word warrior includes putting sentence strips on the bulletin board to display students' chosen words, their definitions, and where the contributor found the special word, including the name of the text and the page number. The 5th-graders then strive to use these words in their writing—"and they *do*, especially if it's *their* word," Rachel shares. The words are of a great variety ("chihuahua," "brute," "formation").

Anchor charts, which are class-made posters distilling important points from units of instruction (from poetry to punctuation), hang on the walls and from heavyweight fishing line strung diagonally across one corner of the room. Earlier in the year, a "symbolism quilt" had hung on the wall. When taken down, the "quilt squares" were placed in a folder. Rachel covered symbolism before the class embarked on the yearlong poetry unit. From one square, she reads: "My symbol is a drum. A drum represents me in three different ways. I'm loud, I don't wait, and I'm noise. I pound for my goals and sometimes reach them. I'm hard-core at my friend's house on video games, just like a drum is hard. That's my paragraph." She concludes, "So, that's Leon." When I queried whether she thought exploring symbolism helped them in writing poetry, she answered, "You know, we talked about those things and I think it did pay off in their poetry. I think it did. They said some pretty deep things." Another result is that six of her students' poems will be published as finalists in a poetry contest that the students entered. One boy in the class, a selective mute, found a voice in poetry. His poem was among the six selected to be published. It begins,

> *"I don't like to talk.*
> *Do you?*
> *They try to make me talk.*
> *Would you?"*

Some of the text on the walls and bulletin boards represent anchor strategy lessons, ones that Rachel and the class refer to over and over, that were introduced during reading and writing workshop. A poem on the back bulletin board about Rosa Parks prompted a discussion about not letting little things get in your way or letting others define you. A quote from Mark Twain, one that draws attention to those who can read but don't, inspired a discussion on reading challenging books and identifying comfort books. A class-generated list of ways to respond to a book provides options for students whenever they finish a book, either in literature group or independently.

Books are everywhere in the room, but the 5th-grader librarian has charge of a tall bookshelf in the corner. The librarian sorts the class library into genres, fiction, nonfiction, and special topics (e.g., Egypt). Egypt is a topic that Rachel knows well, having taught about it and the other African nations for nine years as part of the 6th-grade curriculum. Now, she is glad that she has this collection for another reason. One of her students, Yonne, is a fairly recent immigrant from Nairobi, Kenya. Yonne has been at this school for two years now, but she "misses her home [and] her grandma" and likes to look at these books and other materials that Rachel has brought in. "She writes about it a lot," is the teacher's closing thought.

The books and articles about Africa in the library are nonfiction. Other nonfiction books in the classroom, and a notable collection of books connecting to the social studies curriculum, are available on another bookshelf. Rachel uses these texts to help the students "learn to talk about" and write nonfiction. Social studies is her area of expertise, having taught it to 140+ sixth-graders every year for nine years. Again, one can see the connection between background, beliefs, and pedagogy.

Why Depth and Breadth of Text Are Important

Rosenblatt (1996) invites us to consider reading from an aesthetic and an efferent stance. Different texts may be read for different purposes. Harvey and Goudvis (2000) also note that to become reflective, strategic readers, students must have access to the different kinds of text that invite different strategy use. Allington (2006) emphasizes that "kids need books that they can read" (p. 57). Calkins (2000), Atwell (1987), and others in the field stress the importance of choice and teachers knowing early in the year their students' topical interests and preferences for format. These findings reflect the need to prepare students to be habitual readers of a variety of texts in order to become lifelong learners.

First and foremost, readers need to have that joyful experience of being captivated by the written word. Beers (2003) cautions that just because we, as adult readers, are enthralled by Robert

Cormier's (1974) *The Chocolate Wars* or Walter Dean Myers' (1988) *Fallen Angels,* individual students may not find those texts engaging, for a variety of reasons. In her work with 6th- through 12th-graders who were not engaged as readers, Beers has learned to look for these attributes in fictional text: thin books, short chapters, ample white space, illustrations, well-defined characters, action in the plot that begins immediately, characters close to the readers' ages who face tough choices in an easily defined conflict, and realistic language. Important aspects of nonfiction works include visual features, two-page spreads, differing formats (like magazines, newspapers, Web sites, and instruction manuals), vocabulary defined at point of use, bold print, headings, and high-interest topics. Circling back to Rosenblatt, the reader and the reader's interests are central to the reading process, whether the text is long or short, fiction or nonfiction.

Connecting Language Arts and Content Area Learning

"Ms. Mazzocco, did you know that Ben Franklin invented *'flippers'*? What would make a person invent *'flippers'*?" Rachel had to admit, that, no, she didn't realize that Franklin had applied his ingenuity to aid human swimmers' abilities in this way, and continued the conversation with Leon by telling him a little bit more about Benjamin Franklin. She knew that Franklin had grown up near the ocean, that his mother's family had been whalers on Martha's Vineyard. Maybe these facts would give Leon a clue as to why Franklin had seen a need for such an invention. It became commonplace for students to ask Rachel and each other questions that began with "Did you know that . . . ?" The explanation for these new kinds of questions lay in the application of reading and writing workshop to the social studies topic of study—for example, the Revolutionary War.

The prereading activity is a shared reading from the social studies text, during which Rachel stops and talks quite often. She finds that the social studies text leaves out information. It is an older edition (from 1983), and she quite often needs to make revisions as she reads, such as "Native Americans" for "Indians." She talks about the Freedom Trail in Boston, and finds "virtual tours" on the Internet.

With this background knowledge, the students select books on Revolutionary War subjects and form reading partnerships. With their partners, they "chunk" the book into five parts. At the conclusion of each "chunk," each pair writes a letter to Rachel, telling her about their reading. They also write questions and important facts in their social studies notebooks. Rachel explicitly taught a strategy known as "What's important? What's not?" (Harvey & Goudvis, 2000). She watches carefully to see if they can apply that strategy as they read now.

The students share what they learn by teaching a "lesson" together to the class. For this lesson's objective, Rachel requested that they choose one important thing that they want their classmates to learn from the book. As Rachel observes the students during their planning, she sees such strategies as the KWL chart (Ogle, 1986) being incorporated into lessons. The students also make word finds, crossword puzzles, and posters. The lessons are videotaped, allowing them to review and add information that may have been omitted. In this way, her students learn that teaching, like writing, involves considerable revision.

To conclude the unit, the students apply what they have learned about nonfiction texts. They select a topic from the unit on the Revolutionary War that they find particularly interesting and engaging. Then, after reviewing the features of nonfiction texts, each student tries his or her hand at writing a nonfiction book. This involves making a list of questions, researching answers, asking more questions, and then organizing their ideas into a book-like text.

The structures of reading and writing workshop become the scaffolding for content area learning. In workshop, students and teacher look at the text as a new genre with different attributes and features. The readers gradually move from learning to talk and write about fiction to learning to talk and write about nonfiction. The structures—read-aloud, shared reading, literature groups, journaling, using sticky notes to mark text, asking questions, researching, writing, revising, conferencing with peers and teacher—all successfully transfer to content area learning.

Conclusions—Not Just Mine or Ours, But Theirs

At the close of the school year, I interviewed "focus groups" from Rachel's 5th-grade class. We talked about reading and writing workshop, what kinds of things they did while in workshop, memorable projects, and what connections they could see between the learning from workshop and the learning they foresaw in their middle school futures. Excerpts from one group (Summer, Annabelle, and Benjamin—their self-selected pseudonyms) make clear that the structures and strategies learned in workshop support their learning in other areas and that they realize the connections.

Math

T: What are the most important things, do you think? Do reading and writing help you learn?

A: Yeah, of course.

T: Like how?

A: Like in math. If you're writing a summary about the problem or how you solved the problem, you have to know the steps you take first.

T: Mmhm.

A: You have to know how to describe the numbers.

S: You can't just write, "I solved the problem."

T: Oh. Okay.

A: Yeah. You have to describe the problem and the numbers you calculated or something.

T: So, is that like things you did in workshop?

A/S: Yeah.

T: Can you tell me more about that?

S: So when we're in reading workshop, it's a summary. You read a book and most of the time we have requirements, and one of them is you have to have a summary and you have to have your opinion, so summarize, you have to know how to summarize, which you have to write in math.

Social Studies

S: Well, . . . like when we did our books on the Revolutionary War in reading?

T: Mmhm.

S: We wrote about the Revolutionary War in writing, and we were studying about the Revolutionary War in social studies. It meshed.

T: So it all meshed. That's a good word.

A: But you see, sticky notes and journals help you in writing also.

T:	Okay.

A: Like when we were reading and writing nonfiction, our Revolutionary War books, we had to write down notes about what we read and make them into a paragraph or a nonfiction part of the chapter.

Science

S: Science is a process, too.

T: Like the scientific process and writing process?

S: Actually, when we write we use details in writing, that's like in science . . . and when you read fiction, you look for details.

T: Good point, because you have to be an observer.

S: It's like, okay, and when we went outside and now you have to write down what you see.

A: "I see heat waves coming up from the. . . ."

T: So, you're learning as you're reading . . . to be an observer.

S: Mmhm.

These readers also made comments reflecting their learning in reading and writing workshop and what it means to them to finish a text that they deemed "hard." Benjamin describes the reward he feels when concluding the text: "Man, it's over. I got through it." Finishing that long book encourages the students to face challenges and set goals confidently. Annabelle concluded on this topic, "It's good to be confident when you're reading and in your academic career." They've learned to synthesize while writing summaries, to take notes, to design projects, because, as Summer predicts, "knowing how to do projects will be real important" and, as Benjamin expects, they'll have to do "a lot" of writing in middle school. They know ways "to jump-start" themselves and to ask questions that they, of course, write down.

Note-taking is a topic carefully explored in the students' conversations. They all agree that doing sticky notes has been important and that it could help them in taking notes in their content area classes in the future. In their debate about the use of sticky notes, Summer proposes that "you're not going to write 'This is how I feel about algebra' on a sticky note." Annabelle thoughtfully responds, "I think they're the same in a way, though. Writing notes about what events are important in the story and how you feel about them, and in algebra, you're writing down what you feel that is needed, what's important." They agree that writing sticky notes for fiction and nonfiction are different, but that, in any case, "It helps in academics. In college, you're going to have to take a lot of notes. Like studying how to be a teacher. And how to teach children or students." In the latter comment, Annabelle hints at a future well beyond middle school, one that she feels she is preparing for even now. When I ask, "Then why do you think Rachel has you do sticky notes anyway, if it is so different from one subject to the next?" Summer answers confidently, looking at me directly, "So we can learn to listen to our inner voice." The other two nod in assent. The words Summer uses are familiar to them.

These are, as I have witnessed, the words of the Queen of Room 202. "Inner voice," Rachel shares, "does not stop. It's not there just when you're reading during workshop. We have to realize that. I want my students to learn to listen to their inner voices, no matter what they're reading or writing . . . or doing." In an interview with Nancie Atwell, Nault and Dunaway (1999) record Atwell's advice to teachers using reading and writing workshop, as follows:

Writing and reading teachers have to break through their fear of intervening—we don't have this fear in other subject areas. Our students are children. They need adults who will say, as in math, "Let me show you how I do this. Let's look at how others have done this. Show me how you do it, and I'll help." (p. 5)

Rachel is a teacher who is not afraid to intervene.

Concluding Thoughts

Language arts teaching in the middle grades needs to be purposefully strategic. Reading, writing, talking, listening, thinking, and transmediating between them are the language arts and the arts of language. In reading and writing workshop, as students apply and accomplish these cognitive arts of language, they are actually practicing and refining strategies for a lifetime of learning. The challenge consists of making the connection between the workshop structure and the ability to apply the structure to other areas of learning and life, making the lessons learned tangible and real. Intentionally extending the workshop structure to meet learning needs in such content areas as social studies, science, and math is an initial foray in response to that challenge. At this time, the use of workshop structure in content area learning may be unique and limited to a few classrooms, to a few intuitive teachers with backgrounds somewhat similar to Rachel's. It does not need to be so in the future. We encourage reading across the curriculum and writing across the curriculum, so why not workshop across the curriculum?

References

Allington, R. (2006). *What really matters for struggling readers: Designing research-based programs* (2nd ed.). Boston: Pearson Education.

Atwell, N. (1987). *In the middle: Writing, reading and learning with adolescents.* Portsmouth, NH: Boynton/Cook.

Barnes, D. (1992). *From communication to curriculum.* Portsmouth, NH: Boynton/Cook.

Beers, K. (2003). *When kids can't read: What teachers can do.* Portsmouth, NH: Heinemann.

Calkins, L. (2000). *The art of teaching reading.* Portsmouth, NH: Heinemann.

Calkins, L. (1994). *The art of teaching writing.* Portsmouth, NH: Heinemann.

Cormier, R. (1974). *The chocolate war.* New York: Dell Laurel-Leaf.

DuPrau, J. (2003). *The city of Ember.* New York: Random House.

Ehrenhaft, D. (2003). *The last dog on earth.* New York: Delacorte Books for Young Readers.

Fine, M. (1987). Silencing in public schools. *Language Arts, 64*(2), 157-174.

Five, C., & Egawa, K. (1998). Reading and writing workshop: What is it and what does it look like? *School Talk, 3*(4), 1-4.

Gilles, C. (1991). "We make an idea": Cycles of meaning in literature discussion groups. In K. M. Pierce & C. J. Gilles (Eds.), *Cycles of meaning: Exploring the potential of talk in learning communities* (pp. 199-218). Portsmouth, NH: Heinemann.

Harvey, S., & Goudvis, A. (2000). *Strategies that work: Teaching comprehension to enhance understanding.* Portsmouth, NH: Heinemann.

Myers, W. D. (1988). *Fallen angels.* New York: Scholastic.

Nault, J., & Dunaway, S. (1999). Literacy leaders speak out: Perspectives for the future. *Voices From the Middle, 7,* 2. Urbana, IL: National Council of Teachers of English.

Ogle, D. S. (1986). K-W-L group instructional strategy. In A. S. Palincsar, D. S. Ogle, B. F. Jones, & E. G. Carr (Eds.), *Teaching reading as thinking* (Teleconference Resource Guide, pp. 11-17). Alexandria, VA: Association for Supervision and Curriculum Development.

Roe, M. F. (2004). Real reading interactions: Identifying and meeting the challenges of middle level unsuccessful readers. *Childhood Education, 81,* 9-15.

Rosenblatt, L. (1996). *Literature as exploration* (5th ed.). Chicago: MLA.

Vygotsky, L. S. (1986). *Thought and language*. A. Kozulin, Ed. Boston: MIT Press.

Meet the Authors

Terre Folger has focused her research on literacy learning across grade levels in classrooms and with individual readers and writers. She is presently teaching elementary and middle grade literacy courses at both the undergraduate and graduate levels at Western Carolina University, including reading and writing in the content areas in the middle school, and is working with students and teachers at Asheville High School through an NCQuest grant. Terre also spent more than 20 years in public education as a special needs and regular classroom teacher serving children in grades K-5 in central Missouri.

Rachel Mazzocco is presently teaching language arts at Gentry Middle School in Columbia, Missouri. She has returned to a language arts middle school position after spending two years teaching 5th grade at Benton Elementary and nine years teaching social studies for 6th- and 7th-graders at Gentry Middle School. She graduated from the University of Missouri-Columbia with a B.S. in Education, certified K-9, and received her master's degree through the Education Fellows Program from UMC in 1997. Rachel is an avid reader of adolescent literature and one of her goals is to share her lifelong love of reading with her students. She also shares her teaching methods and strategies with other teachers in her district through ongoing professional development.

Part III

Literacies for Specific Content Disciplines

Chapter 4

Literacy Learning and an Inquiry Curriculum in

Jeff's Middle School
Social Studies Classroom

I n the context of middle school social studies, teachers can approach literacy learning in countless ways. Direct instruction on the use of literacy strategies is one such way. The benefit of this practice is that teachers explicitly address the importance of literacy in connection to the content under study. Students have the opportunity to acquire multiple ways to comprehend and utilize the materials used in the classroom, while also addressing the curriculum requirements. Explicit instruction is one of the best ways to address literacy learning in any content classroom; thus, we would be the last people to fault such a practice. We do, however, find that other ways to promote literacy learning in middle school social studies might produce more involvement.

Through an inquiry curriculum that highlights students' questions, we find that students actively pursue and utilize literacy strategies while also attending to social studies content. One such example of inquiry in a social studies classroom was Jeff's unit on discrimination, which he wanted to pursue during Black History Month. A teacher in a large, predominantly white, middle class, suburban school in Cincinnati, Ohio, Jeff recognized that his students were not as aware of issues of diversity and discrimination as he would like them to be. In the following vignette, we highlight what Jeff did in his middle school social studies classes to address these issues.

Social Studies Vignette

"It's no wonder that many middle school students greet the month of February with assorted grunts and groans," Jeff explained. "They have heard the history and achievements of these few representatives of black history and culture ad nauseam since elementary school." Jeff believes that, too often, instruction addressing Black History Month remains within the "safe" topics of the Civil Rights movement or the Underground Railroad, or such recognizable black leaders as Martin Luther King, Jr., Rosa Parks, or Harriet Tubman. Relying on only these few examples limits African American history to issues of slavery or protest, with no connection to the issues and policies that caused these conditions.

Jeff wanted to mix it up a bit and push his students to think more deeply about the social, economic, and political aspects of discrimination against people of color. Furthermore, he wanted his students to think about how individuals as well as groups of people are discriminated against, along with how discrimination can be initiated by individuals or whole groups. He wanted his students to think about such individuals as Malcolm X or Muhammad Ali, who were targeted as problematic and viewed as

Holly Johnson and Jeff Hoffman

representations of "elements" within society that needed to be controlled. Jeff also wanted his students to pursue their own ideas about discrimination and how actions have the capability of both limiting and expanding opportunity for particular groups or individuals. In his inquiry unit, students became active participants and avid consumers of literacy strategies to address their interests under the umbrella concept of discrimination. Jeff explained his plan for initiating his study on discrimination:

> As a new person in the building, I found, when I asked the other teachers about the topic, that discrimination was generally glossed over in simple discussion. At best, discrimination was something these students had heard of, but to a certain extent had no great grasp of. What does it mean? How does it occur? What are the causes? What are the consequences? Is it inevitable in society? These were the questions I wanted to address, but I also knew that my students might have questions or ideas I had not thought about. More than anything, I wanted to be certain I approached the subject tactfully and did not sound too preachy or, perhaps worse, cavalier. The best means to approach this complex and perhaps touchy subject, in my opinion, was through inquiry-based instruction.
>
> Seeking advice from my mentor teacher, the team language arts teacher, I explained that I had this unique idea for a discrepant event to begin the unit [an event that causes students cognitive dissonance]. I planned to set up a hypothetical discrimination situation within the classroom to give our group of students—almost entirely middle-class suburban white kids—a sense of the dynamics of discrimination and how it is established. I wanted the students to have a chance to emotionally feel it, while also making sure this simulation was done under very controlled circumstances. As is the case with most ostensibly original ideas, my colleague told me that this type of simulation had, in fact, been done before. She then introduced me to Jane Elliott's famous and controversial blue eyes/brown eyes lesson from the 1960s.
>
> Rather than re-create the wheel, we decided that we would simply introduce our students to Elliott's lesson. This was done by showing them a PBS Frontline documentary (www.janeelliott.com) that told Elliott's story and showed the lesson as it was being taught in the classroom to a group of 3rd-graders. I also wanted to introduce our own bogus discrimination scenario within the classroom to allow the students to witness and feel the problems it causes. Knowing how controversial Elliott's lesson was and its probable impact on our own students, the next question to address was in what order to unveil Elliott's lesson to the students: Show the documentary first or blindside them with my own scenario? Since I was new to the building, and certainly didn't want to jeopardize the employment or reputation of myself or my colleague, I somewhat cowardly opted to show the students the documentary first. Astonishingly, it did not matter.
>
> After the students watched the Frontline documentary, we debriefed. I placed them in content area literature circles (described below) and asked them about what took place in the film, using a series of prompts similar to those listed in the content area literature circle section. I then asked them to theorize about why a group of otherwise well-behaved students would turn into a crew of monsters with the simple introduction of a bogus discriminatory plan. Jane Elliott's experiment with her classroom clearly showed the disastrous effects of discrimination and how quickly it eroded her entire class. My students easily made this connection. I then asked them if they felt they would succumb to

this type of hypothetical scenario if it were created in their own classroom. My query was greeted with amused laughter and skeptical comments, such as, "How could we possibly fall for that after seeing this film, Mr. Hoffman?"

That is when I presented my own scenario. I had fabricated a journal article (Figure 1.1), using Adobe Photoshop, that reported new reliable data from a major university stating that brown-haired people were intellectually superior to blonds (thinking on my feet, I suggested to the class that redheads and all other hair colors were just mutant strains of the brunette race and probably as dim-witted as blonds). The students bought into the ploy simply because it came from a seemingly reliable source. Everyone knows that the printed word is always the truth, especially if it is supported by information from a Ph.D. from UCLA!

From a very early age, we have been conditioned to buy into most of what we see and hear. As a teacher, I was aghast at how easily my students bought into my scheme, yet delighted at the fun I knew I was going to have teaching these kids the remainder of the unit. When I later revealed to the class that I created the article, I could see in their faces the realization that they had all learned a great deal that day that transcended this discrepant event.

After their experience, my students excitedly brainstormed areas of interest and questions they wanted answered in connection to discrimination. We talked about racial and ethnic barriers, gender, and social conditions. We transcended the particular eras of the Civil Rights and Underground Railroad movements to include Jim Crow and school desegregation. We thought about the de facto segregation of schooling and housing in current-day America. We talked about popular views on miscegenation and immigration in the past and today. And from there, our inquiries took off! It was now my job to find materials that addressed their questions, and to teach mini-lessons that pertained to particular content and material comprehension.

I must admit that the rest of the unit on discrimination practically taught itself. Yes, I added mini-lessons about literacy strategies to help with their research, their data collection, their burgeoning thoughts and theories, and the ways to publish their findings, but I was practically led by my students and their need to know and to understand. Through inquiry on discrimination, I was able to add to my students' understandings about particular social, political, and economic issues related to the discrimination of people of color throughout U.S. history, while also being sure they utilized great literacy strategies to help with the process.

Figure 4.1
Jeff's Fabricated Research Article

From Jeff's description, it is obvious that such provocative content can produce interest and engagement in the social studies from most middle level students. Is it their age? Their developmental level? Or, is it their desire to know that provokes such interest? Perhaps it is all these. We suggest, however, that a curricular design that allows middle grade students to bring themselves into the social studies classroom may also help arouse their enthusiasm. It may be that inquiry and a workshop environment that allows students to work at their own pace and in their own ways creates such positive activity—and such democratic fervor—in students at the middle level.

In the rest of this chapter, we discuss inquiry as a curricular design well-suited for middle level social studies classrooms. We also discuss general learning invitations that enhance such a design and particular literacy strategies that Jeff used, as well as others that we propose, that advance the literacy development of young people on the verge of participatory social action and awareness.

Inquiry in the Social Studies Classroom

Inquiry as a curricular frame places the learner, rather than the teacher, as central to the learning process. Learners construct or build their own knowledge by focusing on aspects of the larger concept or topic under study that may interest them. They often begin with a question about the topic; with the guidance of the teacher, peers, community members, or experts within the field, they explore numerous sources about this topic until they gain greater understanding or knowledge, or until time constraints necessitate they bring their inquiry to a close.

Utilizing the Gradual Release of Responsibility (GRR) model (Pearson & Gallagher, 1983), which we describe below, teachers scaffold their students' burgeoning independence by introducing, and guiding students through, a continuous cycle of literacy strategies that will help students learn how to learn and produce a product that can articulate what they have learned in their studies. By producing an environment that allows students to wonder and wander or collect and connect information, teachers strengthen their students' abilities to use both literacy and content knowledge. In essence, an inquiry framework provides a variety of learning engagements that foster the development of students as strategic learners (Freedman & Johnson, 2004). Inquiry also becomes the impetus for utilizing reading and writing as tools for learning and for comprehending what students are discovering. In Jeff's classroom, students used a variety of reading, writing, and viewing activities to explore their particular interests under his larger topic of discrimination. Short, Harste, and Burke (1996) suggest that, "Instructionally, curriculum as inquiry means that instead of using the theme as an excuse to teach science, social studies, mathematics, reading, and writing, these knowledge systems and sign systems become tools for exploring, finding, and researching student questions" (p. 261).

Through his use of an inquiry curriculum, Jeff allowed his students to *pose* questions and problems rather than merely answering and/or solving them. For instance, one area of history that often is not addressed in classrooms is the treatment of African Americans during the era known as Jim Crow. A small group of students posed a question about this time period between the Civil War and civil rights, and they were encouraged to explore the topic of Jim Crow because it would naturally fall under Jeff's umbrella concept of discrimination. Other areas of interest as expressed by the students included women's suffrage, treatment of the mentally handicapped, immigration laws, and anti-Semitism. Students had the freedom to explore particular people or small incidents within the history of the world, while Jeff concentrated on mini-lessons that would teach his students literacy strategies to enhance their research. Jeff also was able to address content that he wanted his students to learn that was not being covered by small-group inquiries, such as Japanese internment camps and school-funding practices.

Receiving encouragement and interest from the teacher, and from their peers, motivates students to seek—collaboratively or individually—better understandings of the concepts under study. These understandings often lead to more questions and more critical engagements. Through inquiry, young adolescents move through a variety of learning stances and perspectives as they reach out beyond textbooks and beyond teachers as the "transmitters" of knowledge. This approach differs from traditional schooling practices that suggest students are passive receivers of their teacher's knowledge.

The Inquiry Cycle

An inquiry curriculum typically appears as a cycle that facilitates individual, small-group, or entire-class exploration of a particular topic or question. Regardless of how the teacher may decide to group students for inquiry, the students still have opportunities to work individually, share with a small group, and publish their work for a larger audience. Figure 4.2 is the model we use when discussing inquiry.

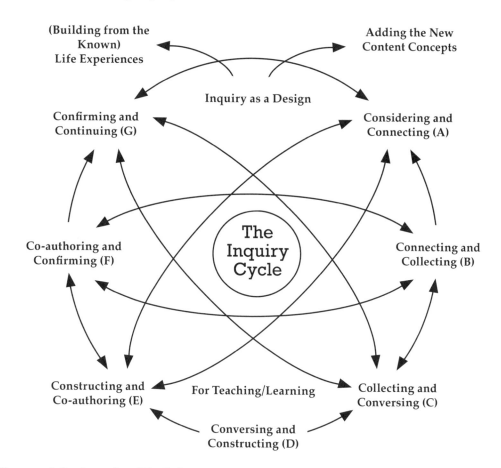

Figure 4.2. Inquiry Model
From Freedman, L., & Johnson, H. (2004). *Inquiry, literacy, and learning in the middle grades.* Norwood, MA: Christopher-Gordon. (p. xvii)

The arrows that point from various stages or phases of the cycle to other phases suggest that the inquiry cycle accommodates movement from all areas of the cycle, and that phases do not have to be completed in a lockstep manner. There are times when we have done our own inquiries and found ourselves "backing up" to a stage we thought we had already completed, only to find out that we need to do more research or that we need to discuss our new understandings or thoughts with others when we just did that the day before. Similarly, we have come to realize that once students are engaged in a question or a topic of interest, they don't stop thinking about it once they have done so for 50 minutes during class time. They stop in the hall between classes to discuss their new ideas, or they go to the library after school. They talk to their parents about what they are learning and surf the Internet to deepen their understandings. They may appear to be doing all the phases of inquiry simultaneously.

Thus, when we show a model of the inquiry cycle with all its phases and arrows, we are only suggesting a cycle with typical stages or phases that most inquirers pass through while learning. To revisit a stage or to jump ahead to another phase may be the way individual learners think and learn. We show this model because it represents all the various stages of inquiry learning. Inquiry provides conditions for students to engage in sustained learning in content learning, which, in turn, requires literacy and literacy development. Additionally, students' literacy development requires the retention and application of strategies that will allow students to learn with increasing independence. All human beings pose questions and problems, investigate possible answers and solutions, search among related and sometimes contradictory resources, and determine what is accurate, what is true, and what is meaningful. As the model shows, the following phases are part of an inquiry framework, which allows for content acquisition, learning independence, and literacy development:

- **Building From the Known/Adding New Content Concepts:** Regardless of what teachers want their students to know, they know the best way to address new concepts is to build from students' prior knowledge. For instance, just after leading students through a discrepant event, which is an event that causes students cognitive dissonance, the teacher explains the concept of cognitive dissonance and then leads students into thinking about other events that would fall under the category addressed through the exercise (in Jeff's example, types of discrimination).
- **Considering and Connecting:** This phase allows students to pose questions and connect to their interests. Typically, this is done through classroom brainstorming and question generation. In Jeff's example, he used a discrepant event to generate thinking and topics of interest in discrimination. Students then pose questions about their interests.
- **Connecting and Collecting:** This phase allows students to begin reading and researching their interests through the use of a variety of materials.
- **Collecting and Conversing:** This phase is usually accomplished through discussion with peers who may be working on a similar topic. It is an informal sharing of what is being learned, as well as a time to ask for guidance and response.
- **Conversing and Constructing:** New concerns or venues for research may surface after informal sharing. Students go back to their topic to deepen their understandings, to clarify their thinking, or to strengthen their research for the consumption of others.
- **Constructing and Co-authoring:** Students publish current understandings through presentations, brochures, poetry, drama, or innovative forms of presentation. It is con-

sidered "co-authoring" because the audience also constructs meaning from the published work.

- **Co-authoring and Confirming:** Assessment and reflection of the inquiry follows, which often depend on the teacher's purpose. Typically, students are asked to do self-reflection on their finished product. This is then combined with peer response and teacher evaluation. The finished product is only part of the student's grade, however. Teachers can ask students to show their understandings and accomplishments from work completed throughout the inquiry cycle.
- **Confirming and Continuing:** Addressing assessments and reflections, making decisions about "where to go from here," ultimately occurs. Decisions can include continuing this inquiry, addressing another question or topic, or moving on to another type of learning.

To facilitate learning, teachers know that content (the facts and knowledge required from the content area) and process (the "how" of student learning or presentation of their learning) must be intertwined. A responsive middle level curriculum and instructional framework integrates the work of the classroom with the needs of the students and the concepts and ideas under study (Arnold, 1993), and an inquiry curriculum allows for both. Figure 4.3 is a visual overview of the connections between middle level students' development, an inquiry framework, and literacy uses.

From our own experiences with inquiry in content knowledge acquisition, we know that an inquiry curriculum creates more engaged, active learners. An inquiry curriculum allows young people to develop as lifelong learners who appreciate the social studies and understand the importance of the historical, political, economic, social, and geographical elements of our world. To create a classroom ready to utilize inquiry, however, we advocate use of the following classroom invitations and learning conditions.

Classroom Invitations for Inquiry-Based Social Studies

Classrooms based on inquiry support teachers' creation of learning environments in which students form networks from classroom materials, the knowledge base within the classroom, and the extensive resources available to them throughout the community (Freedman & Johnson, 2004). Such environments and networks, however, need particular classroom invitations that can produce independence as well as social connections. Four such classroom invitations (or instructional engagements) are:

- The Gradual Release of Responsibility Model of Teaching
- The Development of Critical Literacy, Thinking, and Awareness
- A Workshop Model of Learning
- Content Area Literature Circles.

Each of these classroom elements has the potential to help students take ownership of their own learning and knowledge acquisition.

Gradual Release of Responsibility. In the Gradual Release of Responsibility (GRR) model, the teacher scaffolds knowledge at a pace that fits students' abilities to take ownership of their

Early Adolescence	Inquiry	Literacy
Range of intellectual development	Addresses students' interests, prior knowledge, and backgrounds	Uses a variety of materials for multiple purposes across a range of levels
Moving from concrete to abstract thinking	Scaffolds knowledge from concrete to abstract while providing opportunities for exploration and discovery	Connects abstractions to concrete examples and shifts between simple and complex engagements
Inquisitive	Poses questions and problems	Provides tools for seeking solutions and answers across multiple sources for multiple purposes
Active	Engages and develops self-direction	Sets focus for reading and writing
Social	Collaborates within a community of learners	Shares genres/formats for presenting ideas, resources, strategies, and findings
Focus on Reality and Intertextual Connections	Investigates real-world issues and concepts through use of technology and other resources	Develops comfort with a variety of formats and manners to publish findings
Emotional	Encourages personal connections	Records and shares personal responses
Capacity for Seeing Diverse Perspectives	Views concepts from multiple perspectives, which allows for critical thinking and appreciation of diversity	Uses multiple materials to cover same concept or topic with differing points of view that enhances critical thinking
Focus on Freedom and Equity	Produces a democratic community with a focus on values and ethical choices	Uses GRR of learning strategies, with the potential to choose materials for authentic purposes
Need for Outlets for Energy Release, Variety, and Choice	Enhances the flow of purposeful activity	Uses a variety of literacy strategies and activities
Strive for Independence	Uses a variety of assessments and the creation of responsibility for quality work	Provides self evaluation and assessments of literacy use
Experiment With Identity	Fills a variety of roles within the process	Creates opportunities to experiment with voice and point of view
Need Recognition	Shares knowledge, understandings, and expertise to gain recognition for quality work	Uses expressive language arts processes to be heard and acknowledged

Figure 4.3. Connections
From Freedman, L., & Johnson, H. (2004). *Inquiry, literacy, and learning in the middle grades.* Norwood, MA: Christopher-Gordon. (p. 4)

learning. Often, curricular mandates pressure teachers to cover material rather than teach their students the concepts they want their students to know and understand. The GRR model addresses students' prior knowledge, the concept load of what is to be learned, and assessments that allow the teacher to tailor lessons so that students can become responsible for the content when they are confident of their understandings and learning processes.

For instance, on his unit about discrimination, Jeff did not allow his students to approach their small-group inquiries without his help. He taught mini-lessons that explicitly demonstrated how to assess the authenticity and accuracy of a resource. He performed "think alouds" (described in the strategy section) on some of the essays or articles his students read, to share how he thought about and questioned the reading he was doing. At other times, Jeff would guide a small group through a more complex website so that they could negotiate other websites they found in their research. He also taught them how to cite the materials they were using in their inquiries. He did not do this only once, but rather repeated this lesson a number of times throughout the unit until his students could do it for themselves. When Jeff heard students saying that they knew how to do what was expected of them, he "released" that responsibility to them. Quite often, the GRR has to do with the process of learning, not the content itself. Once his students knew the process, Jeff realized that they would be able to transfer that strategy or skill to another topic in the future with just a short review.

Critical Literacy, Critical Thinking, and Critical Awareness. Critical literacy involves the questioning of power and the various ways that individuals and groups may privilege one group, individual, idea, or way of living over others. Critical awareness pertains to understanding the language and descriptions used to privilege one idea over another, one group over another, one way of living over another. Critical awareness is created from a questioning stance that is also willing to entertain multiple perspectives. We discuss this type of awareness and literacy with young people by using adolescent literature, which codifies ways of living that young people find engaging and relevant. We also use discussion to address the ways that people are represented through characterization, the language used to talk about or describe those characters, and how fiction and reality mirror or conflict with each other (Johnson & Freedman, 2005b). In the social studies, novels and informational texts can be used to address issues of power, representation, oppression, privilege, and, as Jeff did, discrimination. We assert that while discrimination would be a great unit through which to address critical awareness, critical awareness doesn't have to be reserved for such a complex topic. Issues of power and representation can be addressed throughout the curriculum and with the texts available for everyday use (e.g., textbooks).

People often confuse critical literacy with critical thinking skills, which is the cognitive ability to evaluate, analyze, and summarize information. Teachers can address what is also known as higher order thinking skills without ever questioning power or representation. In relation to the social studies, researchers (e.g., Rathes, Jonas, Rothstein, & Wassermann, 1967) have suggested using a more content-specific way of critical thinking about particular topics and concepts. For instance, we would think about concepts in history through the use of cause and effect and context, while thinking about economics might be more about access, supply, and demand. In geography, standards address such elements as thinking about the world in spatial terms (places and regions) or in terms of human and geographical systems. More recently, researchers have asserted that inquiry—and the more general idea of thinking through wondering and questioning inspired by the use of discrepant events—can be used with the skills of critical thinking, such as evaluation, synthesis, application, and inference (Freedman & Johnson, 2004; Short, Harste, & Burke, 1996). Kuhn (1999) asserts that critical thinking encompasses the developmental, cognitive, and metacognitive domains.

By combining these definitions, we find that critical thinking becomes a "habit of mind" (Meier, 1996), which allows for multiple ways of knowing about a particular topic and about the divergent ways different content areas define what knowledge is. Habits of mind encourage students to develop problem-solving and thinking skills that address the following aspects of any situation, problem, or issue:

- **Cause and Effect/Connections:** How did this happen? How is this connected to other things?
- **Point of View/Perspective:** Who is telling/writing this? What other perspectives are there?
- **Evidence:** What are the facts? Where did these facts come from?
- **Suppose:** Wondering about "what if" questions, such as, "What if the community agrees to build an airport?" "What if the school decides that students must wear uniforms?"
- **Debate:** Asking such questions as "So what?," "Who cares?," and "What difference does it make?"

By asking middle level students to become critical thinkers through the use of a "habits of mind" curriculum, teachers ensure that they learn specific content knowledge, while also providing the opportunity for them to become critically aware.

Essential elements of an inquiry curriculum include critical thinking, critical awareness, and critical literacy. By asking students to ask questions (question posing), evaluate the texts they use from various perspectives, and make connections to their lives and to the world, they help students use critical thinking to comprehend the text. In essence, inquiry, along with critical literacy, must involve a question-posing stance, whereby adolescents ponder what is and what isn't revealed within the texts they read and the information they are learning. They also learn to delve more deeply into the text they are reading or viewing. For instance, one group of students studying U.S. history examined the lives of African American women in the Reconstruction era. Using different texts, they found that the lives of these women were similar, yet vastly different. The use of multiple materials allowed the students to have a deeper and broader understanding of the time period, the geographical differences involved, and the perspectives represented.

An Inquiry Workshop Model. Many language arts teachers utilize a reading/writing workshop model for student learning (Atwell, 1987). In a workshop, students work individually or in small groups to improve their reading and writing processes. The teacher facilitates student learning through mini-lessons that address student needs, interests, and specific needs in relation to reading and writing. Just as in a language arts classroom, social studies teachers can create a workshop environment that allows them to teach mini-lessons on social studies concepts, content, and processes as needed for student learning throughout the inquiry cycle. We are not suggesting that social studies teachers leave behind direct instruction entirely, but rather that they allow students more opportunity to become responsible for their learning and acquisition of the social studies content and ways of knowing.

Creating a workshop environment takes planning and resources. With an inquiry curriculum, however, much of the legwork already has been done. For instance, in a workshop, teachers need to start their year by deciding what will be studied and for how long a period of time. Thinking thematically allows for students to generate their own questions about a topic, and then they receive a time line for completion. In Jeff's unit on discrimination, students were given three weeks to work on various examples of discrimination. A workshop environment allows students the time they need to consult various sources, complete their research, and decide upon the presentation model that will suit their current understandings. During any given class period, students may be reading about their interest, discussing their interest with one or two other students, meeting in small groups to discuss their current dilemmas or new information, or planning their presentation or publication.

Many teachers wonder what their role is when students are engaged in an inquiry workshop environment. Ideally, their work should involve facilitating student learning through the teaching of processes for learning (e.g., learning mapping skills, how historians think, what geography consists of, how gross national product is determined, how an aristocracy works); working with small groups when needed; presenting mini-lessons to the entire class or small groups as needed; and managing both the materials and students. While a workshop model seems like a management problem just waiting to happen, teachers instill in their students their expectations in terms of behavior, movement, attitude, and work ethic by defining, clarifying, and modeling what is expected. Once students understand the teacher's expectations, most will behave with decorum, because they are engaged in meeting the academic goals of their groups and they have ownership in their topics. In terms of material management, teachers need to help students find books, websites, and community resources for their students' topics and provide related guidance for reading those materials.

When we think of a workshop environment, we visualize students and teachers working together in a partnership to enhance student learning and find answers to pressing questions. Along with the gradual release of responsibility model, an inquiry curriculum and a workshop environment produce students who take ownership and responsibility for their own learning. We also see teachers who are managers and guides, utilizing their expertise in the field to assist in the transfer of that ownership.

Content Area Literature Circles. Literature circles have been used in language arts classes as a way of giving students opportunities to share their "rough draft" ideas about what they are reading (Short, Harste, & Burke, 1996). Content area literature circles (CALCs) utilize the same idea but address informational texts used specifically in the content areas of math, science, and social studies (Johnson & Freedman, 2005a). Five key questions are used in content area literature circles:

- What have I learned? (Addressing main ideas, key points, and summarization skills)
- What significant language did I notice? (Addressing particular concepts and vocabulary)
- What perspectives are highlighted? (From what stance are the materials written? Addressing critical literacy and multiple perspectives)
- What questions arise for me from this selection? (Addressing question-posing and problem-posing)
- What connections can I make from this selection? (Addressing text to text, text to self, and text to world connections; making inferences and predictions)

Through the use of these prompts, students can begin to discuss elements of the texts they are reading, while also deepening their comprehension and clearing up any misconceptions they may have had. Once students know how content area literature circles work, they can generate their own types of questions and discuss the texts in ways that seem suitable to their purposes.

CALCs consist of no more than five students, who have anywhere from 7-30 minutes to discuss their readings, identify their vocabulary understandings, address topics they may wish to discuss at another time, or clarify their comprehension of a passage. We utilize CALCs in an inquiry curriculum regardless of whether students are working on individual, small-group, or whole-class inquiries. When students are working on small-group inquiries, CALCs are used to support their learning throughout each phase of the inquiry cycle. When students are working on individual or whole-class inquiries, we ask them to meet in CALCs during the more social aspects of the inquiry cycle, such as during the Collecting and Conversing stage when students are asked to share informally what they are learning or when they have questions about what they are learning. We also ask them to use CALCs during the Constructing and Co-authoring phase, which addresses how they should present their inquiries to a larger audience. During this stage, students discuss the format of the presentation or publication, the message they wish to communicate, and the role they will play in the publication or presentation.

Teachers who use content area literature circles acknowledge that learning is a social process, and that adolescents should be given the opportunity to articulate their learning. Jeff used CALCs in his discrimination unit in very specific ways. For his discrepant event lesson, he showed a video on Jane Elliott's simulation of the intellectual superiority of people who had blue eyes. Once the video was over, he asked his students to gather in CALCs to discuss this film by using the following questions:

- How did the teacher's class project affect the students in the 3rd-grade class?
- Did the teacher's project work effectively? Why or why not?
- How did this video change the way you view discrimination?
- Does anyone in class ever feel they have been discriminated against? If so, what happened and how did it make you feel?"

While we ultimately want students to ask their own questions, we use this type of questioning to scaffold student knowledge and their process of learning how to ask their own critical questions.

After the discussion time, members of the CALCs had the opportunity to share their thoughts and feelings with the class. The students were anxious to share their own personal views on the documentary and a lively, engaging discussion ensued. At the end of the discussion, the students were asked to reflect as a group on the question of what they felt would happen if a similar scenario happened to them. As Jeff explained in his vignette, his students believed they would never be duped by such a ploy, especially since they had seen the documentary and had the background information. Of course, Jeff used his blond hair simulation to surprising results.

Content area literature circles are informal ways for students to support each other's learning, assess their own comprehension, and guide each other through inquiry processes that they are attempting. Grouping students by interest, by physical location in the class, and eventually by their own selections, teachers can create a classroom community through a variety of small-group combinations. Teachers must first teach students how to discuss their learning, however, and then scaffold them as they attempt to negotiate the material they are reading or viewing, and then release them to guide each other. Through this process, teachers allow for students' needs to be social while also recognizing that all knowledge is socially constructed through discussion, presentation, reading an author's text, or writing for an audience. CALCs also allow students to become responsible for their own learning and learning processes.

Literacy Strategies Useful in the Inquiry Process

Every content area needs to be mindful of the literacy processes and strategies needed to negotiate the materials used in that content area. In social studies classrooms, students use the textbooks, trade books, journal articles, essays, maps and other visuals, letters and other primary materials to learn. Because it is such a comprehensive content area, social studies teachers should be especially mindful of the communication arts (reading, writing, viewing, listening, speaking, and visually representing through pictures, film, or other media products) and address the "how" of using these arts to acquire the content under study. The International Reading Association (IRA) and the National Middle School Association (NMSA) issued a joint statement, "Supporting Young Adolescents' Literacy Learning" (2002), which states:

> *Continuous reading instruction requires that all middle school teachers understand reading and learning processes, realize the intricate and diverse needs of young adolescents, and know how to help students develop both the competence and desire to read increasingly complex materials across the curriculum. Reading strategies and skills are central to the success of the integrated, multidisciplinary middle school curriculum, and every teacher must possess the knowledge and skills to integrate reading instruction across the curriculum.*

We have used the following literacy strategies in our social studies classrooms because they address the areas that seem to cause the most difficulty for students. Those areas are vocabulary, comprehension, and articulation of ideas through speaking or writing.

Word Walls. The word wall is a great vocabulary strategy. Word walls can be used in a variety of ways and can utilize any type of word list. For his unit on discrimination, for instance, Jeff decided to use a thematic word wall, which meant that he would use words that addressed his theme of discrimination. Other social studies content might best be listed more topically, such as the Civil War or westward expansion or the Aztecs. At other times, word walls can be used for such processes as mapping or for such themes as "Water Words" (such as inlets, marshes, and peninsulas), which Holly used with students so they could learn geography vocabulary.

It is up to the teacher to decide which words to target and how to use the word wall. Sometimes, word walls are generated solely by the teacher; at other times, students are responsible for incrementally developing the word wall vocabulary. It also can be a combination of student and teacher responsibility. Working together is advised since it allows students to gain ownership over their learning of the content under study. Some teachers might use the word wall to generate the official vocabulary students are responsible for throughout the unit of study. Other times, word walls are used as a resource for exposure only, allowing students to use the words as they discuss and write about the topic. Jeff decided to use his word wall as a resource for discrimination so that students would acquire the language through listening and speaking.

After his discrepant event introduction about brunettes and blonds, and before his launching of more complex content, Jeff asked his students to tell him what "discrimination" meant to them. He then asked the students to think of words that come to mind when they hear the word. Using a large dry erase board in the front of the classroom, Jeff wrote each of the words on the board. As the class progressed through that list of words, he asked them to give him their definitions or interpretations as well, and explain how those concepts related to discrimination. After class, Jeff copied the list of words onto cards, which were posted on one of the classroom walls as a resource. The word wall was useful for the students and for Jeff, who used some of the words interchangeably so students would have increased exposure to the words.

At the time of the word wall generation, Jeff used this brainstorming opportunity to gain a quick assessment of his students' knowledge of various aspects of discrimination and discriminatory behaviors and attitudes. Jeff was disconcerted by his students' lack of knowledge, but quickly realized that this exercise could be a great introduction to some of the more delicate aspects of the concept while also an entry to subject matter that many of his students had not thought about critically. It also signaled an alarm that he would have to move at a slower pace than he had originally planned. For the students, it served as a constant visual reference of words they would hear repeatedly over the next few weeks.

KFN Charts. Word walls allow students and teachers to address the vocabulary of a particular historical era, event in time, geographical region, governmental system, or economic process. The need for vocabulary learning is critical for real understanding of social studies content. Because the need is so great, we also find that using KFN charts is an easy way for students to monitor their own vocabulary acquisition. A KFN chart is a matrix that lists either teacher-generated or student-produced words for a specific topic or unit, as well as the columns labeled "known," "familiar with," or "new." Individual students go through the list (whether student- or teacher-generated) at the beginning of a unit or reading selection and mark whether the word and the concept is **k**nown to them, **f**amiliar to them, or **n**ew to them. Figure 4.4 shows a list of words generated for the topic of discrimination.

Students are given the words and then asked to mark their list by deciding if they could not only spell the word, but also use it in a sentence that would make sense, given the meaning of the word. If they have heard of a word, but couldn't really say what the word means, they mark the column labeled "familiar." If the word is entirely new to them, they mark the "new" column. This simple exercise helps them assess their prior knowledge about the content under study, identify word patterns, and track the language used when discussing or writing about that topic, as well as providing a guide for studying. The words that are new to them will need the most energy. The words that are familiar to them need some attention, and the words that are known to them they can use without hesitation. And while learning correct spelling is not the intent of the exercise, we find it is an additional benefit if we draw students' attention to the spelling of specific words for a unit.

Student-produced KFN charts use the same matrix, but individual students make their own lists of words that they believe should be part of a vocabulary list addressing a particular topic. Students can have very different lists, which can be shared with others so all students have the opportunity to build their content vocabulary. Student-produced lists also include "known" words, because we ask students to make sure they are including words that should be a part of

Vocabulary Word	Known	Familiar	New
Bias			
Discrimination			
Prejudice			
Jim Crow			
Privilege			
Oppression			
Dominant			
Subservient			
Suffrage			
Disenfranchised			
Marginalized			
Equality			
Equity			
Social Justice			
Quotas			
Genocide			
Internment Camps			
Concentration Camps			
Slavery			
Anti-Semitism			
Eugenics			

Figure 4.4. KFN Chart for Topic of Discrimination

the language used to discuss the topic at hand.

Using KFN throughout an inquiry cycle or unit is one way to bring the class together if students are working on individual or small-group inquiry questions. The teacher can use a mini-lesson on vocabulary that addresses some of the words on the list, or ask the students to share what they are learning in connection to the vocabulary of the topic or content. Or, small groups can meet together to discuss the language they are learning in relation to the topic; at other times, the teacher can present a mini-lesson on the content that utilizes the words specific to it. For instance, if the teacher wanted to introduce "Internment Camps," a mini-lesson on the plight of Japanese Americans during World War II would be appropriate.

The importance of vocabulary is often overlooked in many content areas. Without explicit attention to the language of the social studies per se as well as to the particular content taught in this content area, we quite often leave students still unsure of what they are learning and reading. Through the use of such vocabulary strategies as KFN charts and word walls, students have opportunities to learn the language necessary to comprehending what they learn in their social studies classrooms.

Think-Aloud in Content Area Literature Circles. Teachers can address content that students are not studying in small groups through the use of mini-lessons, movies, and short stories. After giving background knowledge of the racial strife of the Civil Rights era in connection to the discriminatory scenario his class experienced over blonds and intelligence, Jeff split his students into groups based on physical space in the classroom and asked them to read aloud "Antonio, a Negro," a short essay from the book *Building a New Land: African Americans in Colonial America* (Haskins & Benson, 2001, pp. 5-7). During the reading, members of the small groups were invited to "think aloud" about the text, the concepts it addressed, the language used, and its connection to discrimination.

By thinking aloud, readers model their thinking as they go through a text. They ask questions, wonder about concepts, make connections to other texts or their own lives, and make predictions on both the text and sentence levels. (Sentence-level predictions are based on word substitutions, omissions, or additions that a reader thinks will follow in the sentence because of how he or she uses language.) During a think-aloud session, a reader will also explore comprehension breakdowns and the fix-up strategies (strategies that will help them comprehend the text) that can be used to remedy the lack of understanding. Proficient readers often will model their thinking about a text passage for readers who struggle with comprehension. Jeff Wilhelm (2001) asserts that

> *The most powerful thing we can teach is strategic knowledge, a knowledge of procedures people use to learn, to think, to read, and to write. The most effective way to introduce students to how to use these tools is to model them in contexts of meaningful tasks and then to assist students in their own use of these strategies.* (p. 7)

Asking young people to "think aloud" in small groups lessens the pressure about comprehension ability while also allowing the readers to share their ideas with others. It is the teacher, however, who typically models "thinking aloud" for the entire classroom first. Jeff did this by asking questions about vocabulary, making references to other materials already discussed in class, and utilizing such critical thinking skills as evaluation, analysis, inference, and summarization. Thereby, Jeff shows students how they should approach the texts they read.

To use thinking aloud in content area literature circles, teachers begin by placing students in a small group. Assigning a text that addresses a particular concept, vocabulary, or process, the teacher then invites students to take turns reading one sentence and then pausing to think aloud about that sentence. Asking students to attend to the text on a sentence level introduces thinking aloud so that students aren't overwhelmed by either the material they are reading or the process of thinking aloud. Prompts posted on a bulletin board can help students remember what proficient readers "do" when they read:

- **Question the Author:** Why did the author say this or write it in this way?
- **Make Connections:** How does this connect to my life, to what I have already read, or to what I know about the world?
- **Make Inferences:** What is missing and what am I assuming about what the author is saying?
- **Make Predictions:** What is going to happen next? What do I think should come next in this passage?

- **Summarize:** What have I just read and how would I put it in my own words?
- **Evaluate:** What do I appreciate or like about this? How can I use this information? Why is this relevant to what I should be learning?
- **Target Vocabulary:** What words seem to be important for my understanding of the topic or concept? What words don't I understand?
- **Use Fix-It Strategies:** What should I do if I don't understand what I just read? Should I try reading aloud? Reading slower?

Students can perform think-alouds individually prior to meeting in small groups (Johnson & Freedman, 2005b). The students read silently before meeting with their content area literature circle and write down: 1) the title of the text, 2) why they were reading it, and 3) three thoughts that came to them during their reading that they can share in their literature circles. These thoughts are connected to the prompts listed above so they can become aware of their thinking during reading. After meeting with their content area literature circles, they write down three ideas they learned from others. They conclude the exercise by writing down how discussion helped them understand the content, topic, or concept.

Through the use of such think-aloud sessions, students come to understand the importance of comprehending the material they are reading and recognizing how proficient readers are always thinking during reading. Reading is not merely scanning over the words, but actually attending to what the author is attempting to communicate or share.

Reflective Writing/Quick Writes. After the use of the fabricated article on brunettes and blonds that Jeff used as a discrepant event to start his unit on discrimination, he held a mini-lesson on reflective writing. Students had begun to think about their own ideas of discrimination, so he knew they would have more to share in terms of historical events and authentic examples. Reminding them of the event that launched the unit, Jeff began the lesson by asking his students to comment and reflect upon how they felt when they thought they were being discriminated against because they were blond, or how they felt when notified that they were intellectually superior because they were a brunette. He asked them to ponder what transpired in the classroom when they thought the article was authentic. He then transitioned to a quick-write activity based upon the prompt, "Reflect upon an experience you have had outside the classroom." A quick write is a short piece done on the spur of the moment, and it is not expected to be perfectly organized or used for publication. It is a writing to think activity that allows students the opportunity to work through some of their thinking by seeing it in print.

Before the students began to write their own reflections, Jeff read them a short personal narrative he had written on his own experience with discrimination. The narrative he wrote dealt with a black housekeeper who worked for his grandparents when he was a young child and the feelings he had about her treatment and his participation in that situation. This use of modeling gave the students an opportunity to see their teacher engaged in the writing process and to hear a personal reflection on discrimination. This wasn't just a subject that Jeff was teaching—it was a concept about which he felt strongly and that had affected him as a young person.

After reading his short personal narrative, Jeff's students did a quick write on their own thinking of discrimination, utilizing everything they had learned up to that point, and relating this new knowledge to their own lives. Jeff explained that they would not have to share this writing with the rest of the class, so they should use the opportunity to really take a look at themselves and at the essence of discrimination.

The quick-write reflective essay accomplished two objectives. It created a personal connection to the topic of discrimination and it also created the relevance to discrimination that, up until that time, his students may not have felt outside of the simulation. In this exercise, Jeff hoped to make discrimination a reality that existed in their lives outside the classroom. The whole experience took about 20 minutes. The students wrote for five minutes and then those who wished to do so shared what they had written. Since sharing was not the purpose of the writing, it was not crucial that students participated in this part of the lesson. Jeff collected the papers and commented later to students on an individual basis.

Social studies is a content area that often goes unrecognized in relation to the relevance of all our lives. The use of quick writes in social studies creates relevance, produces reflection, monitors comprehension, and builds personal connections to the topic studied. Jeff believed that taking 20 minutes to write about and discuss what students were thinking was time well spent.

Using a Writing Marathon. One of the final lessons Jeff used in his unit on discrimination was a series of visual and auditory prompts that were meant to serve as a catalyst for the students to create their own longer pieces of writing. In this "Writing Marathon" (Hoffman, 2005), students transferred the writing process from their language arts classroom to their social studies inquiries on discrimination to produce reflective essays.

To begin, students were given approximately 15 minutes to write freely on several prompts that Jeff gave them (including photographs and the song "Imagine" by John Lennon). At the end of the class session, the students selected one of the three prompts to serve as a draft for a more polished piece of writing. The students were given time in class for the rest of the unit to bring the piece to publication. A myriad of student ideas resulted that demonstrated just how differently the students reacted to and absorbed the subject matter from the unit. These ideas were posted on one of the classroom bulletin boards in a gallery technique, and students were given time to check out the pieces so that each student read at least three other pieces from their classmates. The next time Jeff does this unit, he could invite students to create images or select a piece of music for one of their classmates' writings, thus incorporating other sign systems (such as music, drawing, or dance) of the students' choice into the unit.

The writing process has a place across the curriculum, and students should be given the opportunity to use writing in connection to their learning of the social studies. While Jeff used writing as a way of reflecting upon the content, he used another strategy to allow students to produce pieces of writing that included more informational text.

Guided Note-Taking and Summarization. Another type of writing that can be used in all social studies classrooms is note-taking and summarization. During one class session, Jeff gave students the opportunity to witness various forms of discrimination by showing them movie clips from various films (*Birth of a Nation, Remember the Titans, Hairspray, American History X, Malcolm X,* and *Do the Right Thing*). The students took notes and wrote down any forms of discrimination that they saw in the movie clips. Before showing any of the clips, however, Jeff again modeled his own note-taking by doing a modified "think aloud" with the students, using a selection from *Birth of a Nation.* Students got a better idea of what to look for because he modeled this strategy. Jeff stopped the video clips at various times and asked "why do you suppose" and "what if" questions to generate deeper thought. Once Jeff finished his modeling, students were invited to do the same with a second film clip. At the end of the second clip, students shared some of their responses and gave feedback on their peers' responses as well.

The second time Jeff showed video clips, he scaffolded his students' learning by giving them a viewing guide with several questions and prompts on it. These included:

- Why do you suppose . . .
- What if . . .
- Who decides what gets done and how?
- Who is seen as "lesser than" in this clip?
- How is power used in this interaction?
- In what ways are people classified, labeled, or defined in this selection?

Jeff also asked his students to reflect upon the video clips and these questions by writing a brief summary of their responses to the video. They then were asked to go deeper by writing about their thoughts concerning their current understandings of discrimination and its connection to their everyday and academic experiences.

Through guided note-taking, students learn an important life skill. Holly is frequently surprised by the number of students in her education courses who express their anger over not having learned how to take notes in their middle or high school classes. Knowing how to take and organize notes is critical for all students, and can be taught in multiple ways with graphic organizers that either prompt students or outline the information needed to develop a keener understanding of the content under study. With topics that interest them, note-taking is not seen as empty or irrelevant "busy" work, but rather as a beneficial way to manage information.

Graphic Organizers. Graphic organizers are visual representations of content learned. They can address vocabulary, key concepts, such processes as cause and effect, or related information. Semantic maps, one type of organizer, allow students to connect the content they are learning by beginning with the main idea and then adding correlated information and subtopics to it. Concept ladders ask students to organize content in a similar manner by building from either smaller ideas to a main concept, or by taking the larger concept and showing how other, smaller, concepts are subsumed under the topic. Students can use a pyramid diagram by starting with a concept or idea and building information about the topic by adding increasingly detailed layers to the broad foundation.

Note-taking structures, flow charts, and story maps are also graphic organizers. Depending on the teacher's purpose, a number of ways exist for students to use their imaginations to show how information is organized and connected. Jeff used semantic maps with his students that asked them to place "discrimination" in the center of a piece of unlined paper. He then asked them to brainstorm the subtopics that might be connected to this umbrella concept. Students came up with "types of," "language of," "incidents of," "locations of," "policies of," and "fighters of." From these beginnings, students worked in small groups to flesh out the map. At the end of the exercise, small groups displayed their maps on the wall outside their classrooms.

Using graphic organizers allows students to deepen their comprehension of the content while also seeing the connections among the information they are learning. We strongly advocate the use of graphic organizers for most social studies content, but especially so for new or complex concepts with which students are unfamiliar. Beginning by working on organizers partially filled in by the teacher, students eventually will be able to fill in empty organizers and then create their own.

Social studies is a rich content area that addresses a growing amount of information. The use of the above strategies, however, will give students the opportunity to learn this complex information in engaging and organized ways.

Concluding Remarks

The social studies is a content area that can be engaging for any young adolescent. When young people have the opportunity to engage in their own questions while also building their individual repertoires of literacy strategies, they are also creating a foundation for a promising future as well as current academic performance. An inquiry curriculum also allows teachers to address the content they want their students to learn through mini-lessons that connect the larger concept to the smaller examples the students are investigating.

Through the use of an inquiry curriculum, a classroom design based on the reading/writing workshop model, student choice and interest, heterogeneous groupings, and learning invitations (like content area literature circles and critical literacy development), middle level students have the potential to move beyond the role of "student" to become citizens. As teachers create learning environments that enhance student passion, interest, and content acquisition, they also expand the promise of tomorrow.

References

Arnold, J. (1993). Toward a middle level curriculum rich with meaning. In T. Dickinson (Ed.), *Readings in middle school curriculum: A continuing conversation* (pp. 7-23). Columbus, OH: National Middle School Association.

Atwell, N. (1987). *In the middle: Writing, reading, and learning with adolescents.* Upper Montclair, NJ: Boynton Cook.

Freedman, L., & Johnson, H. (2004). *Inquiry, literacy, and learning in the middle grades.* Norwood, MA: Christopher-Gordon Publishers.

Haskins, J., & Benson, K. (2001). *Building a new land: African Americans in colonial America.* New York: HarperCollins.

Hoffman, J. (2005). Marathon writing. Unpublished strategy.

Johnson, H., & Freedman, L. (2005a). *Content area literature circles: Using discussion for learning across the curriculum.* Norwood, MA: Christopher-Gordon Publishers.

Johnson, H., & Freedman, L. (2005b). *Developing critical awareness at the middle level: Using texts as tools for critique and pleasure.* Newark, DE: International Reading Association.

Kuhn, D. (1999). A developmental model of critical thinking. *Educational Researcher, 28*(2), 16-25.

Meier, D. (1996). *The power of their ideas: Lessons for America from a small school in Harlem.* Boston: Beacon Press.

National Middle School Association and the International Reading Association. (2002). Supporting young adolescents' literacy learning. Retrieved March 2006, from: www.nmsa. org/AboutNMSA/PositionStatements/ReadingInstruction/tabid/284/Default.aspx

Pearson, P. D., & Gallagher, M. C. (1983). The instruction of reading comprehension. *Contemporary Educational Psychology, 8*(3), 317-344.

Rathes, L., Jonas, A., Rothstein, A., & Wasserman, S. (1967). *Teaching for thinking: Theory and application.* Columbus, OH: Charles Merrill.

Short, K., Harste, J., & Burke, C. (1996). *Creating classrooms for authors and inquirers.* Portsmouth, NH: Heinemann.

Wilhelm, J. (2001). *Improving comprehension with think-alouds: Modeling what good readers do.* New York: Scholastic.

Meet the Authors

Holly Johnson is currently an Associate Professor at the University of Cincinnati in Cincinnati, Ohio. Her research focus is on middle school students' literacy needs, and she is currently addressing middle school students' reading self-efficacy.

Jeff Hoffman is currently a middle school language arts teacher in Cincinnati, Ohio.

Chapter 5

Literacy in

Jacquie's 6th- and 7th-Grades Math Classroom

Jacquie is a middle school math teacher with 12 years of experience in a western Pennsylvania junior high school, grades 7 through 9. Located approximately 60 miles from the city of Pittsburgh, Jacquie's junior high school enrolls approximately 800 students of varied racial, ethnic, and cultural backgrounds.

Jacquie's educational background includes an undergraduate degree in mathematics with secondary certification and a graduate degree in educational psychology. In addition to teaching junior high school mathematics students, Jacquie teaches 6th-graders who are advanced in mathematical reasoning, number sense, and reading ability. These students are transported to the junior high school each morning. Furthermore, Jacquie provides basic math instruction for struggling 7th-grade students and on-grade-level instruction for high-average learners. In her experience with these various age groups, Jacquie has employed multiple, effective teaching methods that address the diverse needs of her learners.

When asked about teaching in this middle school environment, Jacquie responded, "Most people cringe at the thought of teaching adolescents, but to know them is to love them. They are open to my teaching style and learning activities that I create, yet they are not afraid to tell me, 'That wasn't really fun, Mrs. G.' or 'Next time, you should . . .' "

Each mathematics class period in Jacquie's middle school setting lasts for 40 minutes. Jacquie works with a supportive math team, although she has no paraprofessional support in her math class for struggling students, most of whom have individual educational plans (IEPs). Class size varies from as few as nine students in the basic math classes to as many as 26 students in the mathematically talented group.

Jacquie's classroom invites learners to investigate mathematics in a variety of ways. The walls of her classroom are covered with motivational and philosophical statements about the importance of mathematics in the real world. Jacquie's enthusiasm for math teaching and learning permeates each of her six instructional periods. Regardless of her students' ability levels, she can be heard saying, "Math is your ticket to a good job." Throughout her instruction, Jacquie assists all learners in synthesizing mathematical concepts and reasoning with their everyday lives. This concept is not just philosophical; rather, it is the impetus that guides her mathematics instruction. As Jacquie tells her students, "The more math you learn, the more you want to know."

Jacquie immerses her students in a literacy-rich, positive learning environment and encourages them to read, write, talk, share, question, and investigate mathematical concepts, problem solving, and inquiry strategies. The motto "Mathematics is not a spectator

Susan E. Fello and Kelli R. Paquette, with Jacquie Gentile

sport" creates the foundation upon which all of Jacquie's teaching is constructed. She can be heard saying, "Get off of the bench and get into the game!" Another key quotation reads: "Math is not about numbers or the 'right' answer. Math is about discovery and exploring different ways of thinking" (National Council of Teachers of Mathematics, 1991). Again, this statement supports Jacquie's philosophy of encouraging and promoting students' mathematical success. As identified by Vacca et al. (2006), a teacher's personal belief system and positive attitude are essential tools for facilitating student achievement. Jacquie's personal belief system guides and facilitates the development of students' positive attitudes and encourages students' efforts toward improved mathematical performances.

This chapter will provide a historical perspective of mathematics instruction and an array of research-based literacy strategies to improve middle school students' mathematical learning. Various suggestions will be highlighted for incorporating these strategies into everyday mathematical instruction. The final segment of this chapter identifies the necessary components of talking and writing and illustrates how teachers may effectively implement these ideas into the mathematics classroom.

Incorporating these literacy strategies and techniques into mathematical instruction will help students understand mathematical concepts, solve word problems, and compute basic number equations. Alvermann and Phelps (2002) confirm that students' comprehension and overall mathematical conceptualization will improve with the use of literacy strategies.

Traditional teaching practices focus on the transmission of mathematical knowledge from teacher to student. This practice of *teaching by telling* must be replaced with a more contemporary model for teaching and learning mathematics (Bandlow, 2001; Grant, 1998; Noddings, 1993). This chapter provides instructional methods for an up-to-date mathematics classroom.

Mathematical comprehension transcends beyond students simply understanding a word problem; they must connect mathematics with the real world. Additionally, students need opportunities to discuss and share their mathematical reasoning with peers (Borasi, 1995). Oral language allows sharing of mathematical thinking when solving a problem. Successful math teachers embrace the initiative of incorporating literacy strategies into their daily teaching. This chapter provides guidance for accomplishing this goal.

Historical Background of Mathematical Instruction

Educators, researchers, and theorists outside the mathematics arena traditionally have held an oversimplified view of this content area. Educators often considered mathematics instruction as restricted to a few, limited concepts, such as using the four basic operations, understanding fractions, moving decimal points, and calculating perimeter and area. Today's mathematics instruction goes far beyond this limited view.

In 1920, a few dedicated mathematics educators and researchers saw the need for a consistent set of standards and so founded the National Council of Teachers of Mathematics (NCTM). The organization has weathered several transformations in mathematics education. When the Soviet Union launched Sputnik in 1957, the U.S. government invested heavily in supporting mathematics curriculum development and teacher education. Then, the new math reform of the 1950s and 1960s gave way to the back-to-basics movement of the 1970s (Kilpatrick & Stanic, 1995). In 1980, NCTM issued a position paper titled *An Agenda for Action*. This document called for a more balanced approach to school mathematics that would include problem solving, mathematical understanding, and application to real-world situations (Kilpatrick & Stanic, 1995).

The publication *A Nation at Risk* (National Commission on Excellence in Education [NCEE], 1983) spurred education reform in all areas of the curriculum, including mathematics. According to the report, students in the United States placed fourth academically, after Germany, South Korea, and Japan, respectively (NCEE, 1983). The data led to the designation of the United States as a "second-rate world power" (Kilpatrick & Stanic, 1995). Considering the competitive nature of the global society, improvement in mathematics, the sciences, and technology was examined through a multi-faceted lens. Improving mathematics instruction would improve students' test scores, which, in turn, would make U.S. students fit for intellectual competition. How could this reform be structured? Who would lead the movement?

Once again, the National Council of Teachers of Mathematics was at the forefront. In 1989, NCTM published the *Curriculum and Evaluation Standards for School Mathematics*, which proposed adopting a formal set of standards. The purpose of this document was to ensure quality, pinpoint goals, and promote change. NCTM proposed a specific set of standards to move math instruction toward a classroom in which knowledge must be individualized. The teacher would provide constructivist strategies and activities, while the learner would construct his/her own learning through interactions with other people in the environment (Grant, 1998; Noddings, 1993).

The *Principles and Standards for School Mathematics* (NCTM, 2000) has set the tone for reform in mathematics classrooms across the United States. This document recommended de-emphasizing memorization of isolated skills, basic mathematics facts, and rote memorization. Consequently, teachers were asked to teach from a more constructivist, problem-based approach.

In a reformed mathematics classroom, teachers are learners as much as students are (NCTM, 2000). This cooperative approach to learning provides a framework for understanding mathematics rather than just reproducing mathematical computation. Essentially, the current trend in mathematics education is the creation of a student-centered learning environment (Draper, 2002). With the learner as the focus of the instruction, becoming a literate individual means being able to read, write, and understand mathematical concepts. When asked for a definition of mathematical literacy, Jacquie replied, "Being mathematically literate means being able to apply learned ideas when solving real-world problems."

The history of mathematics education is one of a constant state of flux. The focus for the contemporary mathematics classroom must move beyond the curricular content to that which is important for students. Students must use mathematics in learning how to read, write, listen, speak, and think (Draper, 2002). According to NCTM (2000), the crux of mathematics instruction is that students must realize mathematics is important and has value. Students must be able to articulate their mathematical understanding. Additionally, students must use mathematics to think and solve problems. NCTM (2000) further states that students must be mathematically literate. Therefore, mathematics educators must expand their teaching practices to provide these opportunities (Neilsen, 1998). The use of literacy strategies in the mathematics classroom can assist math educators in this endeavor, thus fostering students' mathematical literacy.

Bridging the Gap Between Past Practice and Literacy Strategy Inclusion

Advocates of infusing literacy education into content courses such as mathematics have met with resistance. Despite efforts to incorporate literacy instruction across all areas of the curriculum, middle and secondary educators have been reluctant to take up the cause (O'Brien, Stewart, &

Moje, 1995). The reason for this is unclear. Many content area teachers, including mathematics educators, may believe that literacy instruction is incongruent with their areas of expertise. In fact, many mathematics teachers view literacy instruction as simply helping students read the textbook (Draper, 2002). Being able to read the mathematics textbook is not the same as being mathematically literate. Students should be able to comprehend mathematical terms and concepts, discuss those terms and ideas fluently with classmates, and apply their mathematical understanding clearly, logically, and sequentially through written or oral communication.

Because of the national standards movement, many content area teachers have become increasingly aware of the role that vocabulary and reading comprehension play in students' understanding of content information (Vacca & Vacca, 2006). In the past, basic vocabulary development and reading comprehension have been taken for granted in middle school education, especially in mathematics instruction. With the publication of mathematics textbooks that require higher reading levels, instruction must move away from rote computation and focus on vocabulary development and reading comprehension (Reehm & Long, 1996). Developmentally, middle school students are at varied reading levels and require differentiated instruction with a rich content in mathematics, as well as in other content areas.

Based on a research review of the last 40 years' worth of scientifically based studies in reading, the National Reading Panel's report (2000) has spurred unrest among educators. Middle school students are reported as often being unprepared to meet content-driven coursework (Vacca et al., 2006), especially in the areas of mathematical reasoning, thought, and concept development. In fact, many students, after four years of high school mathematics, are able to read the mathematics text and yet remain unable to solve word problems (Simon & Stimpson, 1988), the most obvious area for infusing reading instruction in mathematics. Being able to decode the printed text is not the same as being able to read, interpret, and apply the written message.

Fortunately, educators, researchers, and professional organizations have been investigating the role of reading comprehension in all content areas, including mathematics. NCTM has made significant progress in establishing goals, standards, and benchmarks for students to attain at various grade levels in all aspects of mathematics. NCTM's *Standards* (2000) provide clear guidelines for teachers in developing content-based instruction, delivering effective lessons, and assessing students' progress.

In order to understand the role of reading comprehension in the content area of mathematics, math educators must be aware of research-based literacy strategies that support student learning. Researchers, reading specialists, and literacy educators have identified key literacy strategies for comprehension and vocabulary development (Alvermann & Phelps, 2002; Harvey & Goudvis, 2000; Pearson, Dole, Duffy, & Roehler, 1992; Vacca et al., 2006). Examining what good readers do when they encounter expository text passages provides a connection for what students can do when reading mathematical text. According to Harvey and Goudvis (2000), good readers automatically utilize the following strategies: making connections, asking questions, visualizing, making inferences, determining meaning, repairing comprehension, and synthesizing information. Teachers need to instruct students in applying these techniques when reading mathematical text.

Academic Rigor in Today's Mathematics Classroom

A rigorous mathematics curriculum demands thorough instruction to support students' understanding of rich content that meets the state-mandated standards. With the state-mandated testing called for by the No Child Left Behind Act (2001), greater pressure has been placed on the classroom teacher to assess students' performances periodically, to check for potential weaknesses, to determine ample progress, and to hopefully recognize significant yearly gains. Students have never before been asked to perform with such deliberation and consistency.

The instructional changes necessary to comply with these mandates leave little time to add additional concepts and activities that do not support the goal of meeting the state-mandated standards. With increased demands on content, more rigorous instructional practices, and overwhelming assessment needs, teachers commonly lament, "How can so much be accomplished in so little time?"

Many mathematics teachers have judged their role as literacy instructors based on students' successes with textbooks; however, teachers must expand students' concepts of text. According to Neilsen (1998), math teachers must expand the definition of text to include anything that provides readers, writers, listeners, speakers, and thinkers with the potential to create meaning using language or numerals.

Teachers often have limited their interpretations of reading comprehension within mathematics to word problems sprinkled throughout math textbooks. However, middle school math students need to be empowered to think critically about the use of numbers in society, to analyze the reasonableness of statistics, and to validate or invalidate information (Wallace, Clark, & Cherry, 2006). Therefore, literacy strategies should be incorporated throughout mathematics instruction far beyond the word problem. "A learning environment that allows for serious mathematical thinking requires a genuine respect for others' ideas, a valuing of reason and sense making, pacing and timing that allows students to puzzle and to think, and the forging of a social and intellectual community" (NCTM, 1991).

NCTM's *Principles and Standards* (2000) state that "students who have opportunities, encouragement, and support for speaking, writing, reading, and listening in mathematics classes reap dual benefits: They communicate to learn mathematics, and they learn to communicate mathematically." The fact remains that literacy instruction and literacy itself are essential components of mathematics instruction at the middle school level. This philosophical basis is the foundation upon which a mathematically literate classroom is built. Such literacy strategies as visualizing, making connections, determining importance, monitoring comprehension, and graphics organizers enable middle school mathematics teachers to meet this NCTM guideline.

Developing a Literacy Mind-Set

In order to develop a literacy mind-set, teachers first must ask themselves these critical questions: Do I think flexibly and fluently, or do I focus instruction in one particular fashion? Do I use mathematical knowledge and processes confidently, or do I limit my focus to the correct answer? Do I engage in reflective thinking or not? (Rigelman, 2007). Thinking flexibly and fluently, confidently using mathematical knowledge and processes, and regularly engaging in self-reflective practices contribute to the development of a literacy mind-set. Once this mind-set is established, literacy strategies can be employed effectively.

Incorporating literacy strategies into the mathematics instruction is not an additional burden or responsibility, nor is it a novel idea. Having students visualize mathematical concepts, find the important details in a word problem, or make connections with math in the real world are literacy strategies, and an integral part of mathematical comprehension and vocabulary understanding. The mathematical content of the lesson does not change; however, the teacher's delivery style may be altered. The inclusion of reading tools (e.g., reading guides, graphic organizers, or think-alouds) helps students understand the math content. Such topics as the metric system, place value, fractions, percentages, decimals, and ratios are essential and steadfast elements of middle school mathematics programs. It only makes sense, therefore, to encourage students to use literacy strategies to investigate these mathematical concepts and thereby improve students' mathematical understanding.

Effective Literacy Strategies

In order to be strategic, a reader must understand and make sense from the printed word (Vacca & Vacca, 2006). Readers interact with text by making use of their prior knowledge and by employing literacy strategies. In order to help students use literacy strategies in mathematics, an investigation of how successful readers interact with text is pertinent. Researchers agree that the following reading strategies will assist in student comprehension (Harvey & Goudvis, 2000; Pearson et al., 1992). Have students:

- Make text-to-self, text-to-text, and text-to-world connections between what they already know and the new information
- Draw inferences about what they are reading
- Visualize or make a mental image of the reading material
- Ask questions of themselves and their classmates while reading to seek clarification of the information
- Repair faulty comprehension when they self-monitor their comprehension
- Distinguish between important and less-important facts in the text
- Synthesize information with the text and among other familiar texts.

As supported by Siegel and others (1996), readers do not simply take meaning from the text but rather use their knowledge, interests, values, and feelings to generate meaning. This conceptual understanding of what readers do with text can be applied to math. Learners in the mathematical classrooms can develop the same knowledge, interests, values, and feelings through the inclusion of literacy strategies to make connections with mathematical text.

In order to make personal connections, Jacquie capitalizes on her students' musical and sports-related interests when teaching comparative data analysis. After surveying her students, she collects information and creates a narrative compilation of the data. Then, her students read the narrative and analyze the data with Jacquie's assistance. "How many students play only a fall and spring sport? What number of students play three sports? How many students play only a fall sport?" Since the students are unsure, Jacquie models the creation of a three-part Venn diagram with the sports information to clarify the data.

Jacquie converts narrative text using mathematical concepts and creates a visual display. After the large-group instruction on comparing the sports data, students are equipped to prepare individual Venn diagrams, using the information collected about their musical interests. Students illustrate the narrative data through a Venn diagram. The information includes peers who play various instruments, participate in the musical ensemble, and/or sing in the 6th- and 7th-grade chorus.

Jacquie's instructional technique provides students with opportunities to make inferences, ask questions for clarification, and repair their faulty comprehension. When incorporated, these good reader strategies help students learn mathematical terminology and formulate mathematical thought.

To further assist students in analyzing data, Jacquie integrates computer technology into her instruction. Each week, students are assigned to the technology center and create spreadsheets and graphs (bar, circle, and/or line graphs) that represent previously collected data relative to each student's interest. This activity capitalizes on students' interests in computer technology, the visual arts, and interpretation of data. Regardless of students' ability levels, these technological opportunities motivate students to apply mathematical concepts in an interesting, meaningful manner.

Incorporating Literacy Strategies Into Math Instruction

To be a literate person, one must read and write effectively. For the hesitant educator, an excellent starting point for incorporating literacy strategies into the mathematics curriculum is the word problem. Whether teaching 6th-graders how to budget their allowances, instructing 7th-graders to calculate sale prices using percentages, or educating 8th-graders on how to calculate compound interest over a five-year period, basic reading comprehension of the word problem itself is paramount. Middle school teachers often spend excessive amounts of time helping students determine important information in word problems and helping students eliminate non-essential, extraneous phrases. The following five literacy strategies provide an avenue to improve students' mathematical comprehension of word problems, while helping them reach beyond the problem into other areas of mathematical instruction.

Visualizing. The visualizing strategy requires readers to create mental images or make movies in their minds (Harvey & Goudvis, 2000). When students are asked to visualize, their mental pictures are unique and belong to only them. In order to assist students with the visualizing strategy, teachers must provide opportunities and examples of the strategy.

The authors observed Jacquie using developmentally appropriate examples for her 7th-grade students in a basic math lesson on bases and exponents. She described a cheerleading squad creating a base for a cheer, with the smallest cheerleader on the top. She successfully connected the concept of base for the cheerleading squad and the base number in the mathematical problem. The small number at the top, the exponent, is the cheerleader indicating how many of the base number that we will need. Jacquie shouts out, "Give me three fours, give me two fives." Her students readily understand the connection and instead of multiplying 4 x 3 and getting 12, they multiply 4 x 4 x 4 to get 64 and multiply 5 x 5 to get 25.

This simple example illustrates Jacquie's desire to explain mathematical concepts in terms that students could understand. When included in a word problem, the vocabulary words "base" and "exponent" were more understandable, since the students were able to visualize the cheerleading squad as representing those terms. Jacquie thus connected the mathematical terminology to the students' frames of reference. Students visualized a relevant, real-world connection. Rather than defining the words "base" and "exponent" on the chalkboard and expecting the students to complete their math vocabulary books, Jacquie succeeded in teaching the *meaning* of the two vocabulary words. As expressed by Esty and Teppo (1996), "It is difficult to think about, let alone talk about, entities that cannot be represented by some kind of word, symbol, or picture." In mathematics, symbolic language fills a dual role as an instrument of communication and as an instrument of thought by making it possible to represent mathematical concepts, structures, and relationships (Esty & Teppo, 1996; Kaput, 1989).

Making Connections. Teachers must help students make meaningful connections between their experiences and mathematical concepts. Harvey and Goudvis (2000) suggest that the three types of connections are text-to-text, text-to-self, and text-to-world. Text-to-text is when the reader is reminded of a similar situation in another story or literature passage. Text-to-self is when the reader makes a personal connection with the text under investigation. Text-to-world is when the reader applies information to world events.

Jacquie illustrates text-to-self connections while explaining the metric system terminology to her 7th-graders. The opportunity arose to develop their vocabulary when discussing prefixes, such as milli-, centi-, and kilo-, as well as subsequent base words, such as gram, liter, and meter. Making text-to-self connections ensured students' thorough understanding of these prefixes and base words. To illustrate the minute value of a milligram, Jacquie connected milligrams to the dosage weight of her young son's medication, showing the dropper used to administer the medication. Students could connect the weight of the milligrams with medication they have previously taken or those medications that they have seen in their medicine cabinets. When discussing the metric weight of a gram, Jacquie connected it to approximately the same weight of a paper clip. Students could connect the weight of one gram with the paper clip they held in their hands. When introducing "kilogram," Jacquie offered a connection with the weight of one textbook. Then, she asked her 7th-graders, "Are you as heavy as 50 paper clips or 50 text-books?" Jacquie continued, "Pick up your math textbook. Hold it in two hands. Now, hold it in one hand. Balance your textbook on your head. Your textbook weighs approximately one kilogram. If we were to stack 50 math textbooks in the corner of this classroom, it would be equal to the approximate weight of a 7th-grade math student." These text-to-self connections enabled the students to solve various word problems using the metric system. This connection between mathematics and science helps students connect math to its place in the real world (Austin, Thompson, & Beckmann, 2006).

This classroom example illustrates the use of making connections without changing the mathematical content or adding cumbersome activities. In this example, Jacquie's connections were meaningful in that students were able to identify with all of the comparisons that she made to help her students understand metric prefixes and bases. Students should be encouraged to make authentic connections to support their conceptual understanding (Harvey & Goudvis, 2000). The following lesson demonstrates how Jacquie assisted the students with making text-to-text connections between social studies and mathematics.

As Jacquie's 6th-graders were reading about customary measurements in math class, a student enthusiastically blurted, "We were just reading about this in our social studies class! Did you know that before the Industrial Revolution people measured things in weird ways?" Jacquie asked, "What happened during the Industrial Revolution that brought about a need for more exact units of measure?" The student replied, "The industry . . . because of mass-produced products." A discussion quickly ensued on the changing role of measurement due to the Industrial Revolution and the many "weird ways" people used measurement. For example, the height of a horse was measured in hands, the length of a land parcel was measured in shovel handles, and the yards of a bolt of cloth were measured in terms of the length of a person's arm. These antiquated forms of measurement gave way to standardization. The students could easily apply this literacy strategy, since Jacquie had previously modeled making text-to-text connections. Students must distinguish between important and less-important information when engaging in mathematical thought and synthesizing the information with other content areas (Graves, Juel, & Graves, 2004).

Making text-to-world connections can be demonstrated in the following lesson: When Jacquie teaches a unit involving word problems centered on amounts of money, students apply the content of a word problem in an actual activity to develop meaning and understanding. By making connections with students' everyday uses of money, Jacquie provides a clear connection between what the students are reading about in their textbooks, the content of what needs to be learned, and the real world application of these mathematical skills. The middle school level students participated in a variety of activities by creating real-life scenarios that involved people's need to earn, spend, and save money.

For example, following a unit on percentages, students randomly selected a marital status, an annual salary, and a number of dependents. Students had to calculate their salary deductions due to taxes, benefits, and savings plans before being asked to allocate funds for monthly bills and recreational expenses. Critical thinking skills played a key component in a student's decision-making process about earning, spending, and saving monies.

Inviting guest speakers from local financial institutions, participating in a field trip to a local bank, and enjoying a lunch at a local restaurant establishment provided students with a clearer understanding of how mathematics affects their daily lives. Moving beyond the word problem into the realm of personal experience helps students connect what they are reading in mathematics with what they do in real life.

The following scenario further illustrates the concept that mathematics teachers can incorporate all three types of connections into one lesson: After visiting the local home improvement store and buying several metric tools, Jacquie helped her 7th-grade students make text-to-text connections by reading about customary measurements in their math textbooks and the directions for using each tool. The students clearly realized the importance of being able to read about the tools' uses found in the company's directions provided on the packaging. She employed text-to-self connections by having students use the tools and build a model of a house from a scale plan. By applying their understanding of measurement and proportion, students were able to connect the concept to a real-life situation.

For example, students soon learned the true meaning of 5/16 of an inch by using a wrench. Students who had experience with tools were surprised that they were already somewhat familiar with measurement and were able to build upon their knowledge base. Each team of students was responsible for sharing the completed house model. The construction "crews" were required to read a commercially produced floor plan and then convert measurement units and calculate proportions to "build" their part of the model house. When making text-to-world connections, students shared their construction projects with other students. Students created a village displaying each of the individual houses. Each construction "crew" highlighted the novel features of their particular architectural designs. Construction supplies were identified and interior materials were specifically detailed in a written format. Through the constructing process, applicability to the real world was demonstrated. Learning measurement and proportion, utilizing specific vocabulary terms, and providing opportunities for descriptive and narrative writing incorporated a variety of essential real-life math skills. Through the construction process, students made the three connections: text-to-self, text-to-text, and text-to-world.

Determining Importance. A variety of methods can help mathematics students determine what parts of passages are important. As students read mathematical information, they can be taught how to conduct an overview of the entire passage. "Overviewing represents an early entry in the effort to determine importance" (Harvey & Goudvis, 2000). Additionally, skimming and scanning the text prior to reading empowers students to separate important information from non-essential information. Teachers also can model effective ways to highlight important aspects of text passages. While students are reading the text, they can make conscious decisions about what information they need to glean from the text, remember, or learn.

• *Internal text features.* Students can learn to examine the text for features that will help them determine what is important, including italics, bold-faced headings, or such words as "in summary," "additionally," or "the key factors are." Teachers often assume that students know internal text features implicitly; however, teachers must directly teach students these internal text features to assist them with comprehension. When authors write cue words and phrases, such as "for example," "in contrast," "on the other hand," and other similar phrases, the author is encouraging the reader to pause, to highlight key information, or to summarize main ideas, and review previously learned concepts.

In Jacquie's 6th-grade mathematics class, she explained how the layout of the textbook offers clues to important features. The authors incorporated special text features that assist students with reviewing previously introduced concepts. Jacquie facilitated a conversation with her students about how they could utilize this review feature. The authors wove additional sources throughout the textbook to empower students' understanding. When reviewing a concept in chapter 5, the authors may direct the students to refer to chapter 3, lesson 6, wherein the concept was originally introduced. This notation was marked as [3-6]. Jacquie explicitly taught this text feature to her students for their reference and comprehension development. Her goal was to assist middle school learners with reading independence.

• *External text features.* In addition to authors' internal text features, external text features, such as illustrations and photographs, play important roles in enhancing reading comprehension. Authors use diagrams, charts, tables, graphic organizers, and maps to illustrate main ideas. Middle school math students who are visual learners benefit greatly from these aspects of the math textbook. The following example illustrates a real-world application of maps in mathematics. Using state maps and a teacher-created scenario about camping, Jacquie's students learned about proportion, map scale, and distances.

During a lesson on proportions, Jacquie used a set of state maps to help students convert inches to miles. Students first oriented themselves to the map layout and design before planning the camping trip. Given map letters and numbers, students located their hometown and highlighted urban areas, rivers, and national forests in yellow. They followed various state and interstate routes to determine which route was the shortest. Using the scale of miles, the students first estimated and then calculated the actual distance between their hometown and the camping trip destination. They were able to compare their estimations with their calculations. Students also calculated gasoline mileage, elapsed time, and information from charts about costs for camping rentals and facility use.

This real-world example of using maps and charts assisted students when they encountered them in their mathematics textbook. Having had the "virtual" experience, students were provided with background knowledge in dealing with graphic information presented in the textbook.

• *The author's writing style.* Understanding an author's writing style can also assist students when they tackle word problems. Students need to explore the author's meaning and purpose when solving a word problem by focusing on the author's word choice. Students may need help in deciding what constitutes extraneous information or in understanding unfamiliar words or phrases. This concept is illustrated in a middle school math classroom with 7th-grade students.

When Jacquie assists students with understanding an author's wording, she explicitly teaches what the author means. When the author writes, "How are x and y related?" when referring to an equation, students often misinterpret what they are supposed to do. The phrasing makes students think that they should just write a generalization, like "x and y are variables." Jacquie explains that the authors want the learners to write an equation that describes the mathematical relationship between x and y, not just say "x is this and y is this." Jacquie encourages her students not to tell **what** they represent, but to tell **how** they relate mathematically.

• *Vocabulary development.* Word choice is inherent in authors' writing styles. How authors choose to introduce topics, define vocabulary, and build mathematical comprehension defines their writing styles. According to Countryman (1992), students' difficulties with word problems are symptomatic of the larger problem of comprehending mathematical vocabulary. In order to assist students with comprehension of the word problem, teachers must develop students' vocabulary, as well as explain the author's meaning. This does not mean defining words as they appear in a dictionary, but rather exploring mathematical terms and comparing those terms to familiar concepts. Teachers must capitalize on student discussion to assess students' current knowledge base of vocabulary, conceptual understanding, and interpretation of the author's word choice. Identifying important words and phrases within a word problem leads logically to seeking the solution. Mathematics teachers should use a variety of methods to help students determine the important information and to disregard irrelevant information.

Monitoring Comprehension. Monitoring comprehension is a metacognitive thinking strategy. "Metacognition refers to an awareness of and knowledge about strategies for planning, monitoring, and controlling one's own learning" (Block, Gambrell, & Pressley, 2002). Middle school math learners must seek methods of monitoring their own levels of comprehension when faced with calculating answers to mathematical questions. As stated by multiple reading theorists, monitoring and repairing one's comprehension is a vital strategy (Harvey & Goudvis, 2000). Many teachers assume that middle school learners can monitor their comprehension, whether or not they understand the content. In reality, monitoring comprehension should be an explicit skill taught to students in mathematics.

One specific strategy for monitoring comprehension is called SQ3R. Used in a variety of content areas, this strategy also can be adapted for use in a middle school mathematics class. In 1961, Francis Robinson created the SQ3R literacy strategy, which stands for Survey, Question, Read, Recite, and Review (Richardson & Morgan, 2003). Over 40 years later, educators continue to utilize Robinson's SQ3R technique effectively. This simple five-step approach, once taught and practiced, is effective for many learners. In mathematics education, because of the logical and sequential nature of solving problems, comprehension strategies such as SQ3R make overwhelming amounts of text more manageable. Thus, in mathematics education, students can easily implement step-by-step logical processes to monitor their comprehension. SQ3R is merely one study technique that can be utilized in all content area classes.

Supported by the significance of research-based self-monitoring strategies, Jacquie develops and modifies a unique step-by-step method to assist her students when reading math passages and solving accompanying mathematical word problems. Jacquie explicitly teaches a six-step technique that helps her students self-monitor. Jacquie can be heard saying, "What do you do when you just can't 'get it'?" The students have learned to use some combination of the following techniques: 1) Reread the lesson, looking for examples and hints. 2) Look for examples in your notes from class. 3) Go back to the problem after working on other, similar problems. 4) Take a break and return to the problem later. 5) Write down your thoughts and methods that you tried. (Never leave an answer completely blank.) 6) Call a friend to discuss the problem or to get a hint. This structured approach to solving word problems provides consistent support for struggling readers and mathematicians. When students are unaware of "what to do next," this written self-monitoring guide empowers them with an approach to persevere and experience success.

Talking and Writing. In addition to the literacy strategies of visualizing, making connections, determining importance, and monitoring comprehension, talking and writing are essential to the development of students' mathematical understanding. A synergistic pairing of talking and writing enables students to connect the language they know from their own personal experiences and backgrounds with the language of the classroom and of mathematics. Huinker and Laughlin (1996) state that talk fosters collaboration and helps to build a learning community in a classroom. When students have opportunities to talk and write about mathematics, they realize their thinking is valued by their classmates. This process creates a community of learners within a literate, middle school math environment. According to Greenes and Schulman (1996), "Students must communicate with others to gain information; share thoughts and discoveries; brainstorm, evaluate, and sharpen ideas and plans; and convince others."

• *Talking about math.* In order to generate meaningful conversation in math class, teachers can read aloud a variety of picture books suitable for middle school learners (Richardson, 2000). Reading literature in math class helps establish curriculum concepts and apply them to the real world (Carr, Buchanan, Wentz, & Brant, 2001). Reading and discussing mathematical content promotes analysis and critical thinking (Richardson, 2000). Books chosen for reading aloud should contain thought-provoking issues and moral dilemmas that are developmentally appropriate for middle school learners (Carr et al., 2001).

Based on middle school students' need to interact with their peers, Jacquie uses a seating arrangement that is conducive to large-group instruction and group work. Generally arranged in Ls for attention to the chalkboard and board work, the desks are easily shaped into groups of four by swinging the long end of the L into the middle. This quick re-arrangement allows students to talk with their group about mathematics. Students meet to discuss solutions to problems, exchange ideas, do hands-on activities, and share their mathematical thinking. Incorporating group competition also meets the needs of many middle school learners. Teacher-selected teams often work together to review mathematical content. Earning points that lead to tangible rewards is an effective strategy for this age group. Jacquie can informally assess students' understanding while listening to their communication with one another, and the students are motivated to really help each other master the material. Thus, the value of talking in math class is indispensable.

• *Writing about math.* Having students write about their thinking while using appropriate mathematical terminology is an essential literacy skill (Brown, 2005). This writing to learn process differs from learning to write in the earlier grades. At the middle school level, the purpose for writing to learn is meant to be a catalyst for further learning and meaning making (Knipper & Duggan, 2006). Even though most middle school math teachers do not see themselves as teachers of writing, students' use of written expression is imperative in order to describe their thinking processes, methodology for solving problems, and explanations for solutions. This concept of writing in mathematics classes is a relatively new one. As state-mandated tests that evaluate written expression become more prevalent, students will be expected to write and explain how they solved mathematical problems, and so written expression becomes part of the total assessment. Jacquie encourages her students to "**write** to get it **right**."

Concluding Thoughts

Middle school learners are complicated. Because of their unique developmental qualities, varied backgrounds of previous math instruction, and dispositions toward reading, instruction in any content area must be differentiated to meet these individual needs. Middle school students are perceived as learners in transition (Ivey & Broaddus, 2000). The implementation of such literacy strategies as visualizing, making connections, determining importance, monitoring comprehension, and talking and writing in middle school mathematics classrooms helps students make these transitions.

The past practices of a one-size-fits-all mathematics curriculum, limited instructional materials, lack of student ownership, and ineffective use of instructional time negatively affect student performance. Mathematics teachers, like all educators, are eager to investigate and to explore all potential avenues for increasing student understanding and achievement. In a contemporary environment wherein educators must be mindful of state-mandated assessments, district-approved curricula, and school administrators' philosophies, the use of literacy strategies in mathematics instruction benefits students and teachers. These strategies can assist teachers in their quests to improve middle school learners' mathematical understandings.

In developing the next generation of literate individuals, today's mathematics teachers are faced with two critical responsibilities: to match instruction to individual students' growth and to provide a context in which students can become fully engaged (Ivey & Broaddus, 2000). Literacy strategies integrated into the middle school mathematics instruction enable teachers to fulfill these responsibilities. Learning mathematics in a literate environment fosters inquiry and problem solving, promotes self-confidence, and empowers learners to use and understand mathematics. Indeed, being literate in mathematics extends far beyond the traditional word problem.

References

Alvermann, D., & Phelps, S. (2002). *Content reading and literacy: Succeeding in today's diverse classrooms* (3rd ed.). Boston: Allyn and Bacon.

Austin, R., Thompson, D., & Beckmann, C. (2006). Locusts for lunch: Connecting mathematics, science, and literature. *Mathematics Teaching in the Middle School, 12*(4), 182-187.

Bandlow, R. (2001). The misdirection of middle school reform: Is a child-centered approach incompatible with achievement in math and science? *The Clearing House, 75*(2), 69-73.

Block, C., Gambrell, L., & Pressley, M. (2002). *Improving comprehension instruction: Rethinking research, theory, and classroom practice.* San Francisco: Jossey-Bass.

Borasi, R. (1995). What secondary mathematics students can do. In I. Carl (Ed.), *Prospects for school mathematics* (pp. 43-48). Reston, VA: The National Council of Teachers of Mathematics.

Brown, S. (2005). You made it through the test; what about the aftermath? *Mathematics Teaching in the Middle School, 11*(2), 68-73.

Carr, K., Buchanan, D., Wentz, J., Weiss, M., & Brant, K. (2001). Not just for the primary grades: A bibliography of picture books for secondary content teachers. *Journal of Adolescent and Adult Literacy, 45*(2), 146-153.

Countryman, J. (1992). *Writing to learn mathematics.* Portsmouth, NH: Heinemann.

Draper, R. (2002). School mathematics reform, constructivism, and literacy: A case for literacy instruction in the reform-oriented math classroom. *Journal of Adolescent and Adult Literacy, 45*(6), 520-530.

Esty, W., & Teppo, A. (1996). Algebraic thinking, language, and word problems. In P. C. Elliott (Ed.), *Communication in mathematics: K-12 and beyond* (pp. 45-53). Reston, VA: The National Council of Teachers of Mathematics.

Grant, S. (1998). *Reforming reading, writing, and mathematics: Teachers' responses and the prospects for systemic reform.* Mahwah, NJ: Erlbaum.

Graves, M., Juel, C., & Graves, B. (2004). *Teaching reading in the 21st century* (3rd ed.). Boston: Allyn and Bacon.

Greenes, C., & Schulman, L. (1996). Communication processes in mathematical explorations and investigations. In P. C. Elliott (Ed.), *Communication in mathematics: K-12 and beyond* (pp. 159-169). Reston, VA: The National Council of Teachers of Mathematics.

Harvey, S., & Goudvis, A. (2000). *Strategies that work: Teaching comprehension to enhance understanding.* Ontario, Canada: Stenhouse Publishers.

Huinker, D., & Laughlin, C. (1996). Talk your way into writing. In P. C. Elliott (Ed.), *Communication in mathematics: K-12 and beyond* (pp. 81-88). Reston, VA: The National Council of Teachers of Mathematics.

Ivey, G., & Broaddus, K. (2000). Tailoring the fit: Reading instruction and middle school readers. *The Reading Teacher, 54*(1), 68-78.

Kaput, J. (1989). Linking representations in the symbol systems of algebra. In *Research Issues in the learning and teaching of algebra.* In S. Wagner & C. Kieran (Eds.), *Research agenda for mathematics education (4)* (pp. 167-194). Reston, VA: Lawrence Erlbaum Associates and the National Council of Teachers of Mathematics.

Kilpatrick, J., & Stanic, G. (1995). Paths to the present. In I. Carl (Ed.), *Prospects for school mathematics* (pp. 3-15). Reston, VA: The National Council of Teachers of Mathematics.

Knipper, K., & Duggan, T. (2006). Writing to learn across the curriculum: Tools for comprehension in content classes. *The Reading Teacher, 59*(5), 462-470.

National Commission on Excellence in Education. (1983). *A nation at risk.* Washington, DC: U.S. Government Printing Office.

National Council of Teachers of Mathematics. (1980). *An agenda for action: Recommendations for school mathematics of the 1980's.* Reston, VA: Author.

National Council of Teachers of Mathematics. (1989). *Curriculum and evaluation standards for school mathematics.* Reston, VA: Author.

National Council of Teachers of Mathematics. (1991). *Professional standards for teaching mathematics.* Reston, VA: Author.

National Council of Teachers of Mathematics. (2000). *Principles and standards for school mathematics.* Reston, VA: Author.

National Reading Panel. (2000). *Teaching children to read: An evidence-based assessment of the scientific research literature on reading and its implications for reading instruction* (National Institute of Public Health No. 00-4769). Washington, DC: National Institute of Child Health and Human Development.

Neilsen, L. (1998). Playing for real: Performative texts and adolescent identities. In D. Alvermann, K. Hinchman, D. Moore, S. Phelps, & D. Waff (Eds.), *Reconceptualizing the literacies in adolescents' lives* (pp. 3-26). Mahwah, NJ: Erlbaum.

No Child Left Behind Act of 2001, U.S. Public Law 107-110, 107th Cong., 1st session (2002, January 8).

Noddings, N. (1993). Constructivism and caring. In R. D. Davis & C. A. Maher (Ed.), *School mathematics and the world of reality* (pp. 35-50). Boston: Allyn & Bacon.

O'Brien, D., Stewart, R., & Moje, E. (1995). Why content literacy is difficult to infuse into the secondary school: Complexities of curriculum, pedagogy, and school culture. *Reading Research Quarterly, 30*, 442-463.

Pearson, P., Dole, J., Duffy, G., & Roehler, L. (1992). Developing expertise in reading comprehension: What should be taught and how should it be taught? In J. Farstup & S. J. Samuels (Eds.), *What research has to say to the teacher of reading* (2nd ed.). Newark, DE: International Reading Association.

Reehm, S., & Long, S. (1996). Reading in the mathematics classroom. *Middle School Journal, 27*(5), 35-41.

Richardson, J. (2000). *Read it aloud.* Newark, DE: International Reading Association.

Richardson, J., & Morgan, R. (2003). *Reading to learn in the content areas.* Belmont, CA: Wadsworth/Thomas Learning.

Rigelman, N. (2007). Fostering mathematical thinking and problem solving: The teacher's role. *Teaching Children Mathematics, 13*(6), 308-314.

Siegel, M., Borasi, R., Fonzi, J., Sanrige, L., & Smith, C. (1996). *Using reading to construct mathematical meaning.* Reston, VA: The National Council of Teachers of Mathematics.

Simon, M., & Stimpson, V. (1988). Developing algebraic representation using diagrams. In A. F. Coxford (Ed.), *The ideas of algebra, K-12: 1988 Yearbook* (pp. 136-141). Reston, VA: National Council of Teachers of Mathematics.

Stanic, G., & Kilpatrick, J. (1992). Mathematics curriculum reform in the United States: A historical perspective. *International Journal of Educational Research, 5*, 407-417.

Vacca, R., & Vacca, J. (2006). *Content area reading literacy and learning across the curriculum* (8th ed.). Boston: Allyn and Bacon.

Vacca, J., Vacca, R., Gove, M., Burkey, L., Lenhart, L., & McKeon, C. (2006). *Reading and learning to read* (6th ed.). Boston: Allyn and Bacon.

Wallace, F., Clark, K., & Cherry, M. (2006). How come? What if? So what? Reading in the mathematics classroom. *Mathematics Teaching in the Middle School, 12*(2), 108-114.

Meet the Authors

Susan E. Fello is an Assistant Professor in the Department of Professional Studies in Education at Indiana University of Pennsylvania, Indiana, Pennsylvania. She teaches reading methods courses to those seeking elementary teacher certification and graduate reading assessment courses in multiple master's programs. Susan has 35 years of 5th- and 6th-grade classroom experience and a reading specialist certification, and she has published in the following journals: PTA Today, Gifted Child Today, Childhood Education, Early Childhood Education Journal, *and* Pennsylvania READS. *Her research interests include improving students' literacy acquisition in all content areas.*

Kelli R. Paquette is an Assistant Professor at Indiana University of Pennsylvania. Certified as a reading specialist, she teaches undergraduate literacy classes, as well as graduate courses focusing on issues and trends in the language arts. She has published in the following journals: Childhood Education, Early Childhood Education Journal, *and* Pennsylvania READS. *Her teaching experience and knowledge as a 6+1 Writing Traits trainer has greatly improved the literacy development of her elementary learners and has contributed to the knowledge base of her university students.*

The authors wish to thank Jacquie Gentile for her participation in this research investigation. Her middle school math expertise provides the authentic, valid information contained within this chapter.

Chapter 6

Learning Cycles and Arts Integration in

Sarah's Science Classroom

In a West Virginia community, a unique NASA unit spans the 5th-grade science instruction at North Elementary and transitions to the 6th-grade science units at Suncrest Middle School. The teams of science teachers at each school have worked together for many years on this long-term study, which integrates the state science curriculum. Each year, the 5th and 6th grades participate in the NASA field trip. The 5th-graders prepare for a "Mission to the Moon," while the 6th-graders prepare for a "Mission to Mars." A description of some of the actual lessons follows:

The 5th-graders enter the science classroom, buzzing with excited talk. Once the students settle into their groupings, their science teacher introduces them to the integrated curriculum unit packet for the NASA Mission to the Moon. Students are really excited to find out that they will actually participate in a NASA mission. They view the PowerPoint presentation, which was designed by their team of teachers. After the PowerPoint and subsequent discussions, the students process the unit information in a variety of ways. Students read aloud from the textbook as a class, taking turns, with readers picked by the teacher. The teacher then answers questions, explains concepts, and adds mission information details to the discussion. The next day, students review the introductory materials, resources, readings, handouts, texts, and official NASA materials related to the NASA space station mission; then, they watch a video explaining more about their culminating projects. Students then design an original mission patch for their team and write job applications to become candidates for their favorite mission specialist job. This unit spans weeks of study and culminates in a full-day field trip to a NASA Simulation Center for each 5th-grade student.

When they enter the 6th grade, the same students discover that they are continuing the space unit by preparing for a NASA Mission to Mars, which includes a completely different set of mission experiments and specialist activities. As 6th-graders, the students work with an original planning team, create their own original design for a mission patch, view a PowerPoint presentation about Mars, review resource materials about Mars as a class, and read from the textbook out loud as a group. Students engage in processing the information about Mars in a variety of ways. They review the introductory PowerPoint, science resources, readings, handouts, videos, texts, and official NASA materials related to the Mars mission. Students rely on their peers to process and react to what they read, view, and discuss.

Each of these 5th- and 6th-grade units of study culminates in the much-anticipated full-day field trip to

Joy Faini Saab,
Allison Swan Dagen,
and James Rye

the NASA Simulation Center. The 5th-graders participate in a "Mission to the Moon" and the 6th-graders participate in the "Mission to Mars." On mission day, students leave early and take a one-and-a-half hour bus trip to the center. Upon their arrival, the students divide into group A (starting with mission control) or group B (starting with outdoor unit activities). The mission control team members begin their experience by entering Mars Control or the Mars Rover. The Mars Rover consists of a simulation spaceship with a walk-through simulated airlock threshold. Prior to beginning the mission, students put on lab smocks with the real NASA label, signaling the beginning of the mission. Then, students travel to each individualized center area for the particular jobs designated. The centers contain needed materials for the mission, such as desks, microphones, cameras, controls for real working cameras, mission status computers on the wall, working linked computers, communications that link different stations, and a big wall of television monitors that broadcast what each station is doing.

Television monitors in the middle of the computers show images outside the rover (using real film from NASA missions and computer-generated film from Mars). The simulation area also holds a separate room for probes, lab coats, and three isolation stations in separate classrooms (including cranes for dealing with dangerous materials). The remote team station in the middle of the room has a domed ceiling, rubber gloves, rocks, and an examination area; students can manipulate space items through the gloves. The medical team is supported with computers, simulated airlocks, a threshold with rotating door, and a computer. Each group has a booklet for following mission instructions.

When the mission is complete, the students eat lunch and transition to the outdoor activities, which include teamwork physical challenges, or they can stay inside and take written challenges and do puzzles related to the mission. These culminating projects extend the school day by one hour.

Students' reactions to the missions have been extremely positive. They were invested in the preparation and implementation of the missions, they contributed resource materials, they discussed their mission roles and experiments with one another, and they talked to their families about the mission for years afterward.

Teacher Collaboration for Science, Literacy, and the Arts

The thrust for the collaborative 6th-grade science classes at Suncrest Middle School are inquiry-based lessons, with groups of three or four students carefully selected to work together in the scientific process. The science lab groups include special needs students, including those who are learning disabled, mentally impaired, or English language learners (ELLs). The teachers take some time to get to know their students before selecting the groups. They seek to put together students who are able to assist one another, paying close attention to the students' varying strengths and abilities and how they will coordinate.

In formulating working science groups, the teachers will often provide peer support by, for example, grouping students according to their native language. This strategy has turned out to be effective, as teachers have witnessed two students who speak Mandarin working together, enthusiastically conversing in Mandarin while processing the teacher's English instructions for a new science concept. ELLs also have access to electronic translators to help them process new science vocabulary and new science concepts. These can be supportive resources in the acquisition of new and complex science concepts.

Student groups are rotated as differences arise and needs shift. When new science concepts are introduced, teachers scaffold the learning for their students with a combination of PowerPoint presentations, PowerPoint handouts, science textbooks, websites, and additional resource materials. As one teacher pointed out, "Science textbooks automatically challenge students by presenting higher reading levels involving science terms related to each unit of study." The teachers choose appropriate printed media and resource material to clarify new concepts being introduced as they are encountered.

Each student group decides on a reader and a recorder for each science project. These two roles rotate among the students for each project. Students also engage in a cooperative learning technique called "think, pair, share." In this process, the teachers introduce a concept, idea, or question and direct each student to think and write about this idea on their own. Next, the students share their responses with one other student. Once the partners have shared with each other, they join the rest of their science group to compare and contrast the responses of all members of the group.

Collaborative Development of Integration Strategies. All the 6th-grade teachers meet every day to plan cross-curricular strategies for their teaching. Because of this daily 50-minute common grade level team planning time, teachers are able to reinforce their content vocabulary for one another across the curriculum. These teachers feel strongly about reinforcing new vocabulary by using it throughout the day in any class, whenever an opportunity presents itself. With daily team planning, the group of teachers can be consistent with skills, abilities, projects, common themes, vocabulary, and state content standards and objectives across the disciplines.

While working collaboratively, teachers develop PowerPoint presentations to introduce a new unit of study. Additionally, these presentations are then shared as handouts for all students, which is particularly beneficial for those who need to process the information more slowly and thoroughly. Teachers also put content information on audiotapes that can be used by student science groups.

Sarah, a 6th-grade science and math teacher, describes her teaching and the special challenges of the middle school science curriculum. She points out that science texts automatically present higher reading level challenges because of the density of scientific and technical vocabulary used to explain concepts or describe the scientific process.

In a cloze reading activity, the students receive handouts with blanks for every fifth word; they fill in the blanks using resource material and context clues. This exercise seems to help students strengthen their comprehension of the new science content. Students have benefited from the additional written processing of science content and have responded positively to these handouts.

Teachers also work collaboratively to develop nontraditional forms of assessment in which students can demonstrate their understandings of content knowledge in deep and meaningful ways. Therefore, students often demonstrate their understandings while completing creative, arts-integrated projects filled with individual expression as well as science content. These projects are shared with the class, so that other students get a chance to share their perspectives on science content (see Figure 6.1 for specific curricular examples). The students within the group support the editing, tutoring, and review processes during collaborative projects. The groups are always involved in various parts of the scientific process throughout the year, particularly emphasizing analysis, interpretation, and inferences from data. Traditional tests are also given, with learning

Steven's Science Highlights Supported by
Literacy & Arts Meaning Making in His Feeder School System

Suncrest Primary:
1. Created a "water cycle bracelet," twine and yellow bead (sun), brown bead (ground water), tan bead (respiration), green bead (transpiration), clear bead (evaporation), black bead (combustion), and white bead (condensation).
2. Sang "Yellow Submarine"; wrote poems; sang and danced in the rain with umbrellas; explored water tension with bubbles, bubble painting, guided imagery with bubbles, holding imaginary bubbles in your hand; guided clear and polluted water; created a recyclable sculpture (displayed in the library); wrote stories; and drew pictures about types of pollution.
3. Created papier-mâché globes and painted continents on planet Earth.
4. Looked at various interpretations of constellations from various cultures and various times in earth's history inside the portable NASA planetarium brought to your school by the teacher resources NASA personnel.
5. Took an aluminum can and poked holes in it to make a new constellation. Put a candle inside to light up the constellation design.
6. For biology studies, created and maintained a garden outside the school, called the "Owl's Garden." Participated in planting, feeding, weeding, raking, and maintaining a healthy garden.

North Elementary:
1. Created imaginary constellations in a shoebox. Students cut out both ends of the shoeboxes and created their own constellation design by poking the holes in a small piece of black paper measured to cover one end of the shoebox. These were lit by flashlights shone through the other end of the shoebox and pointed at the wall with the lights turned off in the classroom.
2. Mission to the Moon at NASA Simulation Center. Preparation included a mission patch artistic design and study about the moon and the solar system (videos, science textbooks, websites, teacher explanations and diagrams, PowerPoint presentation on mission activities, handouts). Completed a job application; explained what job you wanted and why you thought you'd be good at that job (communications, medical team, life support team, probe, remote team, isolation 1-3, navigation). Whole-day field trip at Moon Mission. The unit took about 2-3 weeks.
3. Learned about atoms and electrons and the periodic table of elements. Did the "Sodium Rap," in which each student created an original piece to teach the other students about their element. Students could choose a song, PowerPoint, poster, game show, rap, drawings, and video to teach the rest of the class. This project

Figure 6.1: Student-Generated Middle School Science Highlights Supported by Literacy & Arts Meaning Making

should include: atomic number, atomic symbol, who discovered it, and general information about the element.

4. Used lessons from Bill Nye the Science Guy throughout the year. Read textbook for related concepts taught in the show.

Suncrest Middle:

1. "Voyage to Mars" at NASA Simulation Center. Preparation included a mission patch artistic design and study about the moon and the solar system (videos, science textbooks, websites, teacher explanations and diagrams, PowerPoint presentation on mission activities, handouts). Teachers assigned jobs to the students based on their observation of them in class (communications, medical team, life support team, probe, remote team, isolation 1-3, navigation). Whole-day field trip in which we completed a "Mission to Mars." The unit took about 2-3 weeks.

2. Greek Unit: studied ancient Greek architecture, building of temples out of common materials (included roof, statue, base, columns, stairs, and pottery). Integrated unit with the social studies, reading, writing, math, and science.

3. Drew a scientist to start the year with the students' perceptions of what a scientist is. Graphed the perceptions of scientists from across the 6th-grade classroom.

4. Conducted many experiments throughout the year: drops of water on a penny (with and without soap), how water tension works, molecules and how they share electrons, the hydrogen electron, drew a molecule, experiments with speed (pushed a marble, a tennis ball, a golf ball, and a basketball down a ramp and graphed how quickly they crossed a certain distance). Read science books, PowerPoints, and handouts to prepare for and conducted experiments.

5. Created a labeled skeleton model called Mr. Bones from plastic milk cartons and spools of thread. Resources included handouts.

6. Hot air balloon project integrated with community hot air balloon festival. Used tissue paper and wire to create a hot air balloon. Community/parents helped to use propane stove to launch balloons on a cold day so the warmer air of the balloon would help it rise easily. Resources included handout, community hot air balloon festival.

7. Role-playing in science experiments in class. Acted as scientists, chemists, climatologists, astronauts, and physicists.

8. Created original art to represent students' understanding of symmetry, mythical architecture, ancient Greek architecture, and genetic concepts.

9. Wrote original poems to teach science concepts.

10. Created an original clay sculpture and biological and environmental descriptions of a new species of animal.

Figure 6.1 (cont'd): Student-Generated Middle School Science Highlights Supported by Literacy & Arts Meaning Making

disabled and mentally impaired students benefiting from the accommodations of extra time and individual attention. Additionally, when requested, ELL teachers will help individual students work through the tests in English.

The science faculty from this West Virginia middle school are certified and trained in various content areas. Sarah has both science and math certifications and her collaborator, John, has science and language arts certifications. When they plan across disciplines, they are able to reinforce content areas more effectively. So, in science class, students are still required to use correct grammatical rules as well as correct mathematical terms and processes. This professional teamwork model also allows for the more consistent use of skills, processes, and content as students move from one class to another.

Meaning Making Through Arts-Integrated Instruction. Middle school teachers spend each year with groups of students who represent unique combinations of personalities, talents, abilities, and cultural influences. These diverse student characteristics reflect the theory that human beings are intelligent in a variety of ways (Gardner, 1983, 2003). Teachers have long recognized this fact, as they have created a variety of teaching methods to reach the different students in their classes. Gardner's theory of multiple intelligences and the National Standards for Arts Education (Consortium of National Arts Education Associations, 1994) contributed to the formulation of innovative methods found at this West Virginia middle school and at the 5th grade of the feeder elementary school. These teachers realized that their students became more engaged in the content when involved with meaning making through the arts.

Children in middle school classrooms are often engaged in traditional, left-brained learning activities dominated by the use of linguistic and mathematical intelligences. They find themselves repeating similar instructional tasks utilizing reading, writing, and mathematical operations. Teachers often organize instruction for large groups of children, in close quarters, preferring quiet and orderly tasks. This is a direct reflection of the type of environment and external testing requirements imposed upon public school teachers. While teachers are not always allowed much flexibility when choosing instructional methods, classroom space, scheduling, and types of assessment, students of all ages deserve the possibility to express their ideas through creative endeavors (Jalongo, 2003; Manning, 2000; Wahlstrom, 2003).

Honoring Students' Multiple Intelligences. The multiple intelligences that students bring to the classroom are linguistic, mathematical, spatial, interpersonal, intrapersonal, naturalistic, musical, and bodily-kinesthetic (Gardner, 1983, 2003). This chapter emphasizes the benefits of using a variety of teaching methods in order to address the multiple intelligences present in any public middle school classroom population. For instance, dance and movement have been acknowledged for their importance in the daily activity of developing students. Studies have revealed the correlation of dance with achievement in a variety of areas, including self-confidence, persistence, reading skills, nonverbal reasoning, expressive skills, creativity in poetry, social tolerance, appreciation of individual/group social development, and such characteristics of creative thought as fluency, originality, flexibility, and elaboration (Catterall, 2002). For instance, with science content, students can communicate effectively the concepts of solid, liquid, and gas through movement.

The authors believe that arts-integrated instruction can reach a wider spectrum of intelligence areas than traditional textbook-oriented instruction can. However, many teachers have not received professional development in this area and may be uncomfortable incorporating arts into the life of the regular middle school classroom. Therefore, opportunities for additional professional development are needed. Teachers who naturally recognize the differences in their students' learning strengths will welcome learning about strategies and techniques for incorporating arts in education (Gardner, 2003; Jalongo, 2003; Reiff, 1999).

Feeder School Collaborative Planning. The teachers at this West Virginia middle school and the feeder elementary school have consistently engaged in professional development opportunities, which have allowed these teachers to add to their effective teaching techniques. Subsequently, their students are challenged with each integrated unit to engage in creative project development to demonstrate their understanding of the state science curriculum. The textbooks are not usually used as the primary focus of each science unit; instead, the text is regarded as a valuable resource for the creative and engaging process-oriented science learning that takes place in and out of the classroom.

Effective Middle School Literacy Instruction

The International Reading Association's (IRA) position statement on adolescent literacy (IRA, 1999) will be used here as a framework for investigating teaching reading in the science content area. The position statement recommends seven principles as critical to adolescents' literacy education. These tenets focus on materials, pedagogy, developmental characteristics, and collaboration. Interestingly, the position paper uses the word "deserves" when describing these principles. Using the terminology of what adolescents "deserve" as opposed to what educators "must do" sets the tone and truly puts the students' needs at the center of these recommendations. Although all seven principles are vital areas to consider when teaching adolescents, three of the seven principles most directly relate to all content area teaching and are expanded upon below.

Adolescent Literacy Principle 1: Adolescents deserve access to a wide variety of reading materials that they can and want to read.

This principle focuses on providing students opportunities to be exposed to a variety of materials for accessing information. The authors cite NAEP trends reported by Campbell, Voelkl, and Donahue (1998), in which 25 percent of the adolescents assessed reported reading five or fewer pages daily in school and for homework. Further, only 25 percent of these 17-year-olds reported reading for fun. Four research-based notions support providing wide access to a variety of materials: time spent reading is related to reading success, time spent reading is associated with attitudes toward additional reading, time spent reading is tied to knowledge about the world, and reading is a worthwhile life experience (Moore, Bean, Birdyshaw, & Rycik, 1999).

The IRA also recommends providing students time to read, choice of materials, and support in selecting materials. How, then, might one go about providing access to a wide variety of materials within the science curriculum?

Most texts used in formal education are just not reader friendly. Issues of reading difficulty, content, and quality of writing are commonly identified weaknesses of content textbooks (Freeman & Person, 1998). Readability estimates are frequently higher than intended grade level and, due to page limitations, content is sometimes presented in a choppy, abbreviated, and superficial manner. Unfortunately, many teachers use their content textbook as the primary, and often sole, source from which students gain information. Given the limitations of most science textbooks, however, using just one source for obtaining information is unacceptable. Even when students are taught explicit strategies for using such text features as headings, boldface words, and organizational text structure, comprehending the text can still be difficult.

In their study of textbook usage by high school students, Lester and Cheek (1997) found that students identified five elements that made textbooks enjoyable and thus readable: graphics/illustrations, topics of interest to teens, organizational patterns, vocabulary, and design. When elaborating on teen interest topics, the respondents explained that they often found it difficult to make connections between the information presented in the texts with their own lives. "Finding a relationship between the textbook material and the 'real world' of a student is essential to achieve understanding in content area reading" (Lester & Cheek, 1997, p. 289). The use of supplemental materials shows great promise for increasing such student connections by providing access to a wide variety of materials.

Students should be exposed to trade materials that supplement content instruction and complement textbook readings. Supplemental materials can be used in the classroom as teacher read-alouds, sustained silent readings, small-group discussions, or large-group assignments. Daniels and Zemelman (2004) recommend using a variety of genres to supplement textbook reading, including reference books, manuals, news stories, historical accounts, profiles, editorials, essays, reviews, biographies, narrated works of nonfiction, memoirs, novels, plays, and poetry.

Ebbers (2002) concurs with the notion of utilizing a wide variety of genres in the content area, especially in science education. Since the term "informational text" may conjure up a negative stereotype of being dull and boring, teachers need to present a variety of nonfiction or informational materials. Ebbers notes that not all informational trade books limit themselves to simply presenting information, as "many writers give us tales of scientists engaged in all stages of inquiry, including the development and explanatory structures" (p. 42). Ebbers also concludes that not all science-based nonfiction or informational texts can be lumped into one category. She identifies the following six genres of informational science texts: reference, explanation, field guides and how-to, narrative expository, biography, and journals. Each of these trade types can be used in a variety of situations, based on the teacher's goals and objectives.

Richardson (2000) provides examples of how read-alouds can be used in the classroom to explore content area instruction. She highlights the theme of nature by using excerpts from Anne Dillard's Pulitzer Prize-winning book *Pilgrim at Tinker Creek* (1974). In one passage, Dillard uses a journal format to describe observations she made while taking a walk along the water's edge in summertime. She writes of watching a listless frog, among a large group that had been "snuffed" by a giant water bug. She describes how the large bug seized its victims with a paralyzing bite and proceeded to suck the fluid from the body. Her account is so well-written (thus a great read-aloud), it clearly has the capacity to pull a reader in and prompt wonderment about what else one can skillfully observe while in the outdoors.

Camp (2000) recommends using twin text sets in the content classroom. Twin text sets are created by identifying one fiction and one nonfiction text devoted to the same topic. Whereas the nonfiction text may present more straightforward information, the structure of the fictionalized text may be more appealing and easier to comprehend. Two examples of such twin text sets are:

Example 1: *Out of the Dust* by Karen Hesse and *The Kingfisher Young People's Book of Planet Earth,* by Martin Redfern

Example 2: *Earthquake at Dawn,* by Kristiana Gregory and *Forces of Nature: The Awesome Power of Volcanoes, Earthquakes, and Tornadoes* by Catherine O'Neill Grace

In addition to printed material, students should be exposed to content area information through use of multimedia formats, which students often find very appealing. As mentioned above, Lester and Cheek (1997) found that students often get frustrated when they cannot make connections between the information presented in their textbooks and their everyday lives. Making connections between students' lives and interests and the content area materials they study requires some creative teaching. In such an effort, Stevens (2001), a literacy specialist, used popular culture as a connection between content information and teen interests. She teamed up with an 8th-grade physical science teacher who was teaching a unit on the basic laws of motion. The two educators brainstormed how to connect the laws of physics to students' everyday lives and decided to test the credibility of particular action sequence scenes in popular movies. After viewing scenes from *Jumanji* and *Raiders of the Lost Ark*, the students were given 15 minutes to write their conclusions about how well the scene adhered to the laws of physics. Stevens reports that during the exercise, the students consulted their textbooks as a resource while writing their conclusions. Two specific responses are presented below.

Movie	Scene	Possible	Why
Jumanji	A hunter shoots a bullet and the bullet stops in the air.	No	Due to the speed the bullet was traveling, it is impossible to stop.
Raiders of the Lost Ark	A plane crashes—and continues to travel through a narrow tunnel.	Yes	After the wings are shorn off, momentum could propel the plane through the tunnel.

Stevens concluded that students were engaged throughout this lesson and did benefit from it. Their motivation to learn can clearly be related to the connection to their "real world" of movie viewing.

In summary, students deserve access to a wide variety of materials that will supplement textbook reading assignments, including such text-based materials as trade books, magazines, and websites. Movies and recordings also can be integrated into the content area classroom.

Adolescent Literacy Principle #2: Adolescents deserve instruction that builds both the skill and desire to read increasingly complex materials.

Adolescent Literacy Principle #3: Adolescents deserve expert teachers who model and provide explicit instruction in reading comprehension and study strategies across the curriculum.

To complete the activities of a graduate level independent study, Becky, a West Virginia teacher who was three credits shy of attaining a reading specialist certification, decided to explore her options for fulfilling the leadership component of her new role by serving as a resource to teachers (International Reading Association, 2000). She decided to develop a four-part series of professional development workshops focusing on content area literacy comprehension. In the first session, Becky planned to have content teachers closely examine their student textbooks, looking at issues of text structure, interest, readability, and accuracy. With the help of the school's librarian, she also identified lists of supplemental texts for the content area teachers. The three sessions that followed were designed to address reading strategies for before, during, and after reading. Becky planned to introduce Word Exploration (Vacca & Vacca, 2005), KWL (Ogle, 1986), and Anticipation Guides (Herber, 1978) as before-reading strategies. Learning Logs (Santa & Havens, 1991), Think Alouds (Davey, 1983), and Concept Definition Mapping (Schwartz, 1988) were selected for the during-reading session. Finally, Becky chose Questioning Answer Relationships (Raphael, 1986) and Discussion Webs (Alvermann, 1991) as after-reading strategies.

Becky created the content of these workshops based on observations of her students' affective, cognitive, and behavior domains; discussions of these observations with other teachers in her building; and knowledge of the research-based literacy strategies she had learned in her coursework at the university. She knew that the students needed to develop their literacy skills in order to be successful with their middle school content area materials. She felt confident that she could lead and support her fellow content teachers as they attempted to implement the comprehension strategies in their classrooms.

In 1937, William S. Gray coined the expression "every teacher, a teacher of reading." Simply put, all teachers need to understand the reading process and be able to apply the skills and strategies that make a successful reader. Every preservice education candidate must learn how to become a teacher of reading and writing and every inservice teacher needs to know how to apply such knowledge in their content classroom so that students can be successful. When asked, however, many content specialists, especially those teaching at the middle and high school levels, do not see "reading" per se as part of their teaching assignment. Many assume the skill has been taught and mastered in the elementary school classroom. Yet many content specialists are working with "unfriendly" textbooks and at-risk or below average readers, many of whom are not motivated by content area subject matter. Unfortunately, although passionate about their area of expertise, many content area specialists lack the tools to help students read and comprehend the texts being used in their classes. Teaching reading comprehension strategies in the content area should be a focus for all teachers. However, content teachers must first have an understanding of what comprehension is, as well as how to effectively teach comprehension strategies and where to go for additional resources.

Pardo (2004) identifies four key components to the comprehension process: reader, context, text, and transaction. Transaction occurs when the reader, text, and context come together. In order to meet the goal of successful comprehension with printed text, a reader must negotiate and process a text's letters, words, sentences, paragraphs, and chapters. Additionally, a reader's background or prior knowledge and motivation play a vital role in comprehending material.

Given recent advances in technology, reading comprehension can no longer be viewed as reading a paragraph and answering the questions presented at the end of the reading assignment. In fact, in a classic study, Durkin (1978) identified only 45 minutes of actual comprehension instruction during 300 hours of observed teaching in classrooms of "the best teachers" (p. 495). The study found that what most teachers were calling comprehension instruction was actually assessing comprehension—typically, answering questions at the end of the reading block. Durkin defined comprehension *instruction* as when the "teacher does/says something to help children understand or work out the meaning of more than a single isolated word" (p. 488). She defined comprehension *assessment* as being when the "teacher does/says something in order to learn whether what was read was comprehended" (p. 490). Durkin's "assessing comprehension" model is, by far, too much the norm in today's content area classrooms.

In addition to activating background knowledge, preteaching vocabulary, and getting students interested and motivated to understand, teachers can support students by teaching about selected text structures and providing time to read (Pardo, 2004). Teachers also can support students by providing explicit direct instruction and modeling of comprehension strategies, teaching children how and when to use such strategies, using multiple strategy approaches, and scaffolding their attempts at applying newly learned strategies.

The National Reading Panel (National Institute of Child Health and Human Development, 2000) recommends the following strategies to improve student comprehension: collaborative learning, question generation, comprehension monitoring, question answering, summarization, and use of story maps and graphic organizers. The Panel also suggests that applying multiple strategies simultaneously is most beneficial to students.

Numerous sources for reading strategies can be found in text-based form and on the Internet. In fact, a recent Google search for "reading strategies" brought up 838,000 hits! Since identifying content-based reading strategies can become an entire text in itself (see below), we have identified a select number of text-based and Internet resources for further investigations.

- Mid-continent Research for Education and Learning (Billmeyer & Barton, 1998; www.McREL. org) publishes a series of resource books on strategic reading in the content areas. The first publication, *Teaching Reading in the Content Area: If Not Me, Then Who?*, is a collection of strategies for informational text. This title was followed up with supplemental content-specific sample texts for science, math, and social studies.
- The International Reading Association publishes the following compendiums of literacy strategies: *Classroom Strategies for Interactive Learning* (Buehl, 2001), *Building Reading Comprehension Habits in Grades 6-12: A Toolkit of Classroom Activities* (Zwiers, 2004), and *Guided Comprehension: A Teaching Model for Grades 3-8* (McLaughlin & Allen, 2002).
- The University of Virginia's Curry School of Education has published *Reading Quest: Making Sense of Social Studies* (the strategies apply to science and math content areas also); see www.readingquest.org.

It is important to note, however, that simply purchasing a text or downloading a template will not make for successful reading instruction in the science classroom. We need to discuss, plan, collaborate, and work together to ensure that students have access to expert teachers providing explicit instruction to increase students' literacy skills. As Keene and Zimmerman (1997) so eloquently state in their landmark text *Mosaic of Thought*, "We must pay attention to the conditions in which we infer and go about creating classroom structures that permit children to discuss, ponder, argue, restate, reflect, persuade, relate, and write about or otherwise work with the words and ideas they read" (p. 161). As content area educators, we need to keep this powerful quote in mind and give our adolescent learners what they deserve.

In addition to reading comprehension, literacy competence includes writing, speaking, listening, viewing, and visually representing (Tompkins, 2005). The *National Science Education*

Standards (National Research Council, 1996) demand that students be scientifically literate. Scientific literacy is much more than is implied by the joining of the definitions for "literacy" and "science." Ebbers (2002) suggests scientific literacy is more that just reading for comprehension: "It means a person can ask, find, or determine answers to questions that derive from curiosity about everyday experiences" (p. 40). She recommends the skillful weaving of the scientific skills of observing, asking questions, predicting, describing, explaining, and investigating with the literacy practices of reading, writing, speaking, and listening.

Effective Science Teaching

Science for All Americans (Rutherford & Ahlgren, 1990) really means science *literacy* for all Americans. Language and the constituents of literacy—reading, writing, speaking, listening, and, more recently, viewing and visual representation—are essential to conducting science and achieving science literacy (Yore et al., 2004). Yore et al. contend that science education needs a paradigm shift that emphasizes strategic language activity and social relevance, which will further strengthen the literacy-science connection.

Science literacy is much more than mastery of a body of knowledge (science as product), just as literacy is much more than reading and vocabulary building. The *National Science Education Standards* (NSES) (National Research Council, 1996) document makes abundantly clear that achieving science literacy requires "doing science"; inherent in that pursuit are a host of science

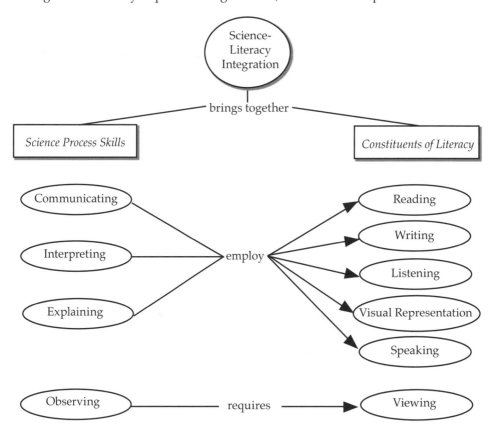

Figure 6.2.
Sample Concept Map of Science and Literacy Connections

process skills that utilize language: explaining, interpreting, and, more broadly, communicating. The concept map illustrated in Figure 6.2 depicts the interrelatedness of the science process skills with various constituents of literacy.

The *NSES* emphasize the importance of "inquiry" as a means to learn the life, physical, and earth and space sciences (National Research Council, 1996, 2000). Doing so involves all of the constituents of literacy: *reading* to ascertain what is already known; *writing* to pose investigative questions and record data; *viewing* to observe what happens when a variable is manipulated; *speaking* and *listening* to engage in discourse ("talk science") with peers while investigating as well as reporting findings; and employing *visual representations,* such as graphs and data tables, in communicating findings of investigation.

In *Nurturing Inquiry,* Pearce (1997) pushes the limits of what is possible in employing writing, speaking, and listening to learn science. Students write reports of their investigations that contribute to a "Book of Discoveries" (Pearce, 1997, p. 39) to inform the investigations of future students, and they partake in a "Kids' Inquiry Conference" (p. 100). He, as does Lake (2000), also emphasizes the importance of reading science tradebooks in conjunction with hands-on activities to inform investigations. Further, Lake, as well as Carin, Bass, and Contant (2005), convey the extensive role of literacy in assessing students' understandings and abilities in science through the use of journals, diagrams, performance assessments (including presentations), and portfolios. These measures provide students with increased, and better, opportunities to show what they know, compared to traditional assessment vehicles (e.g., worksheets and tests).

The use of models in science instruction is perhaps the most robust example of the "visual representation" literacy element. Models attempt to make the abstract concrete. Models as visual representations go beyond physical models (like a human skeleton) to include concept maps (also referred to as mental models), chemical formulae, and simulations (Harrison & Treagust, 1998). Although models are often used for demonstration, a powerful learning strategy is to engage students in making and testing models, such as volcanoes, planes or rockets, and waves. The construction and/or presentation of a model also can be a task given to students as an authentic assessment of what was learned. For example, students might be asked to construct and present models of plant and animal cells, an atom for certain elements, a food web showing the flow of matter and energy, or a portion of our solar system that includes the sun-earth-moon system.

In terms of sequencing the constituents of literacy in teaching science, Carin et al. (2005) remind us that comprehension of science textbooks is dependent on prior knowledge and activating that knowledge. Accordingly, they advocate an approach in which learners first engage in investigation and then read the text. They describe the parallels between good science and reading instruction, both of which ask students to describe events, predict, make inferences, interpret, and conclude.

Freedman (1999) describes innovative strategies as part of "Writing for Understanding" (p. 41). Students can use "Science Daybooks" (p. 42) to record their thoughts, ideas, and questions—which otherwise may be lost—relative to science concepts in daily lessons. "Note Taking, Note Making" (p. 45) engages students' prior knowledge and helps them to be active listeners, making inquiry into the topic of study. For this strategy, students subdivide their paper and write questions and reflections about their notes. This strategy can be integrated with "Science Daybooks," which in turn provides teachers with feedback about students' assimilation of concepts while informing future instruction. Gilbert and Kotelman (2005) determined that teachers find these "science notebooks" can be valuable thinking tools that inform subsequent instruction, augment literacy skills, support differentiated learning, and foster collaboration among teachers.

Instructional Models for Integrating Literacy. A learning cycle model offers multiple opportunities to integrate literacy and science instruction in an inquiry context. Figure 6.3 illustrates examples of literacy integration with the 5-E model—a type of learning cycle—that embeds sequential phases of engagement, exploration, explanation, elaboration, and evaluation (Carin et

5-E Model Phase	Examples of Corresponding Literacy Integration
Engagement	Viewing • Students view a demonstration by the teacher that portrays a discrepant event to generate curiosity. Listening • Teacher reads portion of trade book related to topic to generate interest.
Exploration	Writing • Students write predictions for what will happen when a variable is manipulated. Viewing • Students observe what happens when a variable is manipulated. Speaking • Students discuss with small-group members the potential reasons underlying what happened when a variable was manipulated.
Explanation	Listening • Students listen to their peers as they compare and contrast the findings from the Exploration. Visual Representation • Teacher constructs concept map utilizing input from students to show connections among key lesson concepts.
Elaboration	Reading • Students read background information from a text and procedures for carrying out a controlled investigation that applies lesson concepts. Visual Representation • Students organize data table and construct graphs of their findings from the investigation.
Evaluation	Writing • Students prepare a report of the controlled investigation. Speaking and Visually Representing • Students provide a presentation on the findings of their investigation that includes charts and diagrams.

Figure 6.3
Examples of Literacy Integration With the 5-E Learning Cycle Model

al., 2005; see also the Biological Sciences Curriculum Study at www.bscs.org/curriculumdevelopment/features/bscs5es.html). Figures 6.4 and 6.5 provide actual components of field-tested 5-E learning cycles that engage learners in writing and visual representation.

Science-Technology-Society (STS) instruction—especially the investigation and action model used by Rubba et al. (1995)—is rich in opportunities for students to employ the constituents of literacy in persuading others to take action towards resolving issues and mitigating related problems. Writing, speaking, and visual representation all can be harnessed to persuade others. For example, relative to the STS issue of solid waste, students might develop a brochure to convince others to recycle. Further, students might speak to the local school board about the need for and value of initiating a school recycling program. Relative to the STS issue of global warming, students might be engaged in drawing or constructing a visual representation of how greenhouse gases are building up in the atmosphere, and employ the representation in persuading citizens to carpool, use available mass transit, and plant trees (Rye, Strong, & Rubba, 2001).

Concluding Thoughts

As Paul, a 5th-grade science teacher, points out, "Science seems very vocabulary-driven at this grade level, so I try to do activities that enhance the [concepts] for a particular unit (flip books,

---

Elaboration Phase

1. Bring up the fact that we came to the conclusion that opposites attract. Ask them if they think they could write a story about a magnet.
2. Explain that they are going to create a story about a magnet that is new in town and is looking to make some friends. What kind of friends might he get along with or be "attracted to"? Who might he not get along with or "repel"? Allow the class to discuss.
3. Mention that there is a new boy magnet in town named Murray, and he would really like to make some friends to play with (the name could be changed). The students will agree on what the main character will look like. The character could be portrayed as a bar magnet, horseshoe magnet, circular magnet, etc. Tell the students that they are going to create a picture that shows Murray meeting somebody. Since this is a fictional story, the "people" he meets will be objects. Explain that they must create a picture of Murray meeting an object and that the object can attract, not attract, or repel Murray. Have the students provide text/dialogue for each illustration that shows their understanding of why certain objects attract or repel. Provide the class with an example. Once the class understands the concept, pass out the paper and coloring utensils and allow them to begin illustrating. If time expires, then the lesson will continue the next day. Once the illustrations are done, each student will write a sentence on the bottom of their illustration that explains what is happening. The illustrations will be collected and bound together to form one story.

Figure 6.4
Excerpt From the Elaboration Phase of a Learning Cycle on Magnets That Integrates "Viewing" and "Writing" Aspects of Literacy

(Contributed by Anthony Folden, Preservice Elementary Teacher)

storyboards, anything that illustrates the vocabulary). Also, when doing the hands-on labs, [I make] sure the terms are used constantly when class discussions occur or when results may need to be recorded. When we read from the text in class, I always do some sort of read-aloud, whether it be the kids, a CD/tape, or hearing it from me. That way, I know they have all at least heard it, because some students will never read it on their own, due to learning disabilities or [other difficulties]. Also, doing it this way allows for class discussions throughout the reading."

Sarah, a 6th-grade science teacher, adds, "[We had an] emphasis on integrated curriculum across the [ability] levels. Teachers help the 6th-graders make the cognitive bridge [from one content to another]. The constructivist approach is harder to plan, and we can only plan to a point and then follow the students to where they go [with their projects]. Our daily 6th-grade team meetings help us meet the needs of the students with true, consistent, collaboration. In this way, we are able to be consistent with the curriculum [across all content areas]."

Maxine Greene (1995) discusses the expansive thought that results from the firing up of the imagination. Clearly, these teachers are establishing positive science memories that tap

---

Elaboration Phase

1. Ask students to think about how they would use the information they have collected to make a 3-D model to represent their biome. Would you put mountains in the desert? Would you put snow in the tropical rain forest?

2. Explain to the class that they will need to work together as a group to build a 3-D representation of their biome. They will be given a grading rubric to work from (explain that this is telling them how you will be grading their model).

   a. They will need to represent the landforms (e.g., mountains, plains), climate (sunny, snowy), plants/animals (various animals, coniferous trees, deciduous trees). The inside walls of the box should be painted or have pictures (the art specialist will lead this part—all students will contribute, but the art specialist has the final say and oversees the process).

   b. They will also need to attach a paper to one side of the box describing (recorder's job): average temperature, average rainfall, examples of animals, examples of plants, and types of landforms.

   c. They will attach a picture on the other side of the box of a world map indicating (by color, outline, etc.) the locations of this biome (students may need direction on how to print the picture off the website provided—this will be the web researcher's job).

   d. The top of the box needs to have a label of the biome.

3. Inform students that they can use a variety of materials to complete their model (clay, construction paper, pipe cleaners, paint, pictures, rocks, glue, etc.) and that part of their grade will be based on the colorfulness/interesting design of the model (gathering the appropriate materials will be the job of the materials student).

Figure 6.5
Excerpt From Elaboration Phase of 4th-Grade Learning Cycle on World Biomes That Integrates the "Visual Representation" Aspect of Literacy
(Contributed by Jessica Hartman, Preservice Elementary Teacher)

into the students' imaginations. These fortunate middle school students have experienced meaning making, arts integration, learning cycles, concept mapping, and literacy learning while engaged in exciting science experiences. These students have been given diverse possibilities in their daily expressions of meaning (Jalongo, 2003; Manning, 2000). As a result, they will carry their memorable moments in science learning with them throughout their lives.

References

Alvermann, D. (1991). The discussion web: A graphic aid for learning across the curriculum. *The Reading Teacher, 45*(2), 92-99.

Billmeyer, R., & Barton, M. L. (1998). *Teaching reading in the content area: If not me, then who?* Denver, CO: Mid-continent Research for Education and Learning.

Buehl, D. (2001). *Classroom strategies for interactive learning.* Newark, DE: International Reading Association.

Camp, D. (2000). It takes two: Teaching with twin texts of fact and fiction. *The Reading Teacher, 53*(5), 400-408.

Campbell, J. R., Voekl, K. E., & Donahue, P. L. (1998). *Report in brief: NAEP 1996 trends in academic progress* (Publication No. 98-530). Washington, DC: National Center for Education Statistics.

Carin, A., Bass, J., & Contant, T. (2005). *Teaching science as inquiry.* Upper Saddle River, NJ: Pearson.

Catterall, J. (2002). *Critical links: Learning in the arts and student academic and social development.* Washington, DC: Arts Education Partnership.

Consortium of National Arts Education Associations. (1994). *National standards for arts education.* Reston, VA: Music Educators National Conference/National Association for Music Education.

Daniels, H., & Zemelman, S. (2004). *Subjects matter: Every teacher's guide to content area reading.* Portsmouth, NH: Heinemann.

Davey, B. (1983). Think aloud: Modeling the cognitive processes of reading comprehension. *Journal of Reading, 27*(1), 44-47.

Dillard, A. (1974). *Pilgrim at Tinker Creek.* New York: HarperCollins.

Durkin, D. (1978). What classroom observations reveal about reading comprehension instruction. *Reading Research Quarterly, 14*, 481-538.

Ebbers, M. (2002). Science text sets: Using various genres to promote literacy and inquiry. *Language Arts, 80*(1), 40-50.

Freedman, R. L. (1999). *Science and writing connections.* White Plains, NY: Dale Seymour Publications.

Freeman, E., & Person, D. (1998). *Connecting informational children's books with content area learning.* Boston: Allyn & Bacon.

Gardner, H. (1983). *Frames of mind.* New York: Basic Books.

Gardner, H. (2003). *Multiple intelligences after twenty years.* Chicago: American Educational Research Association.

Gilbert, J., & Kotelman, M. (2005). Five good reasons to use science notebooks. *Science and Children, 4*(3), 28-32.

Greene, M. (1995). *Releasing the imagination: Essays on education, the arts, and social change.* San Francisco: Jossey-Bass.

Harrison, A., & Treagust, D. (1998). Modeling in science lessons: Are there better ways to learn with models? *School Science and Mathematics, 98*, 420-429.

Herber, H. (1978). *Teaching reading in content areas* (2nd ed.). Englewood Cliffs, NJ: Prentice Hall.

International Reading Association. (1999). *Position statement on adolescent literacy.* Available at www.reading.org/resources/issues/positions_adolescent.html.

International Reading Association. (2000). *Teaching all children to read: The roles of the reading specialist.* Newark, DE: Author.

Jalongo, M. R. (2003). The child's right to creative thought and expression: A position paper. *Childhood Education, 79*, 218-228.

Keene, E. O., & Zimmerman, S. (1997). *Mosaic of thought: Teaching comprehension in a reader's workshop.* Portsmouth, NH: Heinemann.

Lake, J. (2000). *Literature and science breakthroughs.* Markham, Ontario: Pembroke Publishers.

Lester, J. H., & Cheek, E. H., Jr. (1997). The "real" experts address textbook issues. *Journal of Adolescent & Adult Literacy, 41*(4), 282-291.

Manning, M. L. (2000). Child-centered middle schools: A position paper. *Childhood Education, 76,* 154-159.

McLaughlin, M., & Allen, M. (2002). *Guided comprehension: A teaching model for grades 3-8.* Newark, DE: International Reading Association.

Moore, D. W., Bean, T. W., Birdyshaw, D., & Rycik, J. A. (1999). Adolescent literacy: A position statement. *Journal of Adolescent & Adult Literacy, 43*(1), 97-112.

National Center for Education Statistics. (1996). *Reading proficiency and home support for literacy.* Retrieved from http://nces.ed.gov/pubs96/web/96814.asp.

National Institute of Child Health and Human Development. (2000). *Report of the National Reading Panel. Teaching children to read: An evidence-based assessment of the scientific research literature on reading and its implications for reading instruction.* (NIH Publication No. 00-4769). Washington, DC: U.S. Government Printing Office.

National Research Council. (1996). *National science education standards.* Washington, DC: National Academy Press.

National Research Council. (2000). *Inquiry and the national science education standards.* Washington, DC: National Academy Press.

Ogle, D. (1986). K-W-L: A teaching model that develops active reading of expository text. *The Reading Teacher, 39*(6), 564-570.

Pardo, L. S. (2004). What every teacher needs to know about comprehension. *The Reading Teacher, 58*(3), 272–280.

Pearce, C. (1997). *Nurturing inquiry.* Portsmouth, NH: Heinemann.

Raphael, T. E. (1986). Teaching question-answer strategies for children. *The Reading Teacher, 39*(6), 515-522.

Reiff, J. (1999, April). *Implementing a learner-sensitive classroom based on brain theory and multiple intelligences.* Paper presented at the meeting of the Association for Childhood Education International, San Antonio, TX.

Richardson, J. (2000). *Read it aloud: Using literature in the secondary content classroom.* Newark, DE: International Reading Association.

Rubba, P., Wiesenmayer, R., Rye, J., McClaren, M., Sillman, K., Yorks, K., Yukish, D., Ditty, T., Morphew, V., Bradford, C., Dorough, D., & Arabas, K. (Eds.). (1995). *Global atmospheric change: The enhanced greenhouse effect, ozone layer depletion, and ground level ozone pollution. A Science-Technology-Society Issue Investigation and Action Unit for the middle grades.* University Park, PA: The Pennsylvania State University. Available online at: www.ed.psu.edu/CI/papers/sts/gac-main.html.

Rutherford, F. J., & Ahlgren, A. (1990). *Science for all Americans.* New York: Oxford University Press.

Rye, J., Strong, D., & Rubba, P. (2001). Global warming and ozone layer depletion: STS issues worth including in social studies instruction. *Social Education, 65,* 90-95.

Santa, C. M., & Havens, L. T. (1991). Learning though writing. In C. M. Sand & D. E. Alvermann (Eds.), *Science learning: Processes and applications* (pp. 122-133). Newark, DE: International Reading Association.

Schwartz, R. (1988). Learning to learn vocabulary in content area textbooks. *Journal of Reading, 32,* 108-117.

Stevens, L. (2001). "South Park" and society: Instructional and curricular implications of popular culture in the classroom. *Journal of Adolescent & Adult Literacy, 44*(6), 548-565.

Tompkins, G. (2005). *Language arts: Patterns of practice.* Upper Saddle River, NJ: Pearson.

University of Virginia Curry School of Education. (nd). *Reading Quest: Making sense of social studies.* Retrieved November 10, 2007, from www.readingquest.org.

Vacca, R., & Vacca, J. (2005). *Content area reading: Literacy and learning across the curriculum.* Boston: Pearson.

Wahlstrom, K. (2003). *Arts for academic achievement: Images of arts infusion in elementary* classrooms. Minneapolis, MN: Center for Applied Research and Educational Improvement, University of Minnesota Press.

Yore, L., Hand, B., Goldman, S., Hildebrand, G., Osborne, J., Treagust, D., & Wallace, C. (2004). New directions in language and science education research. *Reading Research Quarterly, 39,* 347-352.

Zwiers, J. (2004). *Building reading comprehension habits in grades 6-12: A toolkit of classroom activities.* Newark, DE: International Reading Association.

Web Resources for Suncrest Middle School

http://boe.mono.k12.wv.us/SuncrestMiddle/

Suncrest Middle School Website

http://sciencenetlinks.com/resource_index.htm

Science Web link on homepage for Suncrest Middle School, stating a commitment to science for the whole school community, sponsored by Web links from the National Science Foundation, Marco Polo, MCI, AAAS, Science Netlink.

www.edline.net/pages/Suncrest_Middle_School/Classes/05-06-600600-002

Mrs. Corder's 6th-grade science Web link for Suncrest Middle School.

Acknowledgment

A special thanks to Sarah Corder and John Vidovich, science teachers at Suncrest Middle School (a National Blue Ribbon School); Paul Gunter, a science teacher at North Elementary School (an Exemplary School); Jennifer Akins-Moffatt, a demonstration teacher for Monongalia County Schools and former science teacher at North Elementary; and Steven, a middle school student.

Meet the Authors

Joy Faini Saab has focused her research and teaching on integrating the arts in education, international models of excellence in early childhood education, and teaching for creativity. She teaches undergraduate and master's and doctoral candidates at West Virginia University, and has published in numerous journals. She is currently organizing international study opportunities for students at WVU and recently was invited to speak at the International Centenary Conference for Montessori Education in Rome, Italy.

Allison Swan Dagen, a reading specialist and former middle school teacher, currently serves as an assistant professor at West Virginia University. She teaches graduate courses in the literacy studies program. Her recent research has focused on vocabulary assessment and establishing a community of learners in the online teaching environment.

James Rye teaches undergraduate and graduate courses in science education at West Virginia University. His scholarly interests include science-mathematics integration as well as science-technology-society education for investigating human and environmental health issues. He has been an investigator on externally funded projects that foster university-community partnerships, science teacher professional development, inquiry-based learning, and the mitigation of public health problems. He has published in numerous science and teacher education journals.

Chapter 7

Literacy and Movement in Charlita's 5th-Grade Physical Education Classes

This chapter illustrates ways that movement and language can be integrated, while creating a safe, supportive environment that supports a culture of high expectations and active learning. The Association for Childhood Education International (ACEI) supports learner-centered middle schools in which high expectations and active learning are integral curriculum components. Teachers of all content areas must take into consideration students' development and choose curriculum and learning activities appropriate for their developmental stage (Williams-Boyd, 2005). By providing a learner-centered model for adolescents, educators focus on the learners' developmental needs and encourage high expectations for all students (Manning & Bucher, 2000; Williams-Boyd, 2005).

Charlita is a 3rd- to 5th-grade physical education (P.E.) teacher at Diamond Hill Elementary, which is part of the Fort Worth Independent School District (FWISD). Ninety-five percent of the students at Diamond Hill Elementary School are Hispanic and 60 percent are identified as English language learners (ELLs). Despite the challenges students face, a positive learning community is evident to parents, students, and community members as they walk through the doors of Diamond Hill Elementary. This chapter focuses on Charlita's work with 5th-grade students, who are primarily ELLs, and the many ways that she integrates movement and literacy into P.E.

Making Content Learning Comprehensible

Since Charlita's gym class is composed primarily of ELLs, she understands that she must not only teach her subject matter, but also teach language and culture (Johnson, 2005). How can P.E. teachers help students develop English language proficiency? First, teachers must understand the difference between *acquiring* and *learning* a second language. In the 1980s, Stephen Krashen (1982) first distinguished the differences between *acquiring* a language and *learning* a new language. A student who *acquires* a new language learns to speak the language without thinking of grammatical rules while holding an informal conversation. *Acquiring* a language means using the language for real purposes, instead of learning isolated grammar rules (Krashen, 2000). When *learning* a language, isolated drill practice focuses on vocabulary and the rules of grammar. While one may be able to translate sentences from a foreign language book, or even diagram a sentence, real language fluency—that is, communicating in both formal and informal environments—is rarely achieved through such instruction. Krashen explains that the key for ELLs to understand unknown messages, or new content material, is for teachers to

Jan Lacina and Charlita Smith

provide comprehensible input. Comprehensible input enables students to make connections between what they know and what they do not know (Carrier, 2005; Silvina, 2005). Physical education teachers like Charlita make input comprehensible by constantly modeling, using groups to further scaffold directions, and by using graphic organizers to display important vocabulary, shortened sentences, or pictures in a way to lessen the language load (Aukerman, 2007; Carrier, 2005).

Read-Alouds

P.E. teachers also can make learning comprehensible by providing frequent read-alouds (Freeman & Freeman, 2000; Sanacore, 2006), such as reading aloud together activity directions. When teachers read aloud books whose main character the students can identify with, students then are able to make connections to the material and find greater meaning in reading (Wickstrom, Curtis, & Daniel, 2005). Students also begin to connect oral language and print. Charlita specifically provides comprehensible input by drawing on her students' prior background knowledge. She connects their experiences to the lesson, and she uses visuals to reinforce and scaffold new vocabulary.

Teaching Vocabulary in P.E.

Teaching vocabulary prepares students, especially ELLs, for success, by increasing comprehension and enabling students to advance socially and academically (Cummins, 2000; Manzo, Manzon, & Thomas, 2007). Since academic vocabulary and language structures tend to be very different from the vocabulary and language structures used in the ELLs' homes (Heath, 1983; Scott, 2004; Zentella, 1997), Charlita finds fun ways to teach vocabulary and reinforce the words learned during health lessons each week. For ELLs in particular, vocabulary needs to be explicitly taught—and connected to reading, and the physical activity, in meaningful ways (Lacina, New Levine, & Sowa, 2006). In the past, many content area teachers gave students a list of vocabulary words on Monday, and students were told to memorize the words' definitions. During the week, the teacher might provide word scrabbles, worksheets, or vocabulary games to help reinforce the words. Then on Friday, students would be tested on the words in their weekly vocabulary list. For ELLs, or for any struggling reader, such an activity is not effective, since students may not have the background knowledge to connect the word to its meaning. Vocabulary lessons are more effective when teachers plan instruction so that students use the words in meaningful contexts; in such cases, they are more apt to remember the words (Beers, 2003). Charlita finds ways to continually teach vocabulary by actively involving students in movement activities. She finds that vocabulary development is essential for her students' understanding of health concepts, and movement activities provide a fun and meaningful way to teach vocabulary.

Writing Instruction and P.E.

Writing can be easily incorporated into the physical education class in a way that strengthens and enhances regular physical activities. With great emphasis being placed on high-stakes reading and writing tests (Higgins, Miller, & Wegmann, 2007), Charlita wanted to find a way that she could help prepare students for the test while using best practices for teaching. For that reason, she formed a writing pen-pal project with another P.E. class. In addition to this writing project, Charlita finds other ways to integrate writing into movement activities. She explains,

I've done several types of activities that require reading/writing. For my 5th-graders, they had to create their own game. What we did is set out particular equipment. So, they had to, in groups, come up with ideas how to use the equipment. They had to write down the steps, step by step, on how to play the game. They had to then role-play the activity that they designed.

Buell and Whittaker (2001) also support the importance of integrating writing into physical education. Students might record their performance, or participation, after a physical activity. Journal writing and reflection is a way for students to record and document their performance during a physical activity. For example, students might be asked to reflect on their participation and performance, and then set performance or participation goals for the future. Writing also can be used with team sports as students use task cards.

Writing is often not included in the P.E. classroom, since many teachers do not think the gym is the place to write, but this is the result of envisioning only a limited scope for writing (Behrman, 2004). Figure 7.1 presents several writing genres and ways that teachers can integrate writing into physical education lessons.

Genre	Example
Letter	Charlita had her students participate in a writing exchange with another Fort Worth P.E. class. Students wrote about their favorite movement activities.
Diary	Students can record how far they walk or jog in a diary, and then they can graph distance over time.
Poster/Display	Charlita's class competed in a Turkey Trot during the fall semester. Students who were able to jog for seven minutes signed a large paper turkey, and they were then eligible to win a real turkey. Such posters, designed by children, encourage physical activity while also promoting writing.
Editorial	Recently, many school districts have eliminated gym class, as a result of increased pressure from high-stakes tests. At Charlita's school, the early childhood teachers teach their own P.E. classes, and Charlita only teaches grades 3-5 P.E. Students in such schools could write an editorial on the importance of physical education for all ages of children.
Creative Writing	Students could write a poem or narrative piece describing their feelings when competing in a physical activity.
Chat Rooms or Discussion Boards	The Internet provides an excellent resource for writing about and discussing sports or physical activities. Students could post their goals for their next sports competition, or chat rooms/discussion boards could be used as a place to reflect on the strengths/weaknesses of a particular sports competition or physical activity.

Figure 7.1
Writing and Physical Education

Literature and Physical Education

Literature can enhance any content area, and teachers can integrate literacy into the gym in a number of ways. One way for teachers to gain student interest is to highlight books that focus on a student's athletic strength. For example, teachers could spend a few minutes prior to a movement activity reading an excerpt from a book that focuses on the particular activity or sport the students are about to try. By focusing on athletics and books, teachers can promote the importance of maintaining a healthy lifestyle.

Read-Alouds and Book Talks. Reading aloud to students provides opportunities to model fluent reading and, most importantly, it is a way to interest students in a physical education activity (Lane & Wright, 2007; Richardson, 2000). Similarly, when content area teachers promote reading, they show students that reading is important; such enthusiasm influences students' perception of reading. When using literature for a read-aloud in P.E., consider the following recommendations:

- Choose an interesting book, or reading selection, that would engage and interest your students. It should be a selection that relates to a physical education activity and promotes critical discussion.
- Preview the material and select pages/excerpts that would be most interesting for students.
- Practice prior to reading aloud to your class. Students would be most interested in the read-aloud if the reader is expressive and makes eye contact frequently.
- Involve students. By asking questions or having students make predictions, you can actively involve your students in the read-aloud. Most importantly, this is a way to make connections between physical education and literacy.

Silent Sustained Reading. Many schools require teachers to include a time of silent reading within their lesson plans. Silent sustained reading (SSR) is a regular time when everyone in the class reads (Alverman & Phelps, 2005; Parr & Maguiness, 2005). For P.E. teachers, including a time for SSR is difficult, and can be impractical to schedule each day of the year. However, content area teachers may find times when groups of students are working on selective activities at varying paces, and this may be a good time to use SSR. The importance of SSR for P.E. is that students who are particularly interested in sports can read books of interest about that particular sport. SSR also may be initiated as teachers prepare students to participate in a new activity. It can be a time to gain in-depth knowledge about a particular sport. Independent reading is especially important for struggling readers and English language learners. Allowing students the choice to read what they want, and the time to read without academic pressure, is a way to help English language learners move from easier to more difficult material (Alverman & Phelps, 2005); most critically for P.E., students develop confidence in both their reading and physical abilities.

Selecting Books. A large number of excellent fiction and nonfiction books exist that teachers can use for either a read-aloud or SSR. More than anything else, student choice and interest should be considered when selecting books. Prior to a read-aloud or SSR, be sure to read the book to check for its appropriateness. Figure 7.2 includes a list of good books categorized by their particular sport. Although many of the books listed below may interest students, the appropriateness for middle level students needs to be carefully examined, as some content may be

Sport	Books
General Sports	• *Girls in Love* by Cherie Bennett • *Athletic Shorts: Six Short Stories* by Chris Crutcher • *Ironman* by Chris Crutcher • *Sports Stories* by Alan Durant • *River Thunder* by Will Hobbs • *We've Got Spirit: The Life and Times of America's Greatest Cheerleading Team* by James McElroy • *The Runner* by Cynthia Voigt
Baseball/ Softball	• *Throwing Smoke* by Bruce Brooks • *Bull Catcher* by Aiden Carter • *The Crazy Horse Electric Game* by Chris Crutcher • *The Rookie Arrives* by Thomas Dygard • *Cutting Loose* by Michael Z. Lewin • *Extra Innings* by Robert Peck • *My Thirteenth Season* by Kristi Roberts
Basketball	• *Chinese Handcuffs* by Chris Crutcher • *Counting Coup: A True Story of Basketball and Honor on the Little Big Horn* by Larry Colton • *Rebound Capper* by Thomas Dygard • *Last Shot: A Final Four Mystery* by John Feinstein • *Hoops: A Novel* by Walter Dean Myer • *Slam!* by Walter Dean Myer • *Players* by Joyce Sweeney
Football	• *Running Loose* by Chris Crutcher • *Forward Pass* by Thomas Dygard • *Roughnecks* by Thomas Cochran • *The Wimp and the Jock* by John Ibbitson • *Anything to Win* by Gloria D. Miklowitz • *Running Wild* by Thomas Dygard • *Halfback Tough* by Thomas Dygard
Soccer	• *Tangerine* by Edward Bloor • *Home of the Braves* by David Klass • *Going for the Record* by Julie A. Swanson • *Shots on Goal* by Rich Wallace
Swimming	• *Staying Fat for Sarah Byrnes* by Chris Crutcher • *Stotan!* by Chris Crutcher • *Whale Talk* by Chris Crutcher • *Head Above Water* by S.L. Rottman • *Born in Sin* by Evelyn Coleman
Tennis	• *Amazing Grace* by Megan Shull • *Break Point* by Rosie Rushton • *The Kid From Courage* by Ron Berman • *Tennis Ace* by Matt Christopher • *Competitive Tennis for Young Players: The Road to Becoming a Top Player* by Manfred Grosser and Richard Schonborn
Wrestling/ Boxing	• *The Boxer* by Kathleen Karr • *Redhanded* by Michael Cadnum • *Wrestling With Honor* by David Klass • *Fighting Ruben Wolfe* by Markus Zusak • *Wrestling Sturbridge* by Rich Wallace • *Shadow Boxer* by Chris Lynch

Figure 7.2. Physical Education and Books

more appropriate for high school or older students.

A Safe and Supportive Environment. By taking a visual tour of the gym, one can see how a safe and supportive environment can be created in P.E. As students enter the gym, they are greeted by Charlita, who is smiling as she welcomes students to P.E. On their way to their assigned seats on the gym floor, students see brightly colored posters on all four walls of the gym. Some posters describe the different food groups, while others emphasize the importance of exercising and eating right. The rules of the gym are posted, and on a large chalkboard the "strategy of the day" is written. The strategy of the day tells students what strategy they will learn, in addition to noting the day's activities. A chart with writing ideas is posted on one wall, as students have just begun a writing project with another P.E. class in Fort Worth.

On this particular day, Charlita's bilingual assistant, John, places cones throughout the room with words and pictures of a student demonstrating exercise activities. The goal is for students to learn new words by seeing the visual image and by participating in the movement activity. For the ELLs, the pictures accompanying the words support their efforts to transfer what they know about the English language to the P.E. activity.

Seasonal posters are on display, reflecting the fact that Thanksgiving is approaching. This week, students are setting goals to complete a jog in seven minutes, the Turkey Trot. When they complete the seven-minute jog, they sign the turkey and thereby enter a competition to win a real turkey for Thanksgiving. The environment of the gym is inviting, safe, and supportive.

High Expectations for Every Student

A positive attitude and high expectations for her students are integral components of Charlita's teaching philosophy. Charlita explains that she expects her students to be successful, and in doing so, she keeps learning exciting and meaningful. She explains that she wants all of her students to be successful; for that reason, she challenges her students with different types of activities. Charlita teaches health education each Thursday, and she reinforces material from the health curriculum by integrating literacy learning and movement activities. Varying the instructional activities takes extra time and planning, but Charlita finds that students better apply what they understand when instruction is varied and student centered.

Content literacy is included in all aspects of Charlita's class. The gym is surrounded with posters rich with print, and vocabulary is taught through visuals and movement activities. A strategy of the day posted on the chalkboard allows students to read and process how they will participate in various activities in the gym.

On a warm afternoon in October, P.E. begins with a spelling and movement warm-up. Charlita tells students to think back to when they did an activity called chalk talk earlier in the semester. Charlita says, "Do you remember chalk talk?" Students reply in unison, "YES!" Since the students recall the basics of the activity, Charlita turns to the squad leaders, and tells them to review the rules for chalk talk with their squads. Using squad leaders to discuss and review the directions for activities is an integral part of the P.E. classroom. Since the majority of her students are ELLs, Charlita trains squad leaders to translate directions into Spanish for their peers who are not fluent English speakers. While the squad leaders discuss the activities with their squads, Charlita and John check for student understanding as they rotate through the gym. After meeting with each squad for approximately one minute, Charlita calls for each group's attention by telling the squads that it is time to try the activity. She says,

Each person gets a piece of chalk. I'm going to give you a verb, an action verb. Write the word on the floor. Then, when the music plays, you are going to move in any direction, showing me your verb. Squad leaders, please distribute chalk to your squads.

Squad leaders file to the front of the gym to pick up and distribute the chalk. Once each student has chalk in hand, Charlita states that it is time to try the activity, and says the first verb is "skip." Students write the word on the gym floor. Then, Charlita asks the class to spell the word, which they spell in unison. Once the word is spelled correctly, Charlita's assistant turns on the portable stereo; as Chubby Checker's "The Twist" blares through the gym, the students are told to skip to the beat of the music.

Come on baby let's do the twist
Come on baby let's do the twist
Take me by my little hand and go like this
Ee-oh twist baby baby twist
Oooh-yeah just like this
Come on little miss and do the twist.

After three minutes of skipping, the music abruptly stops. Charlita calls out "FREEZE!" Students are told to erase the word. Music blares again, and Chubby Checker sings

My daddy is sleepin' and mama ain't around
Yeah daddy is sleepin' and mama ain't around
We're gonna twisty twisty twisty
'Til we turn the house down
Come on and twist yeah baby twist
Oooh-yeah just like this
Come on little miss and do the twist.

Students twist their bodies to the beat of the music as they erase the word "skip." The activity continues as students act out the verbs "walk," "run," and "jump." Students learn new verbs by acting them out, using the verbs within the context of a sentence, and by spelling the words. Although P.E. is not necessarily the place to learn English grammar and reading skills, Charlita does an excellent job of finding ways to support literacy teachers and their curriculum by reinforcing the importance of language concepts, skills, and strategies.

Promoting Health Through Movement and Literacy

Although movement and learning go hand in hand, and movement is one of the earliest forms of communication for children (Koff, 2000), P.E. instruction has been reduced on many campuses (Landers, Maxwell, Butler, & Fagan, 2001). Nevertheless, research supports the importance of integrating literacy learning into P.E. instruction (Griffin & Morgan, 1998; Hanna, 2001; Marlett & Gordon, 2004; Schram, 1995). Similarly, Leppo, Davis, and Crim (2000) explain the importance for students to demonstrate various movement activities, integrating physical education throughout the curriculum. These researchers explain that *agility, balance, coordination, power, reaction time, and speed are the cornerstones to skill-ful movement patterns and success in playing games. Children need many opportunities to practice these components by participating in a variety of developmentally appropriate activities that include fundamental locomotor, non-locomotor, and manipulative skills. Motor fitness components are the building blocks to skillful participation in a variety of activities and the foundation to a healthful, active lifestyle.* (p. 145)

Figure 7.3 describes ways that teachers may integrate movement within the classroom.

As Leppo, Davis, and Crim (2000) state, creative teachers find ways to integrate movement into almost any activity. Movement activities in gym class allow students to construct meaning in an authentic environment, while helping P.E. become a mindful subject.

Becoming a Mindful Subject

Researchers describe the importance of using movement to teach academics (Buell & Whittaker, 2001; Minton, 2003). Minton (2003) explains that this process is called movement literacy, which is the ability to read, write, or communicate through visual images, sounds, or movements. Body language and movement can be used to communicate different feelings and sensations. What is most important is that input from the environment can be translated and read through movement. Movement literacy is applicable to any content area. For example, Minton (2003) describes movement literacy as a two-part process: "It involves translating concepts into movements and it depends on interpreting the movements and making a connection between concept and the movements that represent the concept" (p. 37).

Minton explains how movement literacy can be integrated into several content areas while giving specific lesson examples. Science teachers can use drifting movements to illustrate the drifting actions of electrons, or students can move their hands back and forth to illustrate the movement of the Earth's tectonic plates during an earthquake. Communicating nonverbally through movement is the first way that infants and toddlers learn a first language, and including movement activities throughout the curriculum helps students develop an understanding of a new idea or concept. Researchers explain that students must first physically respond through "felt thought"; as the concept is learned, such feeling is later expressed in words (Rugg, 1963).

Howard Gardner (1983) popularized the type of learning described as bodily kinesthetic intelligence, which means understanding and learning through body movement. Bodily kinesthetic learning is especially helpful to students who are learning a second language, since they can make direct connections between language and concrete activities (Clancy & Hruska, 2005). Clancy and Hruska (2005) also explain why physical education settings are supportive of English language learners. They contend that P.E. provides the same conditions for language learning as does the first language learning environment, such as

- Physical, active involvement with language
- The use of multiple modalities (e.g., speech, manipulation, modeling) to present information
- Opportunities to demonstrate language comprehension through physical expression
- A setting where success does not depend on language alone
- A low-stress environment for language performance
- An emotionally positive learning environment
- Opportunities to interact with others. (Clancy & Hruska, 2005, p. 31)

Suggested Ways of Practicing the Fundamentals of Movement
(Agility, Balance, Coordination, Power, Reaction Time, and Speed)

Locomotor Motor Skills Development		
Hopping	• Children are scattered in tandem formation around multipurpose area. Each time the whistle blows, children must change direction. • When the whistle blows twice, children must hop to the farthest point of the area. • When the teacher claps, children must stop and stand on one foot.	• Dynamic Balance, Agility, Reaction Time, Speed • Dynamic Balance, Agility, Reaction Time, Speed, Power • Static Balance
Running	• Children run at different paces—slow, medium, fast—keeping time with the tempo of the drumbeat. • Children can run in a forward direction to a slow drumbeat. When the drum stops, the children must stop in place. When the drum begins, the children must run backwards to a slow drumbeat. • The children, initially, swing their arms as they run, then run while keeping their arms still. Afterwards, they compare which method was better.	• Coordination, Speed, Reaction Time, Dynamic Balance • Coordination, Speed, Reaction Time, Dynamic and Static Balance • Coordination, Dynamic Balance
Jumping	• Children long jump their height, plus 6 inches. • Children run and jump as fast as possible. • Children bend their legs and jump as far forward as possible.	• Power, Coordination, Static Balance • Power, Speed, Dynamic and Static Balance, Coordination • Power, Dynamic Balance, Coordination
Skipping	• Children skip, changing directions each time a pair of wooden blocks are hit together. • Children skip in time to music, whose tempo changes periodically.	• Agility, Reaction Time, Static and Dynamic Balance • Reaction Time, Coordination, Speed
Walking	• Children walk, and play follow the leader. • Children change levels each time they hear a different sound: clapping, whistle, drum. • Children march to the music.	• Reaction Time, Agility • Reaction Time, Agility, Coordination, Balance • Coordination, Dynamic Balance
Sliding	• Children slide with a partner. • Children slide in any direction with each drumbeat; then they stop, and begin again.	• Reaction Time, Coordination, Dynamic Balance, Agility • Reaction Time, Agility, Dynamic and Static Balance, Speed, Coordination, Power

Figure 7.3
From Leppo, M. L., Davis, D., & Crim, B. (2000). The basics of exercising the mind and body. *Childhood Education, 76,* 142-147.

By providing lessons that integrate physical education and language development, teachers learn to think about the language used within a lesson and how to best support English language learners—to provide a similar environment in which children learn their first language, an environment that is supportive, interactive, and positive.

Because of the high percentage of ELLs within her school, Charlita became an advocate for incorporating movement literacy within the P.E. classroom. Charlita involves her 5th-grade class in active literacy learning in a variety of ways (see Figure 7.4). She plans specific activities that not only reinforce the health lessons that she teaches each week, but also build on literacy skills that students needed to know.

According to Buell and Whittaker (2001), P.E. teachers often explain that they do not have the time to teach their subject in addition to general literacy. However, instead of teaching students to read and write, effective content teachers can help students learn to read and write to learn.

Game	Literacy Skill	Description
Build a Word	Letter recognition/ Vocabulary	Students are given strips of paper with words from a recent lesson on food groups written on each strip of paper. Students are also given paper plates with different letters written on each paper plate. Charlita calls out a food, and groups of students must spell the word by using the paper plates. Students then must race to match foods with their correct food group. Charlita finds that this movement activity reinforces her health lesson on food groups, and further reinforces new vocabulary.
Chalk Talk	Letter recognition/ Vocabulary	Each student is given a piece of chalk. When Charlita calls out a vocabulary word from a recent health lesson, students write the word on the gym floor. Once the word is correctly spelled, the song "Let's Do the Twist" is played, and students twist to the music to erase the chalk.
Sliders	Vocabulary/Oral language	Students slide their foot across a line as someone else attempts to hit their foot. If their foot is tagged on the toe, the student must answer a math or vocabulary question.
Handshake Warm-Up	Vocabulary/Oral language	Students power walk to music. The teacher stops the music and calls out a word, such as "milking," "fishing," "wave," and the students then act out the word while shaking hands. This activity is especially helpful for English language learners, since it is a fun way to teach vocabulary and oral language.
Skeletal Relay	Vocabulary	After studying the parts of the human skeletal system, students compete to see which group can name all of the skeletal parts. They race to pick up a paper version of the skeletal system and match the correct word to the bone.
Pin Tag	Letter/sound recognition	Each student wears a clothespin that is attached to his/her shirt and has a tag bearing a phonics sound. They must find the word that matches the sound of their letter. They tag the student who is wearing the word.

Figure 7.4
Movement Activities and Literacy

Concluding Thoughts

Physical educators can easily integrate literacy objectives and activities into their content area, as demonstrated by Charlita. When educators integrate literacy into their P.E. lesson objectives and activities, they are supporting English language learners as they transfer language skills across content areas, and they encourage students of all abilities to value reading and writing. All in all, integrating movement and literacy activities in P.E. allows students to construct meaning in an authentic environment, while also allowing P.E. to become a mindful subject.

References

Alverman, D. E., & Phelps, S. F. (2005). *Content reading and literacy: Succeeding in today's diverse classrooms.* Boston: Pearson.

Aukerman, M. (2007). A culpable CALP: Rethinking the conversational/academic language proficiency distinction in early literacy instruction. *The Reading Teacher, 60,* 626–635.

Beers, K. (2003). *When kids can't read: What teachers can do.* Portsmouth, NH: Heinemann.

Behrman, E. H. (2004). Writing in the physical education class. *Journal of Physical Education, Recreation & Dance, 75*(8), 22-32.

Buell, C., & Whittaker, A. (2001). Enhancing content literacy in physical education. *Journal of Physical Education, Recreation & Dance, 72*(6), 32-37.

Carrier, K. A. (2005). Key issues for teaching English language learners in academic classrooms. *Middle School Journal, 37*(2), 4-9.

Clancy, M. E., & Hruska, B. (2005). Developing language objective for English language learners in physical education lessons. *Journal of Physical Education, Recreation & Dance, 76*(4), 30-35.

Cummins, J. (2000). *Language, power, and pedagogy: Bilingual children in the crossfire.* North York, ON: Multilingual Matters.

Freeman, D. E., & Freeman, Y. S. (2000). *Teaching reading in multilingual classrooms.* Portsmouth, NH: Heinemann.

Gardner, H. (1983). *Frames of mind: The theory of multiple intelligences.* New York: Basic Books.

Griffin, J., & Morgan, L. (1998). Physical education—WRITE ON! *Strategies, 11*(4), 34-37.

Hanna, J. (2001). The language of dance. *Journal of Physical Education, Recreation & Dance, 72*(4), 40-45.

Heath, S. B. (1983). *Ways with words: Language, life and work in communities and classrooms.* New York: Cambridge University Press.

Higgins, B., Miller, M., & Wegmann, S. (2007). Teaching to the test . . . not! Balancing best practices and testing requirements in writing. *The Reading Teacher, 60*(4), 310-319.

Johnson, C. C. (2005). Making instruction relevant to language minority students at the middle level. *Middle School Journal, 37*(2), 10-14.

Koff, S. R. (2000). Toward a definition of dance education. *Childhood Education, 77,* 27-31.

Krashen, S. (1982). *Principles and practice in second language acquisition.* New York: Pergamon Press.

Krashen, S. (2000). What does it take to acquire language? *ESL Magazine, 3*(3), 22-23.

Lacina, J., New Levine, L., & Sowa, P. (2006). *Helping English language learners succeed in Pre-K-elementary schools.* Alexandria, VA: Teachers of English to Speakers of Other Languages.

Landers, D. M., Maxwell, W., Butler, J., & Fagan, L. (2001). Developing thinking skills in physical education. In A. L. Costa (Ed.), *Developing minds: Resource book for teaching thinking* (pp. 334-351). Alexandria, VA: Association for Supervision and Curriculum Development.

Lane, H. B., & Wright, T. L. (2007). Maximizing the effectiveness of reading aloud. *The Reading Teacher, 60*(7), 668–675.

Leppo, M. L., Davis, D., & Crim, B. (2000). The basics of exercising the mind and body. *Childhood Education, 76,* 142-147.

Manning, M. L., & Bucher, K. T. (2000). Middle schools should be both learner-centered and subject-centered. *Childhood Education, 77,* 41-42.

Manzo, A. V., Manzo, U. C., & Thomas, M. M. (2007). Rationale for systematic vocabulary development: Antidote for state mandates. *Journal of Adolescent & Adult Literacy, 49*(7), 610-619.

Marlett, P. B., & Gordon, C. J. (2004). The use of alternative texts in physical education. *Journal of Adolescent & Adult Literacy, 48*(3), 226-237.

Minton, S. (2003). Using movement to teach academics: An outline for success. *Journal of Physical Education, Recreation & Dance, 74*(2), 36-40.

Parr, J. M., & Maguiness, C. (2005). Removing the "silent" from SSR: Voluntary reading as social practice. *Journal of Adolescent and Adult Literacy, 49*(2), 98-107.

Richardson, J. S. (2000). *Read it aloud! Using literature in the secondary content classroom.* Newark, DE: International Reading Association.

Rugg, H. (1963). *Imagination.* New York: Harper and Row.

Sanacore, J. (2006). Nurturing lifetime readers. *Childhood Education, 83*, 33-37.

Schram, J. (1995). Physical education and language. *Runner, 33*, 9-10.

Scott, J. A. (2004). Scaffolding vocabulary learning: Ideas for equity in urban setting. In D. Lapp, C. C. Block, E. J. Cooper, J. Flood, N. Roser, & J. V. Tinajero (Eds.), *Teaching all the children: Strategies for developing literacy in an urban setting* (pp. 275-293). New York: Guilford Press.

Silvina, M. (2005). Second language acquisition and first language acquisition loss in adult early bilinguals: Exploring some differences and similarities. *Second Language Research, 21*(3), 199-249.

Wickstrom, C., Curtis, J., & Daniel, K. (2005). Ashley and Junie B. Jones: A struggling reader makes a connection to literacy. *Language Arts, 83*(1), 16-21.

Williams-Boyd, P. (2005). Middle schools that make a difference. *Childhood Education, 81*, 278-280.

Zentella, A. C. (1997). *Growing up bilingual.* Malden, MA: Blackwell.

Children's Literature Cited

Bennet, C. (1996). *Girls in love.* New York: Scholastic.

Berman, R. (2003). *The kid from courage.* La Jolla, CA: Scobre Press Corporation.

Bloor, E. (1997). *Tangerine.* New York: Scholastic.

Brooks, B. (2000). *Throwing smoke.* New York: HarperCollins.

Cadnum, M. (2000). *Redhanded.* New York: Viking.

Carter, A. (2000). *Bull catcher.* New York: Scholastic.

Christopher, M. (2000). *Tennis ace.* Boston: Little, Brown & Company.

Cochran, T. (1997). *Roughnecks.* New York: Harcourt Children's Books.

Coleman, E. (2001). *Born in sin.* New York: Simon & Schuster Children's Publishing.

Colton, L. (2000). *Counting coup: A true story of basketball and honor on the Little Big Horn.* New York: Warner Books.

Crutcher, C. (1983). *Running loose.* New York: HarperCollins.

Crutcher, C. (1986). *Stotan!* New York: HarperCollins.

Crutcher, C. (1987). *The Crazy Horse Electric game.* New York: HarperCollins.

Crutcher, C. (1989). *Chinese handcuffs.* New York: HarperCollins.

Crutcher, C. (1993). *Staying fat for Sarah Byrnes.* New York: HarperCollins.

Crutcher, C. (1995). *Ironman.* New York: HarperCollins.

Crutcher, C. (2001). *Whale talk.* New York: HarperCollins.

Crutcher, C. (2002). *Athletic shorts: Six short stories.* New York: HarperCollins.

Durant, A. (2005). *Sports stories.* Boston: Kingfisher Books.

Dygard, T. (1983). *Rebound capper.* New York: HarperCollins.

Dygard, T. (1986). *Halfback tough.* New York: HarperCollins.

Dygard, T. (1988). *The rookie arrives.* New York: HarperCollins.

Dygard, T. (1989). *Forward pass.* New York: HarperCollins.

Dygard, T. (1999). *Running wild.* New York: HarperCollins.

Feinstein, J. (2006). *Last shot: A final four mystery.* New York: Random House Children's Books.

Grosser, M., & Schonborn, R. (2002). *Competitive tennis for young players: The road to becoming a top player.* United Kingdom: Meyer & Meyer Sport.

Hobbs, W. (1999). *River thunder.* New York: Random House Children's Books.

Ibbitson, J. (1989). *The wimp and the jock.* New York: Simon & Schuster Children's Publishing.

Karr, K. (2000). *The boxer.* New York: Farrar, Straus and Giroux.

Klass, D. (1990). *Wrestling with honor.* New York: Scholastic.

Klass, D. (2002). *Home of the Braves.* New York: HarperCollins.

Lewin, M. (1999). *Cutting loose.* New York: Henry Holt and Co.

Lynch, C. (1993). *Shadow boxer.* New York: HarperCollins.

Miklowitz, G. (1990). *Anything to win.* New York: Bantam Doubleday Dell Books.

Myers, W. (1983). *Hoops: A novel.* New York: Bantam Doubleday Dell Publishing Group.

Myers, W. (1996). *Slam!* New York: Scholastic.

Peck, R. (2001). *Extra innings.* New York: HarperCollins.

Roberts, K. (2005). *My thirteenth season.* New York: Henry Holt and Co.

Rottman, S. L. (1999). *Head above water.* Atlanta, GA: Peachtree Publishers.

Rushton, R. (2002). *Break point.* Great Britain: Piccadilly Press.

Shull, M. (2005). *Amazing Grace.* New York: Hyperion Books.

Swanson, J. (2004). *Going for the record.* Grand Rapids, MI: Eerdmans Books for Young Readers.

Sweeney, J. (2000). *Players.* New York: Marshall Cavendish Corporation.

Voigt, C. (1985). *The runner.* New York: Macmillan Publishing.

Wallace, R. (1997). *Wrestling Sturbridge.* New York: Random House Children's Books.

Wallace, R. (2005). *Shots on goal.* New York: Random House Children's Books.

Zusak, M. (2002). *Fighting Ruben Wolfe.* New York: Scholastic.

Meet the Authors

Jan Lacina has focused her research and teaching on English language learners (ELLs) and on reading and writing instruction. She teaches undergraduate and graduate literacy courses in both the middle/secondary and early childhood programs at Texas Christian University. She is co-author of the book Helping English Language Learners Succeed in Pre-K-Elementary Schools *(TESOL, 2006), and she has published in numerous journals. Jan also writes the "Technology in the Classroom" column that is published in the journal* Childhood Education. *Prior to teaching at the college level, Jan taught ESL in Texas and Kansas.*

Charlita Smith teaches 3rd- through 5th-grade physical education at Diamond Hill Elementary School in the Fort Worth Independent School District (FWISD), Texas. She finds fun ways to blend movement, language, and exercise to teach students lifelong ways to stay healthy.

Part IV

Literacies for All Content Areas

Chapter 8

Sheltered English Instruction:
A Model for English Language Learners in All Content Areas

Lynnette sits at the front of her 6th-grade English class behind a large screen and computer monitor. She begins first period by reviewing what students already know about today's writing topic. Students are beginning a first draft in which they are to make connections to their personal lives and the main character's experiences in the book The Watsons Go to Birmingham.

> *Lynnette: Today, we are going to talk about what it means to be embarrassed. Yesterday, when reading* The Watsons Go to Birmingham, *we read how Kenny was embarrassed. Why was Kenny embarrassed?*

Students slowly raise their hands.

> *José: Wasn't Kenny scared to read out loud because he is not a good reader?*
>
> *Lynnette: Yes, José . . . he really struggled to read. Can anyone tell us why he struggled to read?*

Angelica slowly raises her hand, and when called on, she speaks slightly louder than a whisper and says, "He has a lazy eye."

> *Lynnette: That's right, Angelica! Kenny's lazy eye was one of the reasons why he struggled in school, and he was often embarrassed that he was not a good reader. Today, we are going to write about a time when you were embarrassed, and we are going to be using Dana's [desktop computer]. Now, think of a time when you were embarrassed. Can you tell us about a time you were embarrassed? We are going to think of different ways to begin a paper on embarrassment together.*

The students silently stare ahead . . . either thinking intently or unsure about how to answer Lynnette. She then offers a scenario to help students make personal connections to today's writing topic.

> *Lynnette: What if you were asleep in class, and drool came down your mouth . . . how would you feel?*

Students laugh loudly as they imagine the embarrassment they would feel, but no one has a suggestion of a personal example, and so Lynnette says,

> *What if you are wearing those baggy pants that many kids wear . . . how would you feel if your pants fell down in front of a group of your friends?*

Then the students begin to offer examples of times when they were embarrassed—and make personal connections to the text (from field notes and audio transcription, 3/2006).

Jan Lacina,
Lynnette Mayo, and
Patience Sowa

Integrating content area material, while scaffolding instruction, provides a way for struggling students, especially English language learners (ELLs), to learn academic language while feeling successful during the learning process. This chapter will discuss what research says about teaching ELLs and provide practical classroom examples of methods for teaching language and content.

Research Background

Demographic Changes. The demographics of schools across the United States continue to change; according to the National Clearinghouse for English Language Acquisition (NCELA, 2004), the number of English language learners (ELLs) increased by 95 percent over the past 10 years. Currently, more than 4.7 million students are learning English as their second language in U.S. public schools (NCELA, 2004). At the middle school level, ELLs often only spend part of their day in the English as a second language (ESL) classroom, and the rest of their day is spent in content area classrooms. Despite the change in the school population, merely 12.5 percent of teachers report receiving eight or more hours of training in the area of teaching ELLs (Gruber, Wiley, Broughman, Strizek, & Burian-Fitgerald, 2002). Despite a lack of teacher preparation on how to meet the academic and language needs of ELLs within content area classes, academic and language expectations for students continue to increase—as do the difficulties in trying to teach students academic content while making language comprehensible (Echevarria & Short, 2008; Short & Echevarria, 2005; Valdes, 1998, 2001). The good news is that a wealth of research literature, and practical professional development material, is available for content area teachers who have ELLs as students.

Teaching Language and Content. To effectively teach ELLs, content area teachers must first understand how children and adolescents learn a second language. Chapter 6 explained the difference between acquiring and learning a language (Krashen, 1982, 2000). Teachers also must be familiar with concepts of basic interpersonal conversational skills (BICS) and cognitive academic language proficiency (CALP) (Cummins, 1979, 1980, 2000). BICS is the everyday language that ELLs use for social interaction. Language teachers often refer to BICS as playground talk, since this is the language ELLs use to communicate with their peers on the playground, in school hallways, and in the classroom. Balderamma and Diaz-Rico (2006) also explain that BICS is the language that students hear through the mass media, particularly television. CALP is the use of language skills that ELLs need to be successful academically. Learning a language is a long-term process (Lacina, New-Levine, & Sowa, 2006); although conversational fluency can be obtained within a short time, academic proficiency typically takes from 4 to 7 years—if the students received a minimum of four years of schooling in their primary language (Collier & Thomas, 2002). When students are schooled in their first language, they are more successful in learning a second language.

Over the past 20 years, various language learning theories have changed educators' thinking about how language, particularly English, should be taught and learned. Through the study of the teaching and learning of foreign languages, researchers found that in order to teach any language effectively, it should be integrated with content instruction (Bunch, Abram, Lotan, & Valdes, 2001; Crandall, 1993; Genesee, 1994; Snow & Brinton, 1997). Genesee explains that integrating language development with the teaching of meaningful content serves to motivate language learners. At the same time, teachers of ELLs found that while students were learning English, they were lagging behind their counterparts with respect to their knowledge of the content areas (Balderamma & Diaz-Rico, 2006; Freeman & Freeman, 1988). These findings helped teachers and researchers realize the importance of teaching ELLs the academic language necessary to help them be successful in learning content.

Rosemont 6th-Grade School

Lynnette is an innovative 6th-grade English teacher at Rosemont 6th-Grade School. In Fort Worth ISD, 6th grade is located on its own campus, separate from the elementary and middle school campuses. Ninety-two percent of Rosemont 6th-grade students are identified as low income, based on the number of students qualifying for free and reduced-price lunch. Thirty-two percent of the students are learning English as a second language (ESL). The majority (89 percent) of Rosemont's students are Hispanic (http://just4kids.org/). In just two years, students' scores on the state's reading/language arts exam increased by 10 percent, including an increase of 11 percent by Rosemont's Hispanic students (TEA, www.tea.state.tx.us/cgi/sas/broker). Because of increased academic achievement, the teachers at the school received monetary stipends from the state.

Teachers at Rosemont, like those at many urban schools, face ongoing pressure to prepare students for success on state-mandated tests, even as they contend with problems related to gang activity and discipline. To offer students a safe school environment, Rosemont holds school functions on campus immediately following school. Teachers volunteer their time after school to monitor school dances and other school functions, to ensure that older gang members do not have access to school property or to younger students they may be trying to recruit for gang membership. Students who bring drugs to campus, or threaten peers or teachers, are immediately taken out of the classroom and referred to law enforcement authorities. Dealing with gang activity and serious behavior problems is a way of life for most urban teachers; despite these challenges, the teachers at Rosemont remain committed to teaching their content area material in a meaningful way to students.

Inside a 6th-Grade
Sheltered Instruction Observation Protocol (SIOP) Class

Rosemont is a unique school, since all classroom teachers receive training on how to use a sheltered instruction (SI) model, which integrates language and content area instruction. This model is called the Sheltered Instruction Observation Protocol (SIOP). Researched and developed by Echevarria, Short, and Vogt (2000, 2008), the purpose of SIOP is to help teachers promote the development of the academic language and the content necessary for ELLs to keep up with their English-speaking peers.

While sheltered instruction (SI) is carried out in different ways, the core components of instruction are usually the same. These components consist of district and/or national standards, goals, and objectives; flexible groupings; instructional features; and authentic assessment (Echevarria, Short, & Vogt, 2000; Peregoy & Boyle, 2005). Genesee (1999) states that effective SI should have the following program features:

- Clearly defined language and content objectives
- Supplementary materials
- Scaffolding

- Interaction
- Meaningful activities.

There is variability in types of SI methods. For that reason, Echevarria, Short, and Vogt (1999, 2008) developed SIOP as a research-based model of sheltered instruction. What makes SIOP different is that it can objectively measure effective instruction. The SIOP instrument can be used by administrators, teachers, and SIOP trainers to provide clear feedback to the teachers they observe. SIOP can be broadly divided into three main components: Preparation, Instruction, and Review/Assessment. Instructional indicators under each of these components illustrate effective teaching practices. These instructional indicators are: preparation, building background, comprehensible input, strategies, interaction, practice/application, lesson delivery, and review/assessment. What makes the use of the SIOP particularly advantageous is that it is flexible enough to be used in sheltered and mainstream classrooms. Figure 8.1 illustrates the various components and indicators included in the SIOP model.

Lynnette's strength in the classroom is to scaffold difficult content area vocabulary and instruction to make the content comprehensible for the students in her class. All seven English periods that Lynnette teaches each day are composed of a wide variety of students, including mainstream monolingual students, ESL students, and special education students. Lynnette creates a community of readers and writers in her class by offering ongoing, immediate literacy feedback to students and by creating a safe place where they can take risks. The paragraphs below illustrate how Lynnette uses the SIOP to address the needs of ELLs, and of other students who struggle academically.

Indicator 1: Lesson Preparation
Lesson preparation is an important part of the SIOP model. The first step in preparing for a SIOP lesson involves defining content and language objectives, based on examination of state and/or TESOL standards. Next, teachers must consider the types of supplementary material to integrate within a lesson, such as graphics and models, as well as ways to include activities that are meaningful to students (e.g., letter writing, simulations, debates, etc.) (Echevarria & Graves, 2003).

When working with ELLs in content area classes, teachers need to integrate content area skills and language learning strategies to build academic language. Building academic language is important for all students, but it is especially important for ELL students, because it enables the students to use new English words to express their thoughts and feelings. When academic language is fostered, students feel more confident about expressing themselves in both spoken and written form. Most important, teaching students academic language prepares them for future academic success.

Teachers at all grades in Texas are under increased pressure for their students to perform well on the mandated writing tests. Lynnette finds that she can better prepare students for academic tests by connecting language and content objectives across the curriculum. Lynnette is able to teach difficult content area material while scaffolding language to make language comprehensible to ELLs. Each day, Lynnette centrally displays both content area and language objectives.

Lynnette begins class by pointing to the board and explaining the lesson's objectives for the day. She makes real-world connections to explain why reading and writing are important and relevant to the day's objectives; throughout the year, she emphasizes that learning academic

SIOP MODEL

Teacher Preparation: Teachers begin planning by examining state, and/or TESOL, language standards for instruction. Teachers write clearly defined content objectives on the board for students. These objectives are reviewed at the beginning and end of a lesson. Teachers must consider the students' literacy in their first language, second language proficiency, and the reading level of the materials. Supplementary materials are used to promote comprehension, such as charts, graphs, pictures, illustrations, realia, math manipulatives, multimedia, and demonstrations by teachers and others.

Building Background Knowledge	• Link concepts to students' background experience. This experience can be personal, cultural, or academic. Connections are made to students' prior background knowledge. • Key vocabulary is emphasized. New vocabulary is presented in context. The number of vocabulary items is limited.
Comprehensible Input	• Use speech that is appropriate for students' language proficiency. • Make the explanation of the task clear, using a step-by-step manner with visuals. • Use a variety of techniques to make content concepts clear, such as graphic organizers, realia, or think-alouds. • Focus attention on the most important information. • Introduce new learning in context.
Strategies	• Provide opportunities for students to use learning strategies. Learning strategies should be taught through explicit instruction. • Use scaffolding techniques throughout the lesson. • Use a variety of question types, including those that promote higher level thinking skills.
Interaction	Provide the following for ELLs: • Frequent opportunities for interactions about lesson concepts that encourage higher level thinking skills • Grouping that supports language and content objectives—cooperative groups, buddies, pairs, large and small groups • Wait time for responses • Opportunities for clarification in native language, if possible.
Application	Lessons should include: • Hands-on materials or manipulatives for student practice • Activities for students to apply content and language knowledge in the classroom • Activities that integrate all language skills: listening, speaking, reading, and writing.
Lesson Delivery	• Content objectives are supported by lesson delivery. • Language objectives are supported by lesson delivery. • Students are engaged 90% to 100% of the period. • Pacing of the lesson is appropriate to students' ability level.

Figure 8.1. Adapted from Echevarria, J., & Short, D. J. (2008). *Making content comprehensible for English language learners: The SIOP model* (3rd ed.). Boston: Allyn & Bacon.

language will help her students excel in life. As Lynnette explains,

> [ELLs] must live in the same world I live in. I do not want them to be drop-outs. I expect them to go to college. I think education is their key [for future success]. The more language they know and the higher the level of the language [the greater their chances for success]. . . . Most of them have a social language, [but] they don't have [an] academic [one]. And just getting them to understand that there is a difference is important. That is my job. (From field notes and audio transcription, 2/2006)

Lynnette holds high expectations for her students, and she continually tells them that they can do anything they choose in life.

Indicator 2: Building Background Knowledge

Building background knowledge in a SIOP lesson means explicitly linking students' background experiences to the lesson being taught, in addition to linking past learning to new concepts (Echevarria & Graves, 2003). Lynnette builds on what students already know while making connections to their first language. Making explicit connections to students' first language helps build academic language. For example, when Lynnette introduces new vocabulary, she finds that drawing topics associated to the new word helps students better grasp the new definition. Typically, she finds that by keeping word lists short (Bromley, 2007; Robb, 2000; Vacca et al., 2005) and relevant to the literature being currently read in class, students are more apt to understand that these words are ones they will need to know.

Lynnette chooses nine words from a reading selection and models how to examine the word in the context of a story. When the students read *The Clay Marble,* a book about a family fleeing their Cambodian village during the early 1980s, Lynnette examines the word "refugee." First, she discusses the meaning of the word by thinking of a synonym, an antonym, and then the Spanish equivalent for the word. Next, she examines how the word was used within the book. By explicitly modeling and discussing the word in the context of the book, and linking it to students' native language and experiences, students gain a more thorough understanding of what it means to be a refugee. After analyzing the vocabulary word, pairs of students complete their own circle graphs, which they later discuss as a whole class. By connecting literature, vocabulary, and prior background knowledge, Lynnette finds that students comprehend the story and, more importantly, retain and internalize the new vocabulary.

Teaching vocabulary and making connections to students' background is an ongoing process in Lynnette's class. Analyzing word parts is another strategy Lynnette uses to build background. Research strongly supports the importance of teaching vocabulary by analyzing word parts. Researchers report that 60 percent of multisyllabic words can be inferred by analyzing word parts, and students need to be able to use root, prefixes, and suffixes to help give them a clue to an unknown word's meaning (Bromley, 2007; Nagy & Scott, 2000). This strategy is especially helpful for ELLs, and particularly with multisyllabic terms. Lynnette follows Bromley's (2007) recommendations in creating root word trees for common root words (see Figure 8.3). Lynnette prints a root word on the center of the tree, and then students can find words that use the root word by brainstorming in small groups, and by using the dictionary, glossary, or the Web to help them find words that use the root word.

Beginning in upper elementary school, students begin the transition from learning to read to

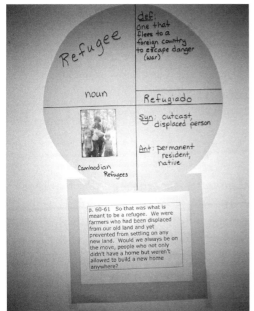

Figure 8.2.
Vocabulary Concept Circle

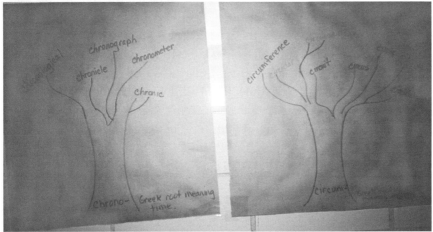

Figure 8.3. Root Word Trees

reading to learn. ELLs may find content area textbooks and grade-level assigned novels difficult to comprehend; the vocabulary is not easy and the syntax is often confusing. As a result, reading and writing in the content areas is a labored and often dreaded experience for many students. Lynnette continually links students' prior knowledge to English content and integrates content area material while connecting with students' prior background. For example, when co-teaching a unit on research writing with her social studies colleague, in preparation for the school district's history fair, she taught students how to research topics, using the topic of Día de los Muertos—the Day of the Dead. To build students' vocabulary knowledge, she purposefully uses cognates to make the connections between Spanish and English words. By connecting literature and vocabulary, Lynnette finds that students better retain the new vocabulary.

Lynnette makes these connections through the use of think-alouds and graphic organizers, and by explicitly teaching vocabulary, using the above-mentioned methods. When working with a class of mainstream students and struggling readers and writers, Lynnette discovered that many of the effective strategies she used with struggling students also work well with ELLs.

Lynnette explains that when working with ELLs

> *You start where they [the students] are. You then realize where they must go. You use*
> *every kind of activity that you can possibly find . . . from making word walls to vocabulary*
> *words, to doing pictures with every vocabulary word. Kids are tuned into computers*
> *and TV. You use the resources that are available to you, and you keep looking until you*
> *find what works for your students.*

Indicator 3: Comprehensible Input

Comprehensible input is achieved through the modification of teacher communication to help students understand the lesson. Teachers can make their lessons more understandable by using linguistic modifications, such as speaking slowly, modeling, using visuals, and total physical response (TPR).

TPR is a method developed by James Asher at San José State University over 30 years ago to aid in the learning of foreign languages (Asher, Kusado, & de la Torre, 1974). In TPR, students respond to commands by using physical movement (e.g., jumping, running, skipping), and once students master producing physical movements to match the commands, they begin to produce commands both orally and in writing (Shrum & Glisan, 2000). Since Lynnette's students are primarily fluent English-speaking students, she does not use TPR as often as would an ESL teacher who works with non-English-speaking students. In particular, Lynnette adapts her lessons to provide comprehensible input through modifying speech and behavior, and by specifically choosing instructional strategies to scaffold instruction of the English content for 6th grade. Figure 8.4 describes ways for modifying speech, behavior, and instructional strategies to provide comprehensible input within content area instruction.

Indicator 4: Learning Strategies

Short, Hudec, and Echevarria (2002) describe learning strategies as the cognitive processes that teachers use to help learners understand new information. ELLs, especially beginning learners of English, have difficulty using learning strategies, since they focus much of their time on translating new vocabulary to their native language. Thus, it is essential for SIOP teachers to explicitly scaffold instruction and instruction strategies, and also to use a variety of question types during a lesson (e.g., literal, analytical, and interpretive) (Echevarria & Graves, 2003).

Think-Aloud is one of the many strategies that Lynnette models in the classroom. Lynnette and a 6th-grade social studies teacher, who collaborate throughout the school year, are currently teaching about the civil rights movement. Students in Lynnette's class read about the context of the movement, including how the movement affected individual families. Lynnette begins the week's lessons by using a think-aloud. Lynnette's lesson demonstrates the importance of accessing and connecting students' background knowledge to literature and prior experiences before beginning a writing assignment.

Students eagerly file into Lynnette's first period class, glancing at the chalkboard, which displays the lesson plan objective and homework assignment. All of the students in this class are fluent English speakers; however, many of the students struggle academically. The class is composed of monolingual English speakers, bilingual students who are no longer categorized by the state as "ESL," and a handful of students who are currently labeled as ESL students. As class begins, Lynnette states the lesson's language and content objectives. She begins with a mini lesson and

Teacher Speech & Behavior	Instructional Strategies	Lynnette's Comprehensible Input
• Uses gestures, facial expressions, and body language • Speaks slowly and clearly • Avoids idiomatic expressions and clichés • Uses simpler syntax and shorter sentences • Emphasizes high-frequency vocabulary • Develops a community of learners	• Integrates visual and graphics into instruction • Communicates using oral, written, physical, or pictoral form • Uses hands-on activities • Integrates cooperative learning • Applies a process-oriented approach to learning • Modifies and adjusts instruction for individual learners	• Lynnette modifies her speech into simpler sentences to make learning comprehensible. • Vocabulary is explicitly taught, and high-frequency words are defined, explained, and related to students' background knowledge. • Lynnette integrates hands-on activities, such as planting an urban garden while reading about an urban garden in a novel. • Visuals and graphics are an important part of each lesson Lynnette teaches, such as the plot diagram and the vocabulary concept—explained in this chapter. • A community of learners is emphasized, along with a process-oriented approach to teaching reading and writing.

Figure 8.4. Comprehensible Input. Adapted from Short, D., Hudec, J., & Echevarria, J. (2002). *Using the SIOP Model: Professional development manual for sheltered instruction.* Washington, DC: Center for Applied Linguistics.

a think-aloud of the research process. Today, she explains the importance of understanding a stand taken by a historical personage and reviews how people develop a personal or political stand, based on their life experiences. Lynnette says

> *Yesterday we talked about the Civil War and how a stand was taken [by Abraham Lincoln]. We also talked about George Washington and what type of stand he took. Remember, Hector, we examined your research topic. What stand did George Washington take, and how did his stand develop?*

After students demonstrate a basic understanding of how people might take a stand, Lynnette begins a mini lesson on how Mother Jones took a personal stand and affected workers' rights. She asks students if they know what a "labor union" is. No one answers. Lynnette knows that she cannot simply give students the answer by providing rote definitions for the social studies vocabulary. She must teach vocabulary in a way that will help students make connections to the literature they are reading, or even more importantly, to their own lives. Since students are unfamiliar with labor unions, Lynnette writes the word on the chalkboard and explains that workers pay a fee to join a union and that the union represents workers to ensure that their rights are upheld; the dues can be used to help workers when they go on strike. Lynnette connects the term to what the students already know about Mother Jones from a book they read. She also asks students why it would be important to be involved in such an organization, and what types of groups are important to students. Next, Lynnette writes the phrase "Miners' Union" on the chalkboard, and asks, "Does anyone know what a mine is?" Lynnette explains the vocabulary word "mine" by discussing Mother Jones and her experience with miners and the Miners' Union. She explains "Mother Jones had an interest in the union because her husband was a miner."

By scaffolding English social studies vocabulary, Lynnette teaches social studies content and the English language. While teaching the mini lesson, Lynnette continually relates the vocabulary and experiences of Mother Jones to the students' own lives. She explains that, as is true for many of the students, Mother Jones' family were immigrants, and their background and experiences in their home country influenced her outlook on life. By making the content comprehensible and meaningful, Lynnette successfully scaffolds difficult content area vocabulary.

Graphic organizers are also helpful learning strategies. Lynnette finds many ways to include graphic organizers in English lessons, and to make the novels students read comprehensible and relevant to their lives. For example, while reading *Seedfolks*, a book that details the lives of diverse residents of an apartment complex as they plant an urban garden, students identify the main characters in the book and important identifying information about each character. She uses the *Seedfolks* graphic to help students keep track of the main characters in the book and how they contributed to the garden (see Figure 8.5). Since the characters come from very

Name _____ Per ____
Seedfolks by Paul Fleischman

Character	Ethnicity	Plant Grown	Why did they grow that plant?	What brings the character to the garden?	What does the character gain from the garden?

Figure 8.5. *Seedfolks* Graphic

different ethnic and language backgrounds, keeping track of the characters' upbringing and why they came to the garden is an important aspect of comprehending this particular book.

In Fort Worth ISD, each unit of study for English is organized based on a theme. Recommended reading strategies to use while teaching the theme, and book, are noted in the district's English curriculum (see Figure 8.6). While reading *The Clay Marble*, students examine the theme "Enduring Understanding." Lynnette explains that family is a concept that students should understand when reading the novel. She says

> *It is a general idea that relates to the novel and could be applied to other novels or their own lives. The students take the Enduring Understanding [theme] and then break it down into three categories—unity, support, and common goals—that are all represented by the concept. Then, we look for quotables—quotes from the novel that support these three categories and relate them to the Enduring Understanding [theme]. After we complete the reading of the novel, we will revisit this poster [see Figure 8.7], which they all have in their folders, and begin thinking about adding other quotes from the remaining chapters and evidence from their own lives under the three categories. We will be writing a compare/contrast personal narrative in which the students will compare their lives with the characters in the novel and will use quotes from the novel to support their comments about the characters.*

Through the use of the graphic organizer (see Figure 8.7), Lynnette finds that students are better able to find evidence, in the form of quotes, to support their opinions. After modeling how to complete the graphic organizer, Lynnette typically guides students through the process as she checks for understanding. Once it is clear that students understand the process, students complete the graphic organizer independently.

Similarly, Lynnette uses a Plot Relationship Chart (Schmidt & Buckley, 1991) (see Figure 8.8) to scaffold comprehension while students read a novel. While reading the *Clay Marble*, students track the actions of the main character and of other characters in the book. Lynnette finds that this chart allows students to make connections between stories and characters. When teaching plot relationships, it is best to choose a story that has clear plot elements. To teach adolescents how to use a plot relationship chart, model how to keep such a chart. First, the teacher needs to show and discuss the elements of a plot relationship, explaining that the characters in most stories encounter some type of problem. The story should show how the character tackles the problem and finds a resolution.

Indicator 5: Practice/Application

The practice/application indicator of the SIOP emphasizes the importance of encouraging students to practice the skills they have learned. Effective SIOP teachers use a variety of activities, and have students not only practice and apply their new content knowledge, but also practice and apply the newly acquired language skills (Echevarria & Graves, 2003; Short, Hudec, & Echevarria, 2002). Practice and application involves integrating all language skills: reading, writing, listening, and speaking.

Practice and application of new writing skills is an especially important part of 6th-grade learning in Lynnette's class, as students prepare throughout the year for next year's 7th-grade state writing test. Modeling, demonstrating, and sharing writing have long been known as ef-

Six Weeks	Themes	Time Line	Novel Unit/ Literature		Student Work/ Writing Portfolio
			English	Reading	
1	Acceptance Individual Courage	*Weeks 1-3*	*Eleven* pp. 26-33	Reader Response Stop & Jot Summing It Up	Personal Narrative
		targeted start date August 29, 2006	*Freak, the Mighty*		
2	Connections Culture and History	*Weeks 1-3*	*The School Play* pp. 402-408	Anticipation Guide Word Wall Get the GIST	Personal Narrative
		targeted start date October 11, 2006	*The Watsons Go to Birmingham*		
3	Family Traditions Home and Heritage	*Weeks 1-6*	*Aaron's Gift Oh, Broom, Get to Work T-A-N-A-E-K-A* Short Story	B-D-A Characterization Foreshadowing Drawing Conclusions Reading Between the Lines	Expository Essay
4	Relationships Cooperation Dependency	*Weeks 1-6*	*Lob's Girl My First Drive With Dolphins* Visual Representation: Party Animals	B-D-A Summing It Up Main Idea Mood Flashback	Personal Narrative
5	Fairness Competition	*Weeks 1-6*	*The Southpaw* pp. 349-353	B-D-A Point of View Fact/Opinion Plot Relationship Chart	Expository Essay
		targeted start date March 20, 2007	*The Clay Marble*		
6	Conflict and Challenge	*targeted start date April 23, 2007*	*Heroes: Gods and Monsters*		Research-based Essay
		Weeks 4-6	*Tuesday of the Other June* pp. 80-88	B-D-A Symbolism Figurative Language Stereotype	

Novel substitutions in case of challenges: *House of Dies Drear* and *Trouble River*

Figure 8.6. FWISD Curriculum

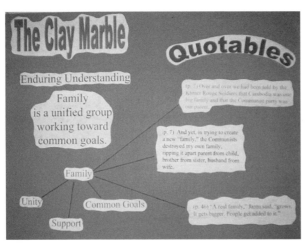

Figure 8.7.
Enduring Understanding

Who	Wanted	But	So	Then

Figure 8.8. Plot Relationship Chart

fective techniques for teaching writing (Calkins, 1994; Cunningham & Allington, 2002; Graves, 1994; Lacina, Griffith, & Hagan, 2006; Ray, 2002). In particular, Lynnette models ways to use technology when writing. She stays current with research in the field of literacy and finds ways to weave technology throughout the English curriculum.

Researchers emphasize the need for teachers to use new literacies when teaching reading, instead of solely teaching traditional foundational literacy skills, such as responding to a prompt with a paper/pencil response. New literacies include the literacies of word processors, the literacies of e-mail, and the literacies of the Internet (Kinzer, 2005; Labbo, 2005; Leu, Kinzer, Coiro, & Cammack, 2004; Teale, Leu, Labbo, & Kinzer, 2002). Leu et al. (2004) contend that new literacies include the skills, strategies, and dispositions necessary to use and manipulate the Internet as new technologies emerge. For example, students must learn how to figure out the meaning of words they do not know in a new way. Instead of necessarily searching the dictionary for unknown word meanings, today's children also must learn to use hypertext links to find the meaning of a word, and how to use such features as spell and grammar check and an online thesaurus. Lynnette models writing regularly through the use of technology. She finds that classroom management is an important aspect of modeling writing using technology. In a well-managed class with regular routines, ELLs develop a sense of comfort in the classroom.

Lynnette sets up her computer prior to the beginning of class, and students are called by row to pick up their computers. Once all computers are turned on, and all eyes are looking at her, she leads students through the process of getting started with writing, by finding the right keys to display their document on the computer screen. She models the process on a large screen that is projected from her computer. Students follow along while Lynnette continually monitors for student understanding. Once all students have their document ready, with their name and class period typed, Lynnette asks students, "How can we begin a story at a time in the past?" Edmund quickly raises his hand and excitedly replies, "We could begin with the date." Lynnette then says, "Okay, I'm going to type the beginning of my piece, using Edmund's suggestion, and you watch." Lynnette types an example of how to begin a story, while writing about a past event. Then, she asks for input from the students, and they generate several ideas for her to type. She types

> *It was March 10, 2005, and I was attending my brother's birthday party. . . .*
> > OR
> *It was March 5, 2004, at Rosemont 6th Grade, and I was in class waiting for the teacher to come to the room.*

Once students seem to understand ways to begin a writing piece using a date, she asks, "Can you begin a story with dialogue?" Several students call out "yes," in unison, and Maria suggests that such a story could even begin with someone laughing. Lyn models using the overhead computer screen, and she types

> *"Oh, no!!!" People were laughing and I was on the ground.*

The students' eagerness to participate by giving examples demonstrates the level of community developed. Lynnette then explains that writers also can begin a piece with a quote, or by describing a situation in which someone is talking. Since students have a firm grasp of how to use multiple strategies for beginning a new writing piece, Lynnette explains,

> *You are going to decide how you will write your story. Your story does not have to be*
> *very long, since we are only writing for about 25 minutes. This is just a free write.*

Students intently work at their computers, and only the clicking sounds of their keyboards can be heard.

Review of key concepts is ongoing throughout Lynnette's lesson; at this point in the lesson, however, she makes sure that students fully understand their task. She reminds students that they can use similar examples to the ones that the class generated, or they can think of different ways to begin their piece. Lynnette walks around the room, checking each student's computer screen to monitor understanding. Then, she reminds students that to begin a new paragraph, they need to remember to press "enter" twice on the computer keyboard. Modeling how to write is not a new concept, but the use of technology is redefining the concept. Students practice and apply what they learned about how to develop a lead (an engaging way to captivate readers' attention and interest), based on what they learned from Lynnette's modeling of instruction. Lynnette ensures that students fully grasp the strategy and the language needed to complete the task at hand. Similarly, students read and respond to their peer's writing, through both sharing orally and in written responses. Effective SIOP teachers make sure that all objectives, content and language, are met as students practice and apply these objectives.

Indicator 6: Lesson Delivery

Planning an effective lesson also is an integral component of the SIOP. Teachers who successfully deliver SIOP lessons ensure that each content and language objective is met and delivered in a lesson. Effective content area teachers take into consideration their students' language needs and examine content area material from a language perspective (Short & Echevarria, 2005). These teachers pose such questions as: To comprehend my textbook, what language skills must students master? Do students need to write cause/effect essays, or narrative ones? Do students need to know specialized vocabulary to understand the reading? When teachers reflect on their students' language needs, they are better able to help ELLs learn academic English.

Student engagement throughout the lesson is also important, and researchers suggest that students should be engaged for 90 to 100 percent of the class period (Echevarria & Graves, 2003; Short & Echevarria, 2005; Short, Hudec, & Echevarria, 2002). As mentioned earlier in the chapter, the pacing of the lesson should be balanced with the students' ability levels. Teachers should make sure that learning is comprehensible, and adjust the lesson pace and instruction to reflect the students' abilities.

Indicator 7: Review/Assessment

The final component of SIOP is review and assessment. Teachers must carefully plan to assess how much their students retained of new concepts and key vocabulary. Review and assessment always should be used to inform future instruction. Echevarria et al. (2008) explain that the review and assessment of lessons should be authentic, ongoing, cyclical, and recursive. Teacher feedback can consist of body language, written, and oral comments on student performance. Feedback must be honest and supportive, while helping students clarify misunderstandings. Short and Echevarria (2005) emphasize the importance of giving students feedback on their language abilities, and they state that content area teachers must not become linguistic experts. A few ways that content area teachers can give students feedback on language is by talking about word choice, strategies for developing speaking/presentation skills, techniques for explaining a solution, or strategies for summarizing text in both spoken and written form.

Lynnette guides students through the writing process throughout 6th grade. She designs meaningful assignments in which she gives students topic and publication choices (see Figure 8.9). She uses holistic rubrics to review and assess student writing, while preparing students for the state-mandated writing test (see Figure 8.10). In all, review and assessment should be ongoing and varied, to best serve the diverse language needs of each student.

Mrs. Mayo's
Book Report Choices

Select one of the following choices to tell me about the book you've chosen. The book MUST be one you have read and taken an AR Test on since February 19, 2007.

Your report will be due on **Friday, March 9, 2007**

1) If you could change places with one of the characters in your novel, who would it be and why?

2) Rewrite a chapter from your novel using another character's point of view.

3) Create a cartoon version of the novel. You should have a minimum of 6 to 8 panels to summarize the novel.

4) Redesign the front and back covers for your novel.

5) Compare and contrast your novel with one you have read in the English or Reading class this year.

BE SURE TO INCLUDE AT THE TOP OF YOUR PAPER

Title of the book
Author
# of pages

ON THE BACK OF YOUR PAPER
Your name, date, and period
List of main characters
Setting of the book
Which choice you are selecting (copy the sentence from the list).

If you are writing, you are expected to have a <u>minimum</u> of one page.

Figure 8.9. Book Report

Name:_____   Teacher: <u>Mrs. Mayo</u>

Date Submitted: _____   Title of Work: _____

Criteria					Points
	1	2	3	4	
Focus and Coherence	Writer shifts from idea to idea abruptly, making it difficult to understand how ideas are related. Composition as a whole has no sense of completeness. A great amount of writing does not contribute to the development or quality of the composition. Composition weakly connected to prompt.	Individual paragraphs and/or composition are somewhat focused. Composition has some sense of completeness.	Individual paragraphs and/or composition are somewhat focused. Composition has some sense of completeness. There is an introduction and conclusion.	Individual paragraphs and/or composition are focused. Composition has a sense of completeness. The introduction and conclusion are meaningful.	
Organization	Sequence of information is difficult to follow. Writer presents ideas in a random or haphazard way. Wordiness and/or repetition stops the progression of ideas.	Progression of thought from sentence to sentence and/or paragraph to paragraph may not always be smooth or logical. Some wordiness, but it does not stop the progression of ideas.	Writer's progression of thought is generally smooth and controlled. Transitions are meaningful, and links between ideas are logical. Wordiness and/or repetition, if present, are minor.	Writer's progression of thought is smooth and controlled. Transitions are meaningful and logical. Organizational strategy enhances the writer's ability to present idea clearly.	
Development of Ideas	Writer presents one or more ideas but provides little development. Development of ideas is vague. Writer presents only plot summary. Writer omits information, creating gaps between ideas.	Writer tries to develop piece by listing ideas or briefly explaining them, limiting the reader's understanding. Writer presents one or more ideas and tries to develop them, but development is somewhat inconsistent. Writer omits small pieces of information that create minor gaps.	Writer tries to develop all the ideas included in the composition. Development overall reflects some depth of thought.	Writer development of each idea has depth of thought, enabling the reader to understand and appreciate the writer's ideas.	
Voice	Writer does not engage reader. Little or no sense of the writer's individual voice.	There may be moments when the writer engages the reader but fails to sustain the connection. Writer has difficulty expressing his/her individuality.	Writer engages the reader and sustains the connection throughout. Writer is generally able to express his/her individuality.	Writer engages the reader and sustains the connection throughout. Writer is able to express his/her individuality.	
Conventions	Writing has 4 or more spelling, capitalization, punctuation, grammar, or usage errors. Writer misuses or omits words and phrases, frequently writing awkward sentences.	Writing has 3 or less spelling, capitalization, punctuation, grammar, or usage errors. Writer may have used some awkward sentences.	Writing has 2 or less spelling, capitalization, punctuation, grammar, or usage errors. Words and phrases used are generally appropriate.	Writing has few spelling, capitalization, punctuation, grammar, or usage errors. Words and phrases enhance the communication of ideas.	
				Total ⟶	

Teacher Comments:

Figure 8.10. Writing Rubric

Concluding Thoughts

It is clear that our linguistically diverse children are lagging far behind their peers in school. Teachers must plan instruction that takes into account this group of students' unique needs, their strengths, and areas where they need improvement. While teachers can use many strategies to help ELLs become academically successful, focusing on language and content, integration of reading, writing, and using technology is one way to bridge the gap between the skills monolingual students are mastering and the skills ELLs need to learn.

Lynnette demonstrates strategies for meeting ELLs' distinct needs, as illustrated in the classroom vignettes. More specifically, Lynnette's teaching represents the type of instruction ELLs need, since she

- Pays close attention to language and content objectives
- Uses appropriate instructional strategies, such as scaffolding, modeling, and linking concepts to students' prior knowledge
- Integrates reading, writing, and technology in classroom instruction
- Holds high expectations for all students
- Develops a sense of community within her class.

Most importantly, teachers like Lynnette provide high-quality instruction to ensure that schools do not leave behind ELLs, or other struggling students, all the while developing a community.

A large number of ELLs throughout the United States receive classroom instruction from content area teachers who have little training in working with second language learners, nor are they familiar with how to make language comprehensible for ELLs (Short & Echevarria, 2005). With the increasing numbers of ELLs in public schools, it is important for content area teachers to find ways to deliver sheltered content instruction to make learning comprehensible to ELLs. Researchers over the past decade discovered that with appropriate preparation and training, teachers can help ELLs master content area knowledge and develop academic literacy skills—which equates to success for everyone.

References

Asher, J., Kusudo, J., & de la Torre, R. (1974). Learning a second language through commands: The second field test. *Modern Language Journal, 58,* 24-32.

Balderamma, M. V., & Diaz-Rico, L. T. (2006). *Teaching performance expectations for educating English language learners.* Boston: Pearson, Allyn & Bacon.

Bromley, K. (2007). Nine things every teacher should know about words and vocabulary instruction. *Journal of Adolescent & Adult Literacy, 50*(7), 528-537.

Bunch, C., Abram, P. L., Lotan, R. A., & Valdes, G. (2001). Beyond sheltered instruction: Rethinking conditions for academic language development. *TESOL Journal, 10*(2/3), 28-39.

Calkins, L. M. (1994). *The art of teaching writing.* Portsmouth, NH: Heinemann.

Collier, V., & Thomas, P. (2002). Reforming education policies for English learners means better schools for all. *The State Education Standard, 3*(1), 30-36.

Crandall, J. (1993). Content-centered learning in the United States. In W. Grabe (Ed.), *Annual review of applied linguistics, 13* (pp. 111-126). New York: Cambridge University Press.

Cummins, J. (1979). Cognitive-academic language proficiency, linguistic interdependence, optimal age and some other matters. *Working Papers in Bilingualism, 19,* 197-205.

Cummins, J. (1980). The construct of language proficiency in bilingual education. In J. E. Alatis (Ed.), *Georgetown University roundtable on languages and linguistics* (pp. 76-93). Washington, DC: Georgetown University Press.

Cummins, J. (2000). *Language, power, and pedagogy: Bilingual children in the crossfire.* Clevedon, UK: Multilingual Matters.

Cunningham, P. M., & Allington, R. L. (2002). *Classrooms that work: They can all read and write* (3rd ed.). Boston: Pearson Education/Allyn and Bacon.

Echevarria, J., & Graves, A. (2003). *Sheltered content instruction: Teaching English-language learners with diverse abilities* (2nd ed.). Boston: Allyn and Bacon.

Echevarria, J., Short, D. J., & Vogt, M. E. (2008). *Making content comprehensible for English language learners: The SIOP model* (3rd ed.). Boston: Allyn & Bacon.

Echevarria, J., Vogt, M. E., & Short, D. J. (2000). *Making content comprehensible for English language learners. The SIOP model.* Boston: Allyn & Bacon.

Freeman, D., & Freeman, Y. (1988). *Sheltered English instruction.* Washington, DC: ERIC Digest. ERIC Clearinghouse on Languages and Linguistics. (ERIC Document Reproduction Service No. ED 301070)

Genesee, F. (1994). *Integrating language and content: Lessons from immersion.* Washington, DC: National Center for Research on Cultural Diversity and Second Language Learning. Washington, DC: Center for Applied Linguistics.

Genesee, F. (Ed.). (1999). *Program alternatives for linguistically diverse students* (Educational Practice Rep. No. 1). Santa Cruz, CA and Washington, DC: Center for Research on Education, Diversity & Excellence.

Graves, D. (1994). *A fresh look at writing.* Portsmouth, NH: Heinemann.

Gruber, K. J., Wiley, S. D., Broughman, S. P., Strizek, G. A., & Burian-Fitzgerald, M. (2002). *Schools and staffing survey, 1999-2000: Overview of the data for public, private, public charter, and Bureau of Indian Affairs elementary and secondary schools.* Retrieved April 22, 2007, from http: nces.ed.gov/pubs2002/21002313.pdf

Kinzer, C. (2005). The intersection of schools, communities, and technology: Recognizing children's use of new literacies. In R. Karchmer, M. Mallette, J. Kara-Soteriou, & D. Leu (Eds.), *Innovative approaches to literacy education: Using the Internet to support new literacies* (pp. 65-82). Newark, DE: International Reading Association.

Krashen, S. (1982). *Principles and practice in second language acquisition.* New York: Pergamon Press.

Krashen, S. (2000). What does it take to acquire language? *ESL Magazine, 3*(3), 22-23.

Labbo, L. (2005). Fundamental qualities of effective Internet literacy instruction: An exploration of worthwhile classroom practices. In R. Karchmer, M. Mallette, J. Kara-Soteriou, & D. Leu (Eds.), *Innovative approaches to literacy education: Using the Internet to support new literacies* (pp. 165-180). Newark, DE: International Reading Association.

Lacina, J., Griffith, B., & Hagan, L. (2006). Developing a writing workshop classroom: Stories from a charter school principal, 2nd grade teacher, and university professor. *The Teacher Educator, 42*(1), 63-75.

Lacina, L., New Levine, L., & Sowa, P. (2006). *Helping English language learners succeed in Pre-K-elementary schools.* Alexandria, VA: Teachers of English to Speakers of Other Languages.

Leu, D. J., Kinzer, C. K., Coiro, J. L., & Cammack, D. W. (2004). Toward a theory of new literacies emerging from the Internet and other information and communication technologies. In R. B. Ruddell & N. J. Unrau (Eds.), *Theoretical models and processes of reading* (5th ed., pp. 1570-1613). Newark, DE: International Reading Association.

Nagy, W., & Scott, J. (2000). Vocabulary processes. In M. L. Kamil, P. B. Mosenthal, P. D. Pearson, & R. Barr (Eds.), *Handbook of reading research* (Vol. 3, pp. 269–284). Mahwah, NJ: Erlbaum.

National Clearinghouse for English Language Acquisition. (NCELA). (2004). *The growing numbers of limited English proficient students, 1991/92-2001/02.* Retrieved April 10, 2007, from wwww.ncela.gwu.edu/practice/itc/elementary.html

Peregoy, S. F., & Boyle, O. F. (2005). *Reading, writing and learning in ESL. A resource book for K-12 teachers.* Boston: Pearson, Allyn & Bacon.

Ray, K. W. (2002). *What you know by heart: How to develop curriculum for your writing workshop.* Portsmouth, NH: Heinemann.

Robb, L. (2000). *Teaching reading in middle school: A strategic approach to teaching reading that improves comprehension and thinking.* New York: Scholastic Professional Books.

Schmidt, B., & Buckley, M. (1991). Plot relationships chart. In J. M. Macon, D. Bewell, &

M. Vogt (Eds.), *Responses to literature: Grades K-8* (pp. 7-8). Newark, DE: International Reading Association.

Short, D., & Echevarria, J. (2005). Teacher skills to support English language learners. *Educational Leadership, 62*(4), 9-13.

Short, D., Hudec, J., & Echevarria, J. (2002). *Using the SIOP model: Professional development manual for sheltered instruction.* Washington, DC: Center for Applied Linguistics.

Shrum, J., & Glisan, E. (2000). *Teachers handbook: Contextualized language instruction.* Boston: Heinle & Heinle.

Snow, M. A., & Brinton, D. M. (Eds.). (1997). *The content-based classroom: Perspectives on integrating langage and content.* White Plains, NY: Longman.

Teale, W. H., Leu, D. J., Labbo, L. D., & Kinzer, C. (2002). The CTELL project: New ways technology can help educate tomorrow's reading teachers. *The Reading Teacher, 55,* 654-659.

Vacca, J. L., Vacca, R. T., Gove, M. K., Burkey, L., Lenhart, L. A., & McKeon, C. (2005). *Reading and learning to read* (6th ed.). Boston: Allyn & Bacon.

Valdes, G. (1998). The world outside and inside schools: Language and immigrant children. *Educational Researcher, 27*(6), 4-18.

Valdes, G. (2001). *Learning and not learning English: Latino students in American schools.* New York: Teachers College Press.

Adolescent Literature

Fleischman, P. (1997). *Seedfolks.* New York: HarperCollins.

Ho, M. (1993). *The clay marble.* Vancouver, BC: Douglas and McIntyre.

Meet the Authors

Jan Lacina has focused her research and teaching on English language learners (ELLs) and on reading and writing instruction. She teaches undergraduate and graduate literacy courses at Texas Christian University. She is co-author of the book Helping English Language Learners Succeed in Pre-K-Elementary Schools *(TESOL, 2006), and she has published in numerous journals. Jan also writes the "Technology in the Classroom" column that is published in the journal* Childhood Education. *Prior to teaching at the college level, Jan taught ESL in Texas and Kansas.*

Lynnette Mayo teaches 6th-grade English at Rosemont 6th Grade in the Fort Worth Independent School District (FWISD) in Texas. Lynnette is the lead English teacher for the 6th grade and is a curriculum writer for the school district and a SIOP trainer.

Patience Sowa conducts research in the areas of teaching ELLs, literacy, multicultural education, and educational technology. She teaches graduate courses in ESL, research methods, and multicultural education at Rockhurst University. As a SIOP trainer, she has conducted workshops with schools in the Kansas City area. She is co-author of the book Helping English Language Learners Succeed in Pre-K-Elementary Schools *(TESOL, 2006).*

Chapter 9

Media Literacy:

Encouraging Critical Thinking
Across the Content Areas

The air in the room is charged with expectancy. At a table sits R. Braden Rod, CEO of the By-the-ROD Ad Agency. Two assistants flank him. A group of professionally dressed young men and women take their places at the front of the room. They introduce themselves, and then launch into the presentation of a new advertising campaign for Buddy Cola. The presentation centers around a 30-second commercial presented on the big-screen television. Rod and his assistants watch and listen intently, making notes and asking questions of the advertising team. An audience of 20 or so observes.

This presentation is being done in a middle school library. The young advertising executives are actually students at J. T. Hutchinson Middle School in Lubbock, Texas, and R. Braden Rod is actually René B. Rodriguez, better known as Coach Rod. These presentations are the culminating event of a two-week-long unit on "Propaganda: An Archetypal Study." According to Rod, the purpose of this unit is to expose students to different propaganda techniques and to engage them in using those techniques, along with archetypes, in the construction of media.

Rod is a middle school language arts teacher with eight years of experience. J. T. Hutchinson Middle School has a very ethnically and economically diverse student population, including students who live in the surrounding neighborhood and students from across the city who elect to attend this school for its emphasis on academics and fine arts. Approximately 70 percent of the students are minorities and a number of students are English language learners who choose to attend the school, even though no services for ELL students are offered. Rod teaches students in both the academically accelerated classes and regular classes with the same mix of high expectations, humor, and encouragement. He knows each of his students as individuals, as evidenced by the interactions observed outside his classroom door prior to each period. Rod greets each student with a handshake and a personal comment. One of the students remarked that being in Rod's class feels like "being at home. He's approachable and gives good advice. Even when I'm having a bad day, I feel like I can leave everything at the door and just learn."

In his classes, Rod designs lessons and projects that meet the diverse learning preferences of his students. Throughout the year he provides students with the opportunity to respond and express ideas in varied media formats, from comic strips to collages, from brochures to Readers Theater. Rod also keeps in mind an overriding goal—to teach skills and processes that will serve students well in future settings beyond life in the classroom. His students frequently comment that Rod teaches them more than English: "He teaches us life lessons."

This chapter offers an in-depth look at Rod's pro-

**Patricia A. Watson
and René B. Rodriguez**

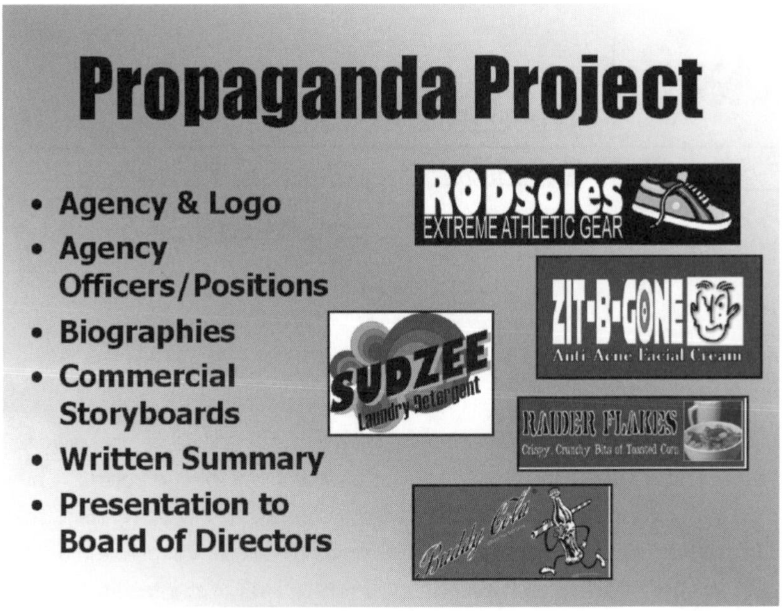

Propaganda Project

- **Agency & Logo**
- **Agency Officers/Positions**
- **Biographies**
- **Commercial Storyboards**
- **Written Summary**
- **Presentation to Board of Directors**

Figure 9.1

paganda unit. This unit exemplifies effective content area literacy instruction. Throughout the unit, students are engaged in the use of literacy processes as they work toward an authentic goal. Students read and author several types of texts and work collaboratively to produce a final product. Through the advertising project, students learn about the concepts of revealed and concealed propaganda. By viewing commercial advertisements, they learn to identify the techniques of propaganda. Although this chapter focuses specifically on a unit taught within a language arts curriculum, media plays a role in the literacies of all content areas. The thinking skills required to be a critical consumer of media complement all subjects, and it is as important to learn about media in a science class as it is in English or history classes.

Students must demonstrate an understanding of propaganda techniques that goes beyond mere recognition. In the production of the 30-second commercials, advertising teams are required to include at least two of these techniques.

Propaganda Techniques	
Testimonials or Endorsements	Fear
Urgency	Scientific Approach
Emotional Language	Exaggeration/Hyperbole
Repetition	Glittering Generalities
Euphemisms	Snob Appeal
Transfer	Plain Folks Appeal
Bandwagon	Something for Nothing

Figure 9.2

Exaggeration

Figure 9.3

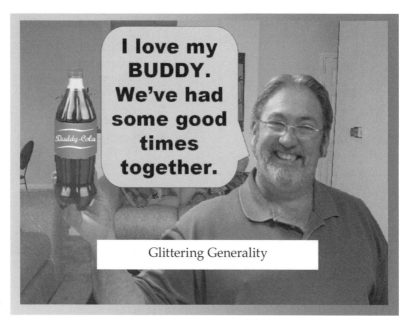

Figure 9.4

The second major understanding students must develop through this project is the use of archetypes. Rod explains archetypes as "patterns that seem to have developed in the minds of mankind from the very beginning" (Rodriguez, 2005, p. 9). He introduces students to the work of psychologist Carl Jung (1964) and his concept of the collective unconscious, images from the primitive mind that are alike for all cultures. Students are asked to demonstrate their understanding of archetypes by incorporating at least one in their advertising design. Rod introduces the students to a variety of archetypes through examples, making this difficult and abstract concept concrete for middle school students by connecting archetypes to their own media experiences.

For instance, he uses *The Lion King* to exemplify the situational archetype of The Quest. The character archetype of The Initiate is exemplified by Daniel from *The Karate Kid* and Elliot from *E.T.*

Situational Archetypes	Character Archetypes	Symbolic Archetypes

1. The Quest
2. The Task
3. The Initiation
4. The Journey
5. The Fall
6. Death and Rebirth
7. Nature vs. Mechanistic World
8. Battle Between Good and Evil
9. The Unhealable Wound
10. The Rituals
11. The Magic Weapon
	1. The Hero
	2. The Young Man From the Provinces
	3. The Initiate
	4. Mentors
	5. Mentor-Pupil Relationship
	6. Father-Son Conflict
	7. Hunting Group of Companions
	8. Loyal Retainers
	9. Friendly Beast
	10. The Devil Figure
	11. The Evil Figure With the Good Heart
	12. The Scapegoat
	13. The Outcast
	14. The Woman Figure
	    • Earthmother
	    • Temptress
	    • Platonic Ideal
	    • Unfaithful Wife
	    • Damsel in Distress
	    • Star-crossed Lovers
	15. Creature of Nightmare
		1. Light vs. Darkness
		2. Water vs. Desert
		3. Heaven vs. Hell
		4. Innate Wisdom vs. Educated Stupidity
		5. Haven vs. Wilderness
		6. Supernatural Intervention
		7. Fire vs. Ice

Figure 9.5

The unit on propaganda and archetypes extends over a two-week period. In this brief time, members of the advertising teams learn a variety of literacy skills and strategies beyond knowledge of the major concepts. Watching the presentations by the advertising team, Rod's high expectations for his students are obvious. The 10- to 15-minute presentations demonstrate the students' use of presentation skills and their integration of research and computer skills. Students take their places before the review team wearing crisply ironed shirts and ties or dresses worn with high heels, their hair is neatly combed, and they hold confident postures. One student in Rod's first-hour class asserted that the advertising assignment was "really fun and different. We got to be creative . . . got to use our potential."

Another student, from the same class, emphasized the stress she was under during the project. "We had four days to do the whole project, then present. We had to rely on computers and other people, and then just hope everything goes right."

When asked to share his teaching philosophy and the motivation behind the advertising unit, Rod makes it clear that media literacy is not something to be taught in a two-week lesson, and then forgotten. Students have multiple opportunities to be actively engaged in learning about media in multiple ways throughout the year. The critical thinking skills necessary for success in the 21st century are incorporated throughout the year as students are asked to interpret, analyze, and, most importantly, produce many forms of media. Students are expected to represent learning through visual and aural images, not just through the written word. Talking about her learning from the propaganda unit, one student said, "He has ruined us completely! We can't watch a commercial or a movie now without seeing the techniques and the archetypes. But it's important. These things play a massive role in our society. It's so easy to get suckered in. Now we're more prepared."

Media Literacy: Beyond the Messages of Printed Text

The definition of literacy is ever-changing. When the United States was first founded, a man was considered to be literate if he could sign his name. As public education became more common, printed texts were in short supply and so school masters and mistresses engaged their young charges in recitation. A literate individual, then, was someone who could recite poetry and Bible verses. In order to be a productive citizen in our current information age, however, individuals are expected to read critically and translate information into varying formats (Braunger & Lewis, 2006). In today's world, literacy goes far beyond traditional print texts. Information comes to us through the images and sounds of our multi-media culture, through television, radio, movies, and the Internet. These multi-media messages have a complex language of their own. Audio-visual communications have their own rules and are multi-layered. In other words, literate individuals today must be media literate as well as text literate. Today's literacy demands that students learn to read and produce these messages using the language of images and sound, as well as spoken and printed text (Thoman & Jolis, 2005).

In 1992, a national media literacy summit defined media literacy as the ability to access, analyze, evaluate, and communicate messages in various forms (Aufderheide, 1993). Most media literacy organizations and experts in North America continue to accept this definition. Media literacy includes the ability to read and comprehend messages in a variety of formats. In addition, media literacy includes the abilities to write, create, design, and produce messages using audio and visual communications as well as the written word. Foundational to media literacy are critical thinking skills, such as connecting multiple ideas across different media, asking critical questions, identifying misleading information, and formulating articulate responses. Media literacy also expands the definition of "text" to include more than written texts. In today's information-filled world, a "text" may include many representation systems and combinations of verbal, auditory, and visual information.

Media Literacy Instruction:
A Necessity in 21st-Century Classrooms

Students and teachers alike often see the classroom and the "outside world" as two separate spaces. Even teachers who actively include content area reading strategies do so with only traditional print texts, ignoring other forms of media or "texts" and continuing this separation of classroom instruction from the rest of everyday life. Today's definition of literacy is more than reading and writing. In this age of the Internet, the critical thinking skills that help young adolescents navigate through traditional texts are even more important to have. In our media-saturated world, middle school students must learn to read the messages that daily inform us, entertain us, and sell to us.

Len Masterman, author of *Teaching the Media* (1990), identified the following six key reasons for including media literacy in the curriculum of our schools:

• *Media Saturation.* As citizens of today's world, we are exposed to more media messages in one day than our grandparents were in a month. A 1999 study by the Kaiser Family Foundation (Roberts, Foehr, Rideout, & Brodie, 1999) found that the typical American child spends close to five-and-a-half hours a day consuming media outside of school. Television is not the only medium that accounts for this saturation. Popular music, radio, newspapers, magazines, computers, and video games also bombard students with messages throughout the day. More than ever, students need the tools and strategies to help them make sense of this barrage of information and persuasion.

• *Media Influence.* In 1974, Wilson Bryan Keys estimated that the average U.S. adult was exposed daily to 100,000 words that were "carefully edited, slanted, and skillfully composed" to sell, propose, and plead for our attention, our sympathy, our loyalty, and most of all, our money (p. 81). By incorporating media literacy into content area literacy instruction, teachers can help learners be in control of their interpretation of these messages, rather than allowing the media to control them (Thoman, 1999).

• *The Manufacture and Management of Information.* In today's information-loaded world, it is critical for students to be able to recognize the source and purpose of information and to be able to evaluate the credibility of sources. Much of what is reported as news is, in fact, based on press releases from both government and business sources.

• *Media Education and Democracy.* The democratic process today is critically influenced by the media. Those who know how to use the media can prevail regardless of public policy or personal integrity. Twenty-first century students need to explore the ways in which political advertising shapes the campaign process, and learn to identify the techniques that are used to manipulate emotions and public perceptions.

• *The Increasing Importance of Visual Communication and Information.* For centuries, literacy has been defined in terms of the written word. To be literate means that an individual could comprehend and produce the basic components of written language. But in today's multi-media culture, the visual image is as important, and perhaps more influential, than the written word. Nevertheless, teachers in today's classrooms continue to privilege the use of written text over the production of visual images as evidence of learning. Media literacy demands that we focus on the understanding and production of visual texts, as well as the written word. It also demands that our students become informed viewers, critics, and consumers of visual information.

• *The Growing Privatization of Information.* While the term "digital divide" has most often been applied to the "haves" and "have-nots" of computer technology, this distinction soon may apply to the information-rich vs. the information-poor as, more and more, individuals are being expected to pay for information, from Internet access to satellite radio. In an interview, filmmaker George Lucas addressed this division as it relates to media education in our schools when he said:

> *When people talk to me about the digital divide, I think of it not being so much about who has access to what technology as about who knows how to create and express themselves in the new language of the screen. If students aren't taught the language of sound and images, shouldn't they be considered as illiterate as if they left college without being able to read and write?* (as quoted in Daly, 2004, p. 38)

For these reasons, media literacy should be a consideration in every content classroom. Every teacher who considers how to incorporate literacy strategies into content area teaching should consider not just print literacy, but also the literacy needed to live in a world of powerful images, words, and sounds.

Media Literacy in the Content Areas: Fostering Critical Thinking

Elizabeth Thoman (1999), founder of the Center for Media Literacy, stated that the goal of media education should be to help students become "competent and literate in all media forms" (p. 50). Media literacy, much like reading comprehension, is not a product but rather a process. It is a way of thinking. Becoming media literate is about knowing how to ask the right questions about what we are watching, reading, or listening to. According to Thoman, the principle of inquiry is central to becoming media literate. Teaching through inquiry encourages students to question and be intellectually curious about the world. Through inquiry, students engage in meaningful research and discussion, a method of learning that is ideally suited to media education. Media messages have many levels and many hidden messages. Learning to ask questions about everything we read, watch, or hear is an essential skill for literate adults in today's media-saturated world.

In most instances, developing media literacy involves two facets: close analysis of media and production of media (Hobbs, 2005). According to Scheibe and Rogow (2004), media literacy education began in the 1970s with the goal of protecting students from the ill-effects of media and teaching them to discriminate between good and bad media content. However, teaching students to be critical of media is not the same thing as teaching students to think critically (Rogow, 2005). Students must not just be taught what an advertisement or a movie means; they must be given opportunities to learn to analyze media for themselves. Recently, there has been a shift towards the goal of empowerment through media, emphasizing critical thinking and production skills. Tyner (1992) cautioned, however, that teachers must guard against curricular planning that is too production-oriented, which tends to minimize the critical analysis component of media education. Students do not, as some people think, learn media literacy skills simply by doing hands-on production.

Rogow (2005) suggested three criteria that educators can use to evaluate their media-related lessons. These criteria are aimed at allowing students to think for themselves. Teachers can examine their pedagogy by asking these questions:

1. Am I trying to tell the students what the message is, or am I giving students the skills to determine what they think the messages might be?
2. Have I let students know that I am open to accepting their interpretation, as long as it is well-substantiated, or have I conveyed the message that my interpretation is the only correct view?
3. At the end of this lesson, are students likely to be more analytical or more cynical? (p. 285)

These three questions will help teachers maintain a focus on student-centered learning, whereby the students construct their own knowledge and abilities to evaluate media messages. The goal is to help students develop a keen eye and analytical mind, not to turn students into sharp-tongued critics who take little pleasure from experiences with media.

Researchers with Project Look Sharp, a media education initiative at Ithaca College, have identified 12 basic principles for incorporating media literacy education into any curriculum:

1. Use media to practice general observation, critical thinking analysis, perspective taking, and production skills.
2. Use media to stimulate interest in a new topic.
3. Identify ways in which students may be already familiar with a topic through media.
4. Use media as a standard pedagogical tool.
5. Identify erroneous beliefs about a topic fostered by media content.
6. Develop awareness of credibility and bias issues in the media.
7. Compare the ways in which different media present information about a topic.
8. Analyze the effect that specific media have had on a particular issue or topic.
9. Use media to build and practice specific curricular skills.
10. Use media to express students' opinions and illustrate their understanding of the world.
11. Use media as an assessment tool.
12. Use media to connect students to the community and work toward positive change. (Scheibe & Rogow, 2004, n.p.)

Project Look Sharp provides teachers with specific curricular planning tools and ideas through material provided on their website at www.ithaca.edu/looksharp.

Rather than be taught as a separate and isolated topic, media literacy education is best woven through the curriculum whenever and wherever possible. Many states in the United States have begun to build media literacy standards into their state curriculum standards in a number of subjects. Examples of state standards can be found at the Media Literacy Clearinghouse (http://medialit.med.sc.edu/statelit.html). For the most part, in the United States, concepts and skills associated with media education are being integrated into existing areas of the traditional curriculum. For example, in language arts classrooms, the definition of "text" has been broadened to include film, television, websites, and even music videos. These texts are examined, discussed, and represented through a variety of verbal, visual, and graphic forms.

The social studies classroom is perhaps the most natural location for media education to be integrated with content area instruction. Many students now get most of the information about their own country and the world from electronic media. Preparing students for responsible citizenship certainly should include an examination of how the media depicts and affects different aspects of a democracy, such as the political process. Discussions of First Amendment rights and the civic responsibilities of media production companies can play a vital role in shaping students' understandings of their own civic rights and responsibilities. Films, both historical fiction and documentaries, have long been used as motivational and enrichment tools by social studies educators. Actively examining these works with a critical eye for the media messages they convey can only strengthen the critical thinking abilities of students in today's social studies classrooms.

Media literacy and the sciences are another natural match for curriculum integration. Thier (2005, p. 260) asserted that "these days, we all have to be able to think like scientists." Students must learn to take an analytical approach to the evidence presented through the mass media. They must learn to gather and evaluate evidence. Science, just like media analysis, requires the strategies of examining assertions for weaknesses and bias. Students of the sciences not only must know the discipline of science, but also must be able to analyze the methods used to present facts and explain how facts can be manipulated to support a particular point of view (Thier, 2005). In the same way, students in the area of health education must learn to "analyze the influence of culture, media, technology, and other factors on health" (Summerfield, 1995). The skills learned through media education can help students analyze messages that promote risky behaviors and the consumption of goods without evident effects on the environment or personal health. Additionally, curriculum integration with mathematics occurs naturally through the use of statistics, surveys, reports, and the analysis and graphical representation of data.

Media Literacy as a Way of Learning: Effective Instructional Strategies

Media literacy is not a content area or a body of knowledge to be taught. Rather, it is a set of skills or a process, much like reading comprehension is a process. Effective media literacy education does not require memorization of facts, but instead requires individuals to learn thinking strategies that will help them interpret the messages they are viewing and producing, in all media forms.

Over time, media experts and educators from around the world have identified the following five key concepts that can be viewed as the foundational ideas for examining and producing media (Share, Jolis, & Thoman, 2005):

1. Media messages are constructed. The messages were created by someone.
2. Media messages are constructed using a creative language with its own rules. Understanding this language increases our appreciation while also making us less likely to be manipulated by media messages.
3. Different people experience the same media message differently. We try to make sense of what we see and hear, filtering it through our own prior knowledge and experiences.
4. Media have embedded values and points of view. The person who created the media decides what is important. Choices are based on the creator's values and beliefs.
5. Most media messages are created to gain profit and/or power. These messages are, to a large degree, created by companies with something to sell. (p. 7)

Providing opportunities and instruction that allow students to access, analyze, evaluate, and communicate media messages can seem intimidating to teachers faced with today's highly structured curriculum frameworks and accountability expectations. The Center for Media Literacy has developed a series of five questions, based on the five key concepts, that can be used to create connections between the critical thinking skills of media literacy and other subject areas. These five questions, if taught repeatedly across different contexts, can become a shorthand for examining how messages are created and analyzing their impact on those who read, hear, and view them. The five organizing questions that can be asked of any media message are:

1. Who created the message? This question prompts students to examine who authored the message and is responsible for the message conveyed.
2. What techniques are used to attract my attention? Through this lens, students examine the format of media messages and how images, sound, color, and persuasive techniques are used to evoke certain responses.

3. How might various people understand this message differently? This question leads students to the realization that media messages are created with specific, targeted audiences in mind and that the messages will affect different audiences with more or less impact.
4. What lifestyles, values, and points of view are represented in, or omitted from, this message? By examining the content of media products, students can confront the different value systems portrayed through the characters who are relaying the media messages.
5. Why was this message sent? This powerful question leads students to recognize that all media messages are created with a specific purpose in mind and that these messages have a powerful influence on many elements of our society. (Share, Jolis, & Thoman, 2005, n.p.)

Jim Burke (2001), author of *Illuminating Texts: How To Teach Students To Read the World*, maintains that a teacher's role is no longer to impart knowledge, but rather to arm students "with a tool belt heavy with strategies and the skill to use them appropriately when reading—and making—texts" (p. 3). Burke's definition of "texts" includes images, the Internet, information, and even standardized tests. McBrien (1999) also discusses how media literacy requires students to have the appropriate tools to read and comprehend the wide variety of written, visual, verbal, and audio texts that bombard them every day. McBrien outlines a five-step pedagogy for arming students with these tools. First, students must understand the historical and contemporary background of a medium in order to understand the reason for the medium's existence. Next, students must be taught to recognize the tools of media production, from camera angles to stereotypes. After students have this basic understanding, they can learn to deconstruct texts. They can examine media to reveal the techniques used to make up a media product. Then, students can learn to evaluate as they consider the messages created through the techniques. This process empowers students to take control of their reactions and to recognize the effects of media on their emotions. The last step is original construction. By creating their own message, students can use their knowledge of tools and techniques to produce media products for their schools and communities.

A close examination of Coach Rod's propaganda unit reveals that he did indeed facilitate his students' progress through these five levels of understanding. The students in his classes emphasized that the final element of construction was crucial to their full understanding of the techniques of propaganda and archetypal images. As one student put it, "Without doing it ourselves, we would have learned it, but we would not have remembered it."

Concluding Thoughts

The four processes built into the definition of media literacy are really the foundational concepts of all literacy in the 21st century; therefore, they should be incorporated into the skills taught in every subject area discipline in today's schools. Students must be able to *access* the tools of our information age and must be able to identify which tools are appropriate and useful, including accessing information through print, computer, and video source. Twenty-first century learners must have the ability to *analyze* messages, from the use of simple categorization through making inferences about the creators of messages they view. *Evaluation* is a tool of necessity in today's information age, when anyone can publish a web page on any topic they choose. If students are given the opportunity and the tools needed to *communicate* their own message, using the media of their choice, then the traditional meaning of literacy is extended to encompass the media that surround our students in their worlds outside of the classroom.

References

Aufderheide, P. (Ed.). (1993). *Media literacy: A report of the national leadership conference on media literacy*. Aspen, CO: Aspen Institute.

Braunger, J., & Lewis, J. P. (2006). *Building a knowledge base in reading* (2nd ed.). Newark, DE: International Reading Association.

Burke, J. (2001). *Illuminating texts: How to teach students to read the world*. Portsmouth, NH: Heinemann.

Daly, J. (1994, September). Life on the screen. *Edutopia Magazine, 1*, 38-41.

Hobbs, R. (2005). Media literacy and the K-12 content areas. In G. Schwarz & P. Brown (Eds.), *Media literacy: Transforming curriculum and teaching. 104th Yearbook of the National Society for the Study of Education, Part I* (pp. 74-99). Chicago: Blackwell.

Jung, C. G. (1964). *Man and his symbols*. New York: Doubleday.

Keys, W. B. (1974). *Subliminal seduction: Ad media's manipulation of a not so innocent America*. New York: New American Library.

Masterman, L. (1985). *Teaching the media*. London: Routledge.

McBrien, J. L. (1999). New texts, new tools: An argument for media literacy. *Educational Leadership, 57*(2), 76-79.

Roberts, D. F., Foehr, U. G., Rideout, V. J., & Brodie, M. (1999). *Kids and media at the new millennium*. Menlo Park, CA: Kaiser Family Foundation Report.

Rodriguez, R. B. (2005). *The art of advertising in the classroom* (conference handout). Lubbock, TX: South Plains Middle School Association Mini-conference.

Rogow, F. (2005). Terrain in transition: Reflections on the pedagogy of media literacy education. In G. Schwarz & P. U. Brown (Eds.), *Media literacy: Transforming curriculum and teaching* (pp. 180-205). Malden, MA: National Society for the Study of Education.

Scheibe, C., & Rogow, F. (2004). *12 basic principles for incorporating media literacy and critical thinking into any curriculum*. Ithaca, NY: Project Look Sharp. Retrieved January 21, 2006, from www.ithaca.edu/looksharp/12principles.pdf

Share, J., Jolis, T., & Thoman, E. (2005). *Five key questions that can change the world: Classroom activities for media literacy*. Retrieved January 19, 2006, from the Center Media Literacy website: www.medialit.org/pdf/mlk/02_5KQ_ClassroomGuide.pdf

Summerfield, L. M. (1995). *National standards for school health education* (ERIC Digest.) Washington, DC: ERIC Clearinghouse on Teaching and Teacher Education. (ERIC Document Reproduction Service No. ED387483)

Thier, M. (2005). Merging media and science: Learning to weigh sources, not just evidence. In G. Schwarz & P. U. Brown (Eds.), *Media literacy: Transforming curriculum and teaching* (pp. 260-268). Malden, MA: National Society for the Study of Education.

Thoman, E. (1999). Skills and strategies for media education. *Educational Leadership, 56*(5), 50-54.

Thoman, E., & Jolis, T. (2005). *Literacy for the 21st century: An overview & orientation guide to media literacy education*. Retrieved January 19, 2006, from the Center Media Literacy website: www.medialit.org/pdf/mlk/01_MLKorientation.pdf

Tyner, K. (1992, Summer). Implementation: The next step. *Strategies for media literacy. Reprinted in Media Literacy Review*. Retrieved February 14, 2006, from http://interact.uoregon.edu/MediaLit/mlr/readings/articles/implement.html

Meet the Authors

Patricia Watson is an Assistant Professor of Language and Literacy at Texas Tech University. Before completing her doctoral studies at the University of Missouri, Pat taught reading and language arts in middle grade classrooms for 18 years. She enjoys collaborating with practicing and preservice teachers in university/public school partnerships. Her most recent work explores teachers' knowledge, attitudes, and beliefs towards literacy in the content areas.

René B. Rodriguez (aka Rod) is currently teaching language arts at Lubbock High School after spending eight years teaching at J. T. Hutchinson Middle School in Lubbock, Texas. Rod has degrees in English and psychology from Sul Ross University. He says his motto is "Dum spiro spero" ("So long as I breathe, I hope").

Part V

Professional Development in Content Area Literacy

Chapter 10

Learning About
Content Area Literacy

Through a Teacher Book Club

My teaching day winds to a close on this sunny, almost autumn Friday. I straighten my room, stack bean bags, put away books, and prepare for team meeting at 2:00, while our students are in their elective classes. I look forward to this meeting, especially today, because instead of discussing the 10 out of 125 students with behavior issues or visiting with parents or administrators, we will meet to discuss chapter one of the Tovani book about content literacy, Do I Really Have To Teach Reading? *I am apprehensive, though excited, about the meeting. I don't know the social studies teacher well. I don't want to overwhelm her during her first year. I wonder if the math teacher will think we are just wasting her time. Content literacy in math? I have no clue how it looks, and I am the reading teacher. I hope the second language arts teacher on the team will have some ideas.*

The teachers enter and we sit in the gathered student desks. All six of us have Tovani's book—a good sign. Some books have Post-its in them. Another good sign. One teacher is smiling; maybe she liked the book. Wouldn't that be great!

And so it begins. Sally, the language arts teacher, jumps in and begins discussing her thoughts. Sally's bubbly personality helps to start our discussion with enthusiasm.

"I love the bulleted information. It's our curriculum, simplified. Our students can't do these things, either. Just like in the book. If students can't make meaning, how are they going to get information?"

I add, "These comprehension strategies are a way we could integrate our curriculum without doing specific units. We teach them in reading and you mention them in your content while you are reading articles. The students will have to start making connections between their reading and all areas."

Debra, the special education teacher, chimes in, "I love the story at the beginning. It is so honest and smart. Kids really are that way. But, look at how they became interested in the lesson after she pulled them in."

"What did you think of the science connection?" I

**Stephanie Wightman
and Carol Gilles**

159

purposefully try to draw in Stacy, the science teacher. She flips through the pages and mentions that the article on viruses could become part of her unit.

This was the beginning of our first book club. Not everyone had read the chapter but everyone participated. Some enthusiastically joined in the discussion, while others listened more. All agreed to read chapter two by next Friday.

I had really wanted it to go well, and I wondered what each of them was thinking. Did some teachers not like the book? Did some respond in the way they did because they have never been in a book club before? Did they not know what to do? Will three or four strong teachers carry us? Should I back off and not get so excited about the book? Will motivation grow as the weeks go by? Or will people feel less motivated? Only time will tell.

Stephanie's comments (above) reflect her excitement and anxiety as she and her teammates began discussing content area reading strategies during team meeting. In this chapter, we closely examine how this teacher book club began, what actions helped it to flourish, and what barriers hindered the collaboration. In addition, through teacher interviews, we report the teaching strategies and understandings that persisted the following year.

Longview (a pseudonym), Stephanie's school, houses grades 6 and 7. It is located on the north side of town in a middle-income residential area and enrolls children from low- to middle-income families. About 45 percent of the student population of 764 qualifies for free and reduced-price lunches. White students make up 65 percent of the population, while 35 percent are African American. Longview is considered the most diverse middle school in this Midwestern community of about 80,000. About 20 percent of the students on the team read below grade level. Six teachers make up the team—one each from social studies, science, mathematics, and special education, as well as two language arts/reading teachers.

Over the last three years, testing has become top priority in the district. The school administration strongly emphasizes the importance of literacy for each and every student. The main state assessment is the communication arts exam, which the 7th-grade students take in the spring of each year. The test emphasizes reading and writing skills in fiction, nonfiction, and poetry. While the burden of test preparation lies on the language arts/reading teachers, the faculty and principal realize that teachers in the content areas classes can and should play a larger role in student test preparation. Teachers know that content area strategies are valuable tools for deeper learning (Keene & Zimmermann, 1997; Robb, 2000; Trabasso & Bouchard, 2002). Since approximately one-third of the state test involves nonfiction reading, the strategies taught in the content area can be applied on the test.

While content teachers are aware of the important role they play in strengthening reading and writing strategies, they are already overwhelmed by the required curriculum set by the school district. In this district, mathematics teachers are required to test in "windows"; they must cover a certain amount of material in a certain time frame, leaving no time for additional curricular choices. In addition, many content area teachers in the building speak of "not wanting to be reading teachers." Their frustration stems from the perception that focusing on content literacy takes time away from their subject areas. Content literacy quickly became a taboo phrase among the teaching staff, because it was viewed as a "drop-everything-you-know-and-teach-reading" idea.

So, Stephanie was faced with a problem. The administration wanted the middle school teams to work together on content literacy. The teachers knew it was important, but they were already overloaded. As team leader, Stephanie was in a position to encourage discussion about this topic, to share her new learning from a university course, and to gain a better perspective on what literacy could look like in a content class. Could she convince the content area teachers that this was something that would benefit everyone?

As the team met in the late spring of 2004, Stephanie made a conscious effort to include content literacy as a primary focus for the upcoming school year. This decision stemmed from countless discussions of the skills their population of students needed to work on. To Stephanie, it seemed that the students had difficulty going beyond the surface of any fiction or nonfiction piece. Instead of focusing only on testing, Stephanie wanted to incorporate content literacy in ways that would help increase students' comprehension, while not sacrificing content. She wanted to give struggling readers quality reading instruction across the curriculum that would allow them to better understand their content area and progress as readers. At the same time, she wanted to continue to push the average and advanced readers to dig deeper into their reading and be more thoughtful. Stephanie had participated in several professional book clubs around the district and valued the knowledge gained from the book and the talk among other teachers. She thought a teacher book club, one day a week, might be a way to introduce content literacy and promote team discussion around a common curricular idea, in addition to having the normal team discussions about students and modifications in school procedure and behavior.

Stephanie knew that she needed to gain the support of the team members. Over the summer, the team gained a new social studies teacher. Stephanie hoped to bring her on board right away. She felt it was important to meet individually with the science, special education, language arts, and social studies teachers over the summer to discuss each person's idea of content literacy and develop a plan of attack for the upcoming school year. She also wanted to help promote positive thinking about content literacy and the challenge ahead. As a language arts/reading teacher, Stephanie knew she had to spearhead the idea of content literacy and provide resources to help everyone work together. Coming to an understanding of how content literacy could be effectively incorporated into an already overfull curriculum would be her challenge. She knew that each teacher's input could inspire changes as a team.

Gaining Support From the Teachers for the Book Club

Stephanie met with Debra, the special education teacher, at a coffee shop in early August. They worked well together and Stephanie valued Debra's support. A veteran teacher, Debra radiated warm personality and enthusiasm for teaching at meetings. As they sat, Debra pulled out Tovani's book. She had already read the first few chapters during the summer.

"I think our team could do this. This book is short and the stories will interest other members." Debra flipped through the book and thoughtfully shared her insights.

"Do you think we can get everyone involved?" Stephanie countered. Ensuring that others buy in to the project is a constant problem and she did not want to alienate herself by forcing people to do something undesired or stressful.

"You mention the book club and I will back you up by telling them what a great book this is. You know I will talk it up," Debra said. Stephanie had one person on board.

Stacy, a second-year science teacher, met with Stephanie about a week later to discuss potential science/language arts integration. A very organized person, Stacy preferred high school instruction, but took a middle school position and hoped to enjoy the experience as well. Stacy's laid-back personality helped to ground the team during stressful times. In her classes, she frequently assigned readings with questions for the students to answer. Stephanie thought that content strategies would complement Stacy's teaching style, already filled with reading opportunities for the students.

Stephanie approached the topic by saying, "I was thinking we could do a book study this year, during our team meeting, so we wouldn't have to spend additional time at school. What do you think?" Stacy said the idea sounded good to her.

"Let me show you some of the books we were thinking about," Stephanie said as she pulled a stack of content literacy books and let Stacy flip through them. "Debra liked the Tovani book. Do you think that one would be a good one, or would another book work better?"

"I think the Tovani book would work well. It's short and it looks like there are parts about science in here."

"Great. Half of us wants this book, so I will talk with Tom (the building principal) and see if he would order it for us."

Tom was excited about the idea of book clubs. All six teams at the school were going to meet once a month with the literacy specialist to discuss content literacy strategies, and a book club could only help to deepen their understanding. The book club would be a good use of team meeting time.

After several individual discussions during the summer and then several group meetings, all members supported the decision to begin a book club. Because the team met daily, they were able to reserve each Friday to discuss the book *Do I Really Have To Teach Reading?* by Cris Tovani. Tom ordered six copies for the team and the group started reading the book the second week in September, almost immediately after school began. The team members jumped in, feet first! Since no other team in the school had tried a book study during team meeting time, Stephanie used her knowledge about literature study/literature circles (Campbell-Hill, Schlick-Noe, & King, 2003). She outlined the same model for book study as she used with her language arts students:

> *Meet.*
> *Set a purpose.*
> *Talk.*
> *Set a reading goal for next week.*

With a vision to learn more and teach better, the team began its work.

Highlights of Book Club Meetings

The sessions were collegial throughout two months of meetings about Tovani's book. Team members frequently brought food and comfortably discussed the book's ideas. Stephanie and the others enjoyed this time because it was a change from behavior and school policy discussions. The book club became a time for them to discuss what they love: teaching. Collaboratively, they set small reading goals, such as reading about 10 pages a week. Although the group occasionally strayed from the discussion, they always returned to talk of the reading and new discoveries. In addition to discussing the book, the team shared stories about classrooms, new strategies they tried, and applications to the curriculum. Stories from each other's classrooms enriched the book discussions.

One Friday, Jane, the first-year social studies teacher, brought in a test the students had just completed. Having recently studied content literacy at the university, Jane had integrated many reading strategies in her units completed for college classes. The transfer of these strategies to her classroom was easy. This time, she designed the test to mirror the different types of learning students had done in class. For one question, Jane asked the students to draw a picture of the Trojan horse and explain why it was important. Chapter one of Tovani's book highlights the strategy of students drawing representations of their thinking as a way to understand the reading more deeply. The team members smiled as they viewed the students' pictures. Some were simple, others intricate, but all demonstrated thinking about the topic. Stephanie loved Jane's idea of using drawing as one way to extend thinking and continued to use this strategy in her class as well.

When six people read the same book, each person finds different quotes or ideas that highlight her individual understanding. As she read chapter one, Stephanie thought everyone would point out the boxes along the side of the text. The boxes outlined such comprehension strategies as background knowledge, inference, and questioning. Debra, for example, focused on the story at the beginning. Her background was teaching special education students, who often act bored with instruction. Debra loved the way Tovani drew the students in with everyday experiences that connected to the real world.

Sally, on the other hand, was fascinated by Tovani's interest in teaching content reading. She wanted to help her students read math, and so she used math as an example throughout the rest of the book discussions. Sally could relate to students' difficulties in reading math texts because of her own struggles. She proceeded to try out different reading strategies during the daily study hall she taught. An outgoing person, Sally began many of the book club meetings with examples from her experiences helping students with math.

Stephanie enjoyed watching other book club members, like Sally, take ownership of the book and lead discussions. Even though Stephanie used book clubs with her students, the discussions helped her understand more fully how book clubs *really* worked. Each teacher came to the table with different backgrounds and understandings, and together they created new meanings (Barnes, 1992; Pierce & Gilles, 1993). Stephanie would have never highlighted the parts that Debra and Sally found useful, yet through the discussion she began to value them and thus expand her own knowledge base.

The book club helped each team member to view the book through each other's eyes. When Sally contributed her perception of reading math texts, the discussion changed Stephanie's and Sally's understanding of math instruction even if it did not immediately affect their learning. When Stacy, who struggled with fiction reading herself as a child, discussed her frustration, Stephanie began to wonder about her reading students. Which students shared those same frustrations? How could she help those students? These types of conversations helped everyone see how content literacy was embedded in every content area, and they began to feel that they were all, in a sense, responsible for the larger curriculum.

Two or three weeks into the book group, the science teacher, Stacy, assigned a class reading on the devastating Galveston hurricane of 1900. She looked through several informational texts and carefully chose an article that matched her curriculum. Stephanie was excited about her willingness to try a lay audience article with her students. Like many science articles taken from high-level informational texts, the article was long (six pages) and difficult. During study hall, Sally and Stephanie broke down the article, using the content literacy strategies of previewing and questioning the text. These two strategies helped the students better understand the article and be more successful. The students were able to understand how a reader breaks down a difficult text and the teachers could see how they can support one another.

Midway through Tovani's book, Jane became convinced that reading strategies helped her students learn the content more effectively. Consequently, she took the time to create guides for previewing a text and required students to do a variety of tasks during their reading, such as questioning and summarizing. Jane worked hard to define a purpose each time they read, and was able to create tests that incorporated drawing pictures and captions. The students responded well to her assignments and frequently scored well on tests. Their success reinforced Jane's willingness to use content strategies.

Although the group made steady progress, they had frustrating moments as well. Teaching involves planning lessons each day. Because teachers don't want to constantly "redesign the wheel," they borrow ideas from one another. Borrowed ideas may work well with one class or one situation, but not so well with others. Such was the case with Stacy, who tried a comprehension strategy that didn't work well with the text. The group had discussed the "probable passage" (Beers, 2003) pre-reading strategy, in which students have a list of words and categories to sort and then are asked to write a statement about what they think the reading would be about. The strategy was originally used with fictional texts, but the group discussed how it could be adapted to nonfiction works.

Who knows why it didn't work? Perhaps the students didn't understand the categories, or Stacy had different expectations from her students. Regardless, both the students and Stacy were frustrated. Stacy felt she had wasted her valuable time. The lesson the book group took away was that implementing strategies was a lot more difficult than they had anticipated. They also learned that teachers couldn't just borrow someone else's ideas; they have to think through what the product will look like and then work backward (Marzano, Pickering, & McTighe, 1993). Stephanie also realized how deep the understanding of these comprehension strategies must be to create successful lessons. Not only do teachers need to know a wide variety of comprehension strategies, they also need to know the purpose for each one, and then match the strategy to particular learners' needs. For example, creating a graffiti poster for the American Revolution may be helpful if the teacher's purpose is to brainstorm information about the topic, but will be less useful if the teacher's purpose is to help students understand the sequence of events that led to the war.

For Stephanie, the highlight of all the meetings came when the principal visited the team meeting. He came to share administrative ideas, not to talk specifically about the book study, but the conversation soon turned to the book study. Each teacher was able to articulate a strategy she had tried, explain how it helped reading instruction, and make plans for future learning. The team knew they were the only team in the school trying a book club during the meetings, and everyone on the team seemed proud of their collaboration. Although the principal was delighted to see that his purchase of the books and his assignment of the team time for book study paid off, equally important was the teachers' articulation and public display of the progress they had made in their own classrooms with content literacy.

Applying Our Learning: The Content Strategies

The book club continued from September to December, when it disbanded because the members had completed the book. Of course, the team continued to meet weekly to talk about the students, and they later moved on to read two other books, *Discovering Gifts in Middle School: Learning in a Caring Culture Called Tribes* (Gibbs, 2001), about building community, and *The Five Dysfunctions of a Team: A Leadership Fable* (Lencioni, 2002), about teaming. Even after the first book club concluded, both the science and social studies teachers remained interested in using the strategies to support their content instruction. They frequently brought their class reading to the team meeting and asked for the group's response. Stephanie wanted to support their efforts and volunteered to help, because she was concerned that creating these reading assignments would take too much of their valuable time. Consequently, Stephanie was spending hours sifting through books to find ideas on how to introduce or teach the different pieces.

In order to consolidate the strategies, Stephanie decided that she would create a notebook of content reading strategies that the team could use during the discussions. She also could use the notebook as part of a final paper she was completing for her class on "Struggling Readers" from the university. Stephanie wanted this notebook to be a useable, quick reference for the team, where all could post their thoughts about the strategies and thus keep it dynamic and current.

With the idea established, Stephanie sifted through resources to find content literacy ideas to place in the notebook. She wanted the notebook to begin with ideas taken from many resources and graphic organizers. She decided to categorize these strategies as pre-reading, during reading, and post reading. After reviewing different strategies, she typed a synopsis with reference pages where a teacher could find more information about the strategy. (See Figure 10.1 for a sample of the content strategies.)

The content literacy notebook was a moderate success. Stephanie referred to it frequently when assigning nonfiction pieces to her students. When teachers asked for help with a particular strategy, Stephanie and others would flip through the notebook for thoughts and ideas. People from other teams also borrowed the notebook when brainstorming strategies.

Sally was impressed with a strategy involving a "map" of a nonfiction page (Allen, 2004). The teacher creates the map for a specific nonfiction article. It cannot be generic. When creating the layout, the teacher puts empty boxes where the pictures are located in the article and lines to represent the article's text and captions. Students are encouraged to read the article and take notes about the text in the boxes and on the lines. The purpose is to help students read the entire text, including the picture and captions (see Figure 10.2 for an example). Sally tried the map strategy with success.

Stacy also tried the strategy of Word Sorts (Bear, Invernizzi, Templeton, & Johnston, 2004) with her class. She typed words involving a science concept on a piece of paper, then had the students cut out the words and sort them into categories. She spoke animatedly at a team meeting about the different ways the students sorted the words. Some found creative categories that were related to science concepts, while others sorted the words based on their beginning letter. Stacy enjoyed watching the students work and learned a great deal about how they think in the process.

Applying Our Learning: The Science Unit

Stephanie knew that in order to gain deep understanding of the reading strategies, she needed to apply them to a specific area. So, she decided to apply them to an unfamiliar area, a science

Pre-Reading:
Word Sorts

The teacher finds 15-20 words or phrases that are an important part of the upcoming reading. Each of these words or phrases is cut apart and the students sort them into groups. After sorting, the students can write a paragraph predicting the content of the reading.

Rasinski, T., & Padak, N. (2003). *Effective reading strategies: Teaching children who find reading difficult* (3rd ed.). New York: Prentice Hall.

After-Reading:
Text Reformulation

Upon completion of a reading, the students are asked to create a different type of text using the same information. ABC books, poems, news articles, comic books, or short stories are all examples of what a student could do. Fortunately-Unfortunately, If-Then, Cumulative and Repetitive are all text structures that could work in text reformulation.

Beers, K. (2002). *When kids can't read: What teachers can do*. Portsmouth, NH: Heinemann.

During Reading:
Sketch to Stretch

During this activity, the teacher stops the class during their reading and has them sketch their thinking on a piece of paper. After a minute or two, the teacher can have the class discuss their reading with a partner. This strategy can help visual learners understand the text.

Siegel, M. G. (1984). *Reading as signification.* Unpublished doctoral dissertation. Indiana University, Bloomington.

Name:_____

Sketch to Stretch

Use your sketches to summarize your reading.

_____
_____
_____
_____

Figure 10.1. Sample Content Strategies

Article Titles: "Bubonic Blunder?"

Strategies

Pre-Reading: Map
Students could use the text map organizer to predict what the text may be about.

During-Reading: Map
Students could read the piece as a whole class, in pairs, small groups, or individually and use the organizer to summarize their thinking.

After-Reading: Gist
Students could complete the gist summary, and in two sentences or less, summarize the article based on the notes from the text map.

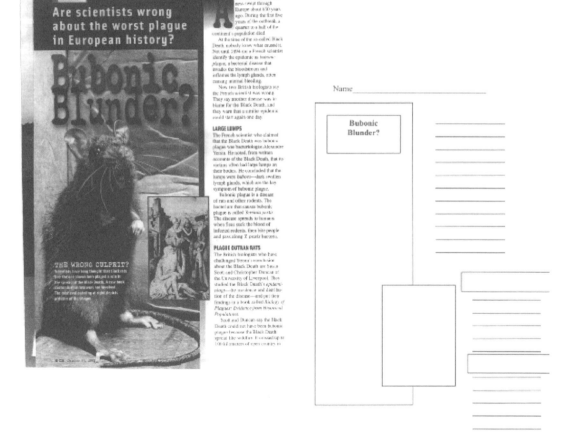

Figure 10.2. Mapping a Nonfiction Page

unit on disease. The unit forced her to think in new ways. Stephanie pulled together potential reading excerpts from a variety of sources at a variety of levels and matched the readings with possible instruction strategies. She worked through potential activities, well aware of the risk when instruction is not individualized. For the disease unit, she pulled together lessons with specific students and reading levels in mind because she had the same students. For example, Stephanie knew the 6th-grade class had generally high-level readers, so most of the strategy lessons were created to promote interest in the topic and many of the readings were on level. But 20 percent of the students read below grade level, so she included pieces for them to read as well.

Stephanie also knew that the notebook served as a model for the team to see how the strategies could support one another. Often, strategies were used in a fragmented manner. Using the disease unit, Stephanie learned how particular strategies enhanced specific content and built on one another. For example, she used a book pass to introduce the disease unit, followed by a KWL chart to encourage questioning and activation of background knowledge. She then introduced more specific articles with pre-reading, during reading, and post reading strategies to focus the learning. (See Figure 10.2.)

While Stephanie was pleased with the unit, neither she nor the science teacher ever used it. With all the scheduled events and end-of-year special projects, time just ran out.

What Are the Lasting Learnings From the Book Club?

A year later, Stephanie interviewed the book club members (except the mathematics teacher) about their experiences. Since Stephanie and Stacy had left the school, Stephanie was not sure if the book club had made a lasting change in teachers' behaviors. She was delighted to find that the other teachers reported that the book club was a positive experience, overall. Jane, the first-year social studies teacher, explained how she continued to use the strategies:

> Of course, I'm actually using some of the strategies this year, while doing some reading on Africa. We previewed it by asking questions from the title and then we looked at what kind of format the text was in. Then we looked at the pictures and we figured out what we could get from the pictures. And then we actually read it with the questions . . . the whole topic was about desertification, so we discussed it and actually ended up defining it from what we read, because it wasn't clearly stated in the article. . . . I think it helped the kids truly understand it.

One can easily see that Jane uses the strategies to guide her students' textbook reading.

Sally, who enjoyed the book club because it was from "the perspective of teachers who don't teach reading," continues to work with her students to read and understand math concepts during her class and academic lab. She also was quite insightful about a change she had made:

> When I first started the book, I had heard that [phrase] accessible text, meaning find something "on their level," find something easy. But not find something they know so well [that] they know its patterns and they can read it. They understand the whole thing to the point where they can explain how it is working . . . then we teach them how to transfer [those strategies] to texts that they don't know. We can teach them better how to use all the strategies that we want readers to use.

Sally's thinking has come a long way. Now she is using easier texts to point out the strategies and patterns in text that help kids to understand the content. Students practice the strategies in easier texts, and then transfer the use of those strategies to more difficult texts.

Debra, the special education teacher, enjoyed sharing with the teachers: "I got to listen to other teachers who had used [the strategies] and tried to learn what worked for them and what didn't, and I walked away with a wealth of knowledge." She still uses the two-column graphic organizer and also helps her students learn that each person reads differently, depending upon the materials: "I still use the *read like a scientist* [strategy]. I'm teaching science this year with behavior-disordered kids, so we talk about how you read differently as a scientist than you would in math or social studies. We also use the organizers in the book."

Besides using many of the specific strategies, Stephanie also continues to use the Strategy Notebook with her 5th-graders. She has used at least four strategies from the notebook and frequently shares those strategies with other teachers at her new school. They like the brief, easy-to-find information.

Insights From the Book Club Experience

In reflecting about the power of the book clubs, the instructional notebooks, and meeting during team time, placing the work within the professional literature about teachers working collaboratively on such projects is necessary. Little (1982) found that successful site-based reforms occur when the organizational structure supports conversations about teaching, professional growth, and collegiality. The principal showed this level of support when he gave the team books to study from and the time to study. The book group gave team members opportunities to "engage in frequent, continuous and an increasingly concrete and precise talk about teaching practice" (Little, 1982, p. 331). Lieberman (1988, 1995) and Darling-Hammond and Sclan (1996) remind us that when professional development opportunities are built into the day, they are more successful. The team chose the book club time (during team meeting on Friday) and they chose the book.

The content book clubs and instructional notebooks were a huge undertaking for Stephanie. She now realizes that not everyone is as excited about reading instruction as she is. We believe that one of the reasons that many teachers were more successful with the book discussion than others is that not every teacher "bought in" to the book club idea. Stephanie worked hard to foster buy-in through her conversations throughout the summer. She worked slowly, over several months, and made sure that team members vocalized their thoughts before beginning the book club. Perhaps some of the momentum was lost because Stephanie did not involve other team members in creating the content literacy notebook and unit. Ownership is key to collaboration. As Clark and Florio-Ruane (2001) maintain, "When teachers are not involved in framing the goals and means for their continuing professional education, they naturally feel put upon, manipulated, and not taken seriously as professionals" (p. 5). When Stephanie began, she believed that all of the team members had bought in. But even ownership carefully established is fragile. One cannot assume that it will continue automatically. Instead, opportunities to affirm ownership must be provided all along the way. As we reflect on Stephanie's story, we realize that creating the notebooks could have provided another opportunity to reaffirm ownership.

When Stephanie interviewed team members, she asked how book clubs could be improved. Several team members suggested a voluntary book club instead of a mandatory one, thereby ensuring that every person who was in the book club wants to be there. Team teachers who didn't choose to be part of the book club could spend the same time tackling a different project that would be relevant to their subject area or the team's needs. Thus, everyone could be engaged in smaller groups for the benefit of the students on the team. It is interesting to us that even with all the activities Stephanie did at the beginning of the process, teachers still saw the group as "mandatory." Was that because it was during the school day? Because the principal bought the books? Because it fit nicely with their work with the reading specialist? Stephanie will never know, but again it shows the fragile nature of ownership.

One insight of the team was that just because content literacy is introduced in multiple classrooms, it doesn't mean that students will automatically work harder or become better readers. Modeling and scaffolding reading strategies are vital elements of the process. However, some content teachers are not familiar with modeling and scaffolding. Others may feel that it takes time away from covering content. Midway through the second quarter, Stephanie could sense that at least one teacher was getting tired of content reading talk. Having release time for observation or team teaching, so the team could work together teaching some of these content literacy concepts, might help to deepen their learning even more. This would allow them time to "inquire and reflect, listen and respond, rise and stumble" (Robb, 2000). They would not just talk about content area literacy and share strategies, but actually coach one another.

Another important insight for the team and Stephanie was that the book club encouraged everyone to build on one another's ideas. Just as team members pointed out different parts of each chapter, they applied their learning differently in the classrooms and discussed the outcomes during book club meetings. Jane said, "I liked hearing what other people were doing in their classes . . . because I may read something, and you may read something and we'll take it two totally opposite directions."

Sharing personal narrative and classroom stories also was important. First, sharing stories and personal narratives gave teachers a chance to articulate what they know and believe, while negotiating difficult experiences (like Stacy's failed strategy) (Harris, 1995). Sharing classroom stories within a safe place helps teachers to shape and reshape who they are as teachers.

Second, sharing personal narratives gave team members a better sense of the "big picture." Classroom teaching is often done in isolation. Teachers often concentrate on just their subject within the confines of their classrooms. Listening to the stories about team members trying new strategies opened the doors of their classrooms. It offered them a safe place to talk about students' learning and a common vocabulary. They shared insights about students, strategies, and techniques. More important, it helped them understand how content literacy was embedded in every content area and it made these teachers feel that they were a part of, and responsible for, a larger curriculum. As Sally, the language arts teacher, reminded us, "It was a way for teachers to see how what we're doing fits into what they are doing. And even how what we're doing is the basis for being successful in what they are doing." The team book clubs gave teachers the time during the school day and a safe place to discuss learning, creating a situation that is at the heart of teaming.

As these teachers worked together, they were able to understand that content area reading strategies weren't just a fragmented "add-on." Instead, they were tools, just like chalk or textbooks, to help their students understand the content more completely. Stephanie reflects:

A year has passed since our book club discussions about content literacy. I hand out the paper with six boxes to my 5th-grade students. I explain to them I will read aloud the first two paragraphs of their nonfiction piece and then stop. Next, we will sketch out our thinking. As the students draw their ideas, I think briefly about the tests Jane gave last year where the students sketched a Trojan horse. Different topic, but the same exercise in thinking. We go through the entire reading, stopping periodically to sketch the text. Upon completion, I ask my students to summarize their reading. For the first time all year they do this without questions, but with understanding of what they read. Although I am in a different place, last year's learning is with me, and for a moment I wish the book group could meet again, so I could share this small success.

Concluding Thoughts

As teaching reading in the content classes became a shared building goal, Stephanie and her middle school team decided to read and discuss *Do I Really Have To Teach Reading?*, by Cris Tovani, as a book club. Stephanie spearheaded the idea while carefully fostering teacher buy-in through individual discussions with each team teacher. For two months, teachers read small portions of the book and met weekly to discuss the reading. As the teachers grew in their understanding of content literacy, they made a commitment to apply their learning in their classrooms. When teachers shared their classroom ideas and lessons in the context of a book club discussion, the talk became rich with ideas for lessons and assessment. Stephanie was amazed at how her team teachers' interpretations and applications of the reading deepened her own understanding of content literacy. Stephanie's team teachers felt the same. When Stephanie interviewed her teammates a year later, the teachers mentioned the strategies used in their classrooms as the same strategies they had read about, discussed, and tried as a part of their book study. Using teacher book clubs is an important way to help practicing teachers learn about and use content area reading strategies.

References

Allen, J. (2004, November). *Tools for teaching content literacy.* Missouri International Reading Association Conference. Lake of the Ozarks, Missouri.

Barnes, D. (1992). *From communication to curriculum.* Portsmouth, NH: Heinemann.

Bear, D. R., Invernizazi, M., Templeton, S., & Johnston, S. T. (2004). *Words their way.* Upper Saddle River, NJ: Pearson Prentice Hall.

Beers, K. (2003). *When kids can't read. What teachers can do.* Portsmouth, NH: Heinemann.

Campbell-Hill, B., Schlick-Noe, K., & King, J. (2003). *Literature circles in middle school.* Norwood, MA: Christopher-Gordon Publishers.

Clark, C., & Florio-Ruane, S. (2001). Conversation as support for teaching in new ways. In C. Clark (Ed.), *Talking shop: Authentic conversation and teacher learning.* New York: Teachers College Press.

Darling-Hammond, L., & Sclan, E. M. (1996). Who teaches and why: Dilemmas of building a profession for twenty-first century schools. In J. Sikula, T. J. Buttery, & E. Guyton (Eds.), *Handbook of research on teacher education* (2nd ed., pp. 67-101). New York: Macmillian.

Gibbs, J. (2001). *Discovering gifts in middle school: Learning in a caring culture called tribes.* Windsor, CA: Center Source Systems.

Harris, D. L. (1995). *Composing a life as a teacher: The role of conversation and community in teachers' formation of their identity as professionals.* Unpublished doctoral dissertation, Michigan State University, East Lansing.

Keene, E., & Zimmermann, S. (1997). *Mosaic of thought.* Portsmouth, NH: Heinemann.

Lieberman, A. (Ed.). (1988). *Building a professional culture in schools.* New York: Teachers College Press.

Lieberman, A. (1995). Restructuring schools: The dynamics of changing practice, structure and culture. In A. Lieberman (Ed.), *The work of restructuring schools: Building from the ground up* (pp. 1-17). New York: Teachers College Press.

Lencioni, P. (2002). *The five dysfunctions of a team: A leadership fable.* New York: Wiley.

Little, J. (1982). Norms of collegiality and experimentation: Workplace conditions of school success. *American Educational Research Journal, 19,* 325-340.

Marzano, R. J., Pickering, D. J., & McTighe, J. (1993). *Assessing student outcomes.* Alexandria, VA: Association for Supervision and Curriculum Development.

Pierce, K., & Gilles, C. (1993). *Cycles of meaning.* Portsmouth, NH: Heinemann.

Rasinski, T., & Padak, N. (2003). *Effective reading strategies: Teaching children who find reading difficult* (3rd ed.). New York: Prentice Hall.

Robb, L. (2000). *Redefining staff development.* Portsmouth, NH: Heinemann.

Siegel, M. G. (1984). *Reading as signification.* Unpublished doctoral dissertation. Indiana University, Bloomington.

Tovani, C. (2004). *Do I really have to teach reading? Content comprehension, grades 6-12.* Portland, ME: Stenhouse.

Trabasso, T., & Bouchard, E. (2002). Teaching readers how to comprehend text strategically. In C. C. Block & M. Pressley (Eds.), *Comprehension instruction: Research-based best practices* (pp. 176-200). New York: Guilford Press.

Meet the Authors

Stephanie Wightman is a 6th-grade reading and language arts teacher in Columbia (Missouri) Public Schools. She loves the creativity and ingenuity found in 6th-graders and works to enhance their unique attributes, using a combination of multi-media and drama in her teaching. Stephanie is also a doctoral student at the University of Missouri and enjoys instructing future educators in the undergraduate teacher development program.

Carol Gilles is an Associate Professor of Reading/Language Arts at the University of Missouri, Columbia. A middle-level classroom teacher for over 20 years, Carol now researches in the areas of adolescent literacy, using talk to learn more deeply, children's literature, and induction programs for teachers. She has written three books and many articles. She enjoys working with fine doctoral students like Stephanie!

Chapter 11 | Content Area Tools

A carpenter's bag holds a variety of tools, such as hammers, mallets, pliers, and scrapers. The experienced carpenter knows when and how to use each tool to create, and finish, a project. The same is true for effective content area teachers. Their tool bag includes a variety of teaching techniques and strategies to increase students' content area learning. Collecting a bag of tools takes knowledge of what research says works, plus teacher expertise and experience. The purpose of this chapter is to describe and illustrate instructional content literacy tools that can be easily integrated into any content area. Although we do not cover each strategy noted in the book, we provide a research base and simple-to-follow steps for many commonly used content literacy strategies.

The following tools provide a framework for improving content area instruction and learning by connecting strong research support to practical classroom implementation. We recommend varying instructional tools to meet the needs and interests of the diverse learners within the classroom. Teachers—not policymakers or individual school districts—must be the instructional decision-makers about which tools work best for the students they teach. Teachers know their students, and the strategies needed to teach their content area subject matter, better than anyone else.

INQUIRY-BASED INSTRUCTION

Research Base

The idea of structuring learning around inquiry is grounded in the work of Lev Vygotsky and John Dewey (Freedman & Johnson, 2004). The theoretical base for inquiry learning assumes that learners acquire new knowledge and construct new understandings by connecting the new learning with prior experience and knowledge. Based on Dewey's theories, inquiry is an active process and thinking is the natural activity of humans (Tanner, 1988). In inquiry learning, students ask questions and pose problems, then use reading and writing as tools in the search for answers and solutions.

Description

Instruction based on inquiry takes advantage of students' natural curiosity. Learning through inquiry requires that students (and their teachers) be immersed in the study of a theme, topic, or problem. In the inquiry process, students construct new knowledge by connecting with prior experiences, posing questions, and planning and carrying out research or investigations. Learning is extended through discussion and conversation. Findings, conclusions, and

Jan Lacina and
Patricia A. Watson

insights are shared through presentations and publications.

Procedure

Inquiry-based instruction is always structured to move from the known to the new. The teacher's role is to guide students toward learning. Almost any topic can become the foundation for inquiry if it interests the students. At the heart of inquiry learning is the idea that students participate in the planning, development, and evaluation of projects and activities.

The inquiry cycle can be structured around either a whole-class focus or individual student explorations of topics that they find personally significant. The inquiry cycle is recursive rather than linear, with students moving back and forth across each part of the cycle. A number of different versions of the inquiry cycle can be found in different disciplines; however, most of the models have the following elements in common:

- **Asking/Posing Real Questions**

Initial experiences in the inquiry cycle allow students to make connections to what they already know. Students are encouraged to make connections through read-alouds, browsing books, listening to music, sharing stories, observing, and examining artifacts. Students then share their connections through writing and conversations.

Students move toward more depth with their inquiry by asking questions of the texts they encounter. They choose aspects of the theme or topic that are personally interesting to them. Helping students find their questions can sometimes be difficult, depending on their levels of development and sophistication. Teachers should guide students towards questions that are answerable and have sufficient depth to warrant an extended investigation.

- **Investigating/Finding Resources**

The focus of this portion of the cycle should be on finding multiple sources that might lead to the answers, solutions, or understandings sought. Students sometimes get caught in the search to find "the answer." They must be taught skills that will allow them to collect parts of the answers from multiple sources. They also must learn to organize this information and to be critical consumers of the texts they read.

During this time, the teacher may offer mini-lessons on aspects of the investigation, such as interviewing, note-taking, and reading informational materials. Students explore the topic from multiple perspectives and through multiple types of texts.

- **Interpreting Information/Discussing/Creating New Knowledge**

In this stage of the inquiry cycle, students deepen their learning through discussion with the teacher and their peers. Students communicate to share their ideas, analyze and interpret their data, and defend their results. They identify information that is relevant to their problem or question, making sense of multiple pieces of information. They also may identify new questions that arise.

Whether students are investigating topics individually or as a group, they need opportunities to discuss their learning with others. Through talk, students are often able to synthesize their findings into new thoughts and understandings. At this point in the inquiry cycle, learners share their new ideas with others. They compare notes, discuss conclusions, and share experiences. Teachers may structure group engagements to encourage this social interaction.

- **Sharing Learning/Reporting Findings**

In this stage of the cycle, learners report their findings and reflect on the path they followed to arrive at this answer. The finished product can be any of a wide variety of products, from a paper to a web page to a collage or a multimedia presentation. The goal is for learners to transform their new understandings into a form that others will enjoy and learn from.

During this stage, the teacher may teach mini-lessons on effective presentation through a variety of formats. Through these lessons, students can learn to consider audience, identify important content, and develop presentation skills.

Examples

See Chapter 4: Literacy Learning and an Inquiry Curriculum in Jeff's Middle School Social Studies Classroom, for an example of an Inquiry-based Instruction.

References

Freedman, L., & Johnson, H. (2004). *Inquiry, literacy, and learning in the middle grades.* Norwood, MA: Christopher-Gordon Publishers.

Tanner, L. N. (1988). The path not taken: Dewey's model of inquiry. *Curriculum Inquiry, 18*(4), 471-479.

READ-ALOUD

Research Base

In 1992, Elley compared the reading scores of 9- to 14-year-olds from education systems in 32 different countries and found that teachers in high-scoring countries frequently read aloud to students. Read-alouds are appropriate in all content areas. Through read-alouds, content area teachers can model many different purposes and contexts for reading. Teachers who read aloud model enjoyment from reading, reading from a variety of materials, and connections they make between content area topics and reading for pleasure. Teachers also can demonstrate fluent and expressive reading (Richardson, 2000).

Description

Many teachers, remembering their own school careers, think of reading aloud in terms of the traditional chapter-a-day sharing of a novel. While this is a valuable practice, opportunities for reading aloud extend far beyond this conventional method. Reading aloud in content classes can, and should, include a variety of types of reading. Teachers can use what Teri Lesesne (2003) calls a "read and tease," in which only a short piece of text is read, from a few sentences to a single chapter. Read-alouds also can be used to introduce a unit or subject to the class. Both of these practices are intended to spark student interest in a text or topic. Read-alouds can serve as models for students in writing particular types of texts, from narrative description to lab reports.

Procedure

- Choose texts that will stimulate discussion of content area material. Selections may be chosen to build background knowledge or encourage students to question or apply new knowledge.
- Preview and practice the text before reading.

- Before you begin to read, always introduce the title of the book, the author, and the illustrator.
- Use expression while reading. Even middle school students enjoy character voices and sound effects.
- Adjust your pace. A good rule of thumb is to read slower than you think is necessary. Many readers read too quickly. Listeners need time to process information.
- Teach by example. Share texts you enjoy and share your pleasure with students.
- Don't feel like you have to tie every read-aloud directly to classwork. Middle school students often develop a strong interest in current events and appreciate the sharing of news clippings and excerpts from books and magazines related to the general content of the class.

Examples of Texts for Content Area Read-alouds:

Math

Clements, R. (1991). *Counting on Frank.* Milwaukee, WI: Garth Stevens Publishing.

Schwartz, D. M. (1985). *How much is a million?* New York: Scholastic.

Science

Editors of YES Magazine. (2004). *Fantastic feats and failures.* Tonawanda, NY: Kids Can Press.

Fleischman, J. (2002). *Phineas Gage: A gruesome but true story about brain science.* New York: Houghton Mifflin.

Social Studies

Freedman, R. (2004). *The voice that challenged a nation: Marian Anderson and the struggle for equal rights.* New York: Houghton Mifflin.

Keller, L. (2002). *The scrambled states of America.* New York: Henry Holt.

Language Arts

Frasier, D. (2000). *Miss Alaineus: A vocabulary disaster.* New York: Harcourt.

Medina, T. (2002). *Love to Langston.* New York: Lee and Low Books.

References

Elley, W. D. (1992). *How in the world do students read?* The Hague, The Netherlands: International Association for the Evaluation of Educational Achievement.

Lesesne, T. S. (2003). *Making the match.* Portland, ME: Stenhouse.

Richardson, J. S. (2000). *Read it aloud! Using literature in the secondary content classroom.* Newark, DE: International Reading Association.

KAMISHIBAI: JAPANESE STORYTELLING CARDS
Research Base

Kamishibai is a variation of text reformulation (Beers, 2003). This strategy allows students to read a passage and then put the expository passage into the framework of a narrative example. Text reformulation encourages readers to think critically about the text. As students work to present the meaning of the text in a new format, they return to the text, reread portions, question whether something was important or not, and share their interpretations with other readers. Examples of text reformulation are Alphabet Books, Fortunately-Unfortunately Stories, and cumulative stories, like "The House That Jack Built."

Kamishibai adds an element of visual representation to the text reformulation. Creating visual representations in response to expository texts helps students to connect to the content and deepens their understanding of the subject. Visual representations are a unique form of communication. As students use images to interpret a text, they are encouraged to think critically about the meanings conveyed by the images as well as the text itself (Bustle, 2004).

Description

Kamishibai (pronounced *ka-mee-shee-bye)*, translated literally, means "paper drama." This form of storytelling originated in Japanese Buddhist temples, but became popular in the mid-20th century when storytellers rode from village to village on bicycles. The storyteller would announce his performance with wooden clappers and then present the stories using a set of illustrated boards, displayed on a small stage attached to the back of his bicycle. The storyteller also sold candy, awarding the best seats for the performance to the children who purchased his wares. The stories were often serials, with new episodes being added on each visit to the village. The storyteller used special voices and sound effects to bring the story to life.

Although the rising popularity of radio and then television brought an end to the itinerant storytelling tradition, a renewed interest in the practice has developed, through libraries and schools in Japan and the United States.

Procedure

Students can work individually, in pairs, or in groups. For group work, students may be assigned different tasks or roles for drawing, scripting, and presenting the story. For using kamishibai with expository texts, students should first read and outline the text, looking for sections that lend themselves to retelling.

- Choose a section of text with strong visual images that is long enough to divide into at least eight scenes. Kamishibai can be used to retell historical events in social studies, steps in an experiment in science, or even the sequence of a word problem in math.
- Plan out the sequence by creating a storyboard. Make a rough draft, quickly sketching the scenes with a pencil. Newsprint folded into sections or fan-fold computer paper works well for this activity. The kamishibai "story" should contain 8 to 12 sketches.
- Using the outline, begin creating the cards. Use 8" x 12" or 11" x 14" cardstock or art board. Vibrant color is essential, so drawing in pencil and then using brightly colored felt markers to outline and fill in works well. Keep in mind that the scenes will be viewed from a distance and that the details will be added through the script as the story is told.
- Write the script for the scenes. Use the text frequently, but tell the story in your own words. Use vivid description. Divide the story to match the scenes on the story cards. Print or type the text in a large font so it can easily be read by the presenter.
- Rehearse the story several times. Bring it to life with character voices and sound effects. Practice until the story is almost memorized, because your eyes should be on the audience, not the cards.

Examples

Lee, G. (2003). Kamishibai: A vehicle to multiple literacies. *Voices From the Middle, 10*(3), 36-42. A middle school teacher describes how she uses kamishibai in her classroom.

National Clearinghouse for U.S.-Japan Studies: www.indiana.edu/~japan/kamishibai/index.html.

Kamishibai play in English and Japanese

Say, A. (2005). *Kamishibai man.* New York: Houghton Mifflin.

See wonderful examples of the art in this beautiful picture book.

References

Beers, K. (2003). *When kids can't read: What teachers can do.* Portsmouth, NH: Heinemann.

Bustle, L. S. (2004). The role of visual representation in the assessment of learning. *The Journal of Adolescent and Adult Literacy, 47*(5), 16-23.

GRADUAL RELEASE OF RESPONSIBILTY

Research Base

Pearson and Gallagher (1983) developed and popularized the gradual release of responsibility (GRR) framework. Researchers found that effective readers use a variety of strategies when reading, such as activating prior background knowledge, asking questions, and inferring (Freedman & Johnson, 2004). The GRR is a framework to use while teaching struggling readers the same comprehension strategies that proficient readers have mastered. When using GRR, teachers provide explicit instruction through teacher modeling and guided practice. Then, students are invited to try the strategy on their own through collaborative practice, independent practice, and application. The goal of GRR is independent application of strategies.

Description

The gradual release of responsibility framework (GRR) indicates a progression from teacher modeling to a shared reading and writing experience with students, and eventually to independent practice. Shanahan (2005) clearly explains that the GRR framework moves from "I do it," in which the teacher models the strategy, to "We do it," in which the teacher guides the students to practice the strategy while reading. Finally, the "You do it" occurs when the teacher assigns a text excerpt for the students to read and practice the strategy independently. This framework focuses on students' prior knowledge, the concept to be learned, and individual lessons, thereby enabling each student to be responsible for content area learning. Shanahan (2005) recommends that teachers need to use both narrative and expository texts when teaching strategies using the GRR framework.

Procedure

- Model the particular strategy.
- Use the strategy in a large-group setting, with the teacher directly participating for direction and support.
- Expect students to use the strategy in small-group settings. The teacher monitors the group, and checks for student understanding.
- Finally, expect each student to use the strategy independently. The teacher monitors students by observing them and reviewing their work.

Example

Figure 11.1 illustrates the GRR process, from teacher modeling to student/teacher-guided practice, to independent practice by the student. For a detailed example of the GRR in practice, please refer to Chapter 4: Literacy Learning and an Inquiry Curriculum in Jeff's Middle School Social Studies Classroom.

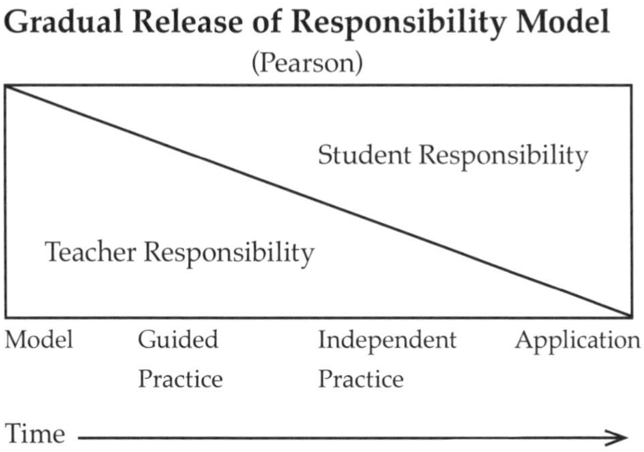

Gradual Release of Responsibility Model
(Pearson)

Figure 11.1. Gradual Release of Responsibility Model (GRR)

References

Freedman, L., & Johnson, H. (2004). *Inquiry, literacy, and learning in the middle grades.* Norwood, MA: Christopher-Gordon Publishers.

Pearson, P. D., & Gallagher, M. C. (1983). The instruction of reading comprehension. *Contemporary Educational Psychology, 8*(3), 317-344.

Shanahan, T. (2005). *The national reading panel report: Practical advice for teachers.* Naperville, IL: Learning Point Associates.

CONTENT AREA LITERATURE CIRCLES

Research Base

Harvey Daniels (2002a, 2002b, 2003) popularized literature circles, in which choice is a key feature. Students choose the books they want to read and discuss. Teachers prepare students for circles by creating a classroom community in which students assume responsibility for their learning. Another key feature of literature circles is that the literature should be on the students' reading level. Good books to choose are ones that have interesting plots, well-developed characters, rich language, and a thought-provoking theme. Lastly, it is critical that teachers have already read the books, so they can provide effective, and convincing, talks to introduce the books.

Description

Literature circles typically take about three weeks to complete, and mini lessons are taught during the same block of time. The mini lessons used by many teachers focus on reading strategies or literature circle procedures. Teachers decide on topics for mini lessons at times when they are most relevant (Abel & Lacina, 2004). Teachers generally begin the year discussing in detail the roles within literature circles. Many teachers provide hand-outs, or have students refer to a chart displayed on the wall for the specific roles (see Figure 11.2). For a detailed example of how to implement content literature circles in the middle school classroom, please refer to Chapter 4.

Steps To Implement Content Area Literature Circles

- Provide a book talk, in which you highlight at least 5-8 excellent content area books.
- Determine which students will work together as a literature circle, and keep groups to no more than five students.
- Ask the group of students to vote on a book they would like to read and study together.
- Distribute, and discuss, the literature circle tasks, or use the questions posed in Chapter 4 to guide student discussion of the readings.
- Enjoy reading and responding to excellent literature!

Literature Circle Roles	**Word Wizard** You are responsible for analyzing unfamiliar or challenging words in the selection. You will need to identify three difficult words, guess what they mean, and then actually look them up in the dictionary. Please include the page numbers where the words can be found so your group members can discuss the words.
Literary Luminary You are responsible for choosing two passages from the reading selection to share with your group. These passages may be chosen because you find them interesting or funny. You can share these passages with your group by choosing someone to read them aloud or by reading them aloud to the group.	**Reporter** You are responsible for summarizing the selection read. You need to summarize the main events that happened in the story. After sharing the summary, you will encourage group discussion and clarification when needed.
Connector The Connector is in charge of sharing the connections you make as your read the selection. You can make text-to-self, text-to-world, or text-to-text connections. After sharing these connections, give the rest of the group time to share any connections they made as they read the text.	**Discussion Director** Your job is to form discussion questions. You will also be responsible for encouraging group discussion among members. Most importantly, you will serve as a leader for your group by making sure that everyone participates.

Lacina, J., New Levine, L., & Sowa, P. (2007). *Helping English language learners succeed in pre-K-elementary schools.* Alexandria, VA: Teachers of English to Speakers of Other Languages.

Figure 11.2. Literature Circle Roles

Questions To Guide Discussion for Content Literature Circles (as described in Chapter 4):

- What have I learned? Address main ideas, key points, and summarization skills.
- What significant language did I notice? Address particular concepts and vocabulary.
- What perspectives are highlighted? From what stance are the materials written? Address critical literacy and multiple perspectives.
- What questions arise for me from this selection? Address question-posing and problem-posing.
- What connections can I make from this selection? Address text-to-text, text-to-self, and text-to-world connections, as well as making inferences and predictions.

Additional Resources

Alger, C. L. (2007). Engaging student teachers' hearts and minds in the struggle to address (il)literacy in content area classrooms. *Journal of Adolescent & Adult Literacy, 50*(8), 620-630.

Johnson, H., & Freedman, L. (2005). *Content area literature circles: Using discussion for learning across the curriculum.* Norwood, MA: Christopher-Gordon Publishing.

Rallo, C., & Roessing, L. J. (2006). Teacher to teacher: What text have you found most successful with your students? *English Journal, 95*(3), 16-17.

References

Abel, C. D., & Lacina, J. (2004). Implementing literature circles: An interview with a middle school teacher. *Focus on Middle School, 17*(2), 1-8.

Daniels, H. (2002a). Expository text in literature circles. *Voices from the Middle, 9*(4), 7-14.

Daniels, H. (2002b). *Literature circles: Voice and choice in book clubs and reading groups.* Portland, ME: Stenhouse Publishers.

Daniels, H. (2003). How can you grade literature circles? *Voices from the Middle, 11*(1), 52-53.

THINK-ALOUD

Research Base

Think-aloud has been a well-used strategy at the middle level since the 1980s. Research on the use of think-aloud shows that this type of instruction improves comprehension-monitoring abilities (Baurmann, Selfert-Kessell, & Jones, 1992). Other researchers found that think-aloud improves students' summarization and studying skills (Rinehart, Stahl, & Erickson, 1986), while other researchers note the benefits of think-aloud in teaching students to generate questions (Rosenshine, Meister, & Chapman, 1996).

Description

Poor readers often have not learned the skills needed to comprehend a text. A think-aloud is a way for a teacher to model effective reading strategies to students, while demonstrating the think-aloud process to help students become more strategic readers. The example we included in this chapter is teacher-directed; however, we also note below a student-centered variation. For further descriptions of how to implement think-aloud, refer to Chapter 8.

Procedure

- Discuss with students the ways for thinking-aloud. Show a copy of the Think-Aloud List (see Figure 11.3).
- Read aloud a content area text excerpt from a chapter, while stopping at different times to model think-aloud. As you are thinking aloud, have the students take notes on your thoughts, referring to the Think-Aloud List.
- After you read the text excerpt, discuss the types of statements you made during the think-aloud, as students discuss the notes they took.
- Once students feel comfortable with the process, move to a more student-centered approach of practicing think-aloud. Pair students in groups of two, and have them refer again to the Think-Aloud List.
- One student will serve as the reader/think-aloud guide, and the other students will monitor that student's comprehension process. Similar to the process followed above, the reader will read a text selection while thinking aloud. The other student will refer to the Think-Aloud List to monitor comprehension and meaning construction.
- After pairs practice, follow up with a whole-class discussion to assess group understanding of the thinking process (Zwiers, 2004).

Example

<table>
<tr><th colspan="6">Think-Aloud List
Strategies for Comprehending Text</th></tr>
<tr><th>Connecting</th><th>Summarizing</th><th>Making Inferences</th><th>Generating</th><th>Using Context Clues</th><th>Fixing Up</th></tr>
<tr><td>Makes self/world connections, or makes connections to other texts.</td><td>Connects summaries to the author's purpose or main ideas.</td><td>Examines text evidence and makes inferences. Makes predictions based on text evidence. While reading, confirms/disconfirms inferences.</td><td>Asks well-founded questions while reading the text, and points out answers to questions while reading.</td><td>Notes context clues used to figure out words while reading.</td><td>Notes times when meaning is unclear, and uses fix-up strategies to solve confusion (look back, look ahead, examine text structure, examine graphs/illustrations or words in bold).</td></tr>
</table>

Adapted from Zwiers, J. (2004). *Building reading comprehension habits in grades 6-12: A toolkit of classroom activities.* Newark, DE: International Reading Association.

Figure 11.3. Think-Aloud List

Resources

www.englishcompanion.com/pdfDocs/exthinkaloud2.pdf (Jim Burke offers a detailed example of how he uses think-aloud when teaching English)

Walker, B. (2005). Think-aloud: Struggling readers often require more than a model. *The Reading Teacher, 58*(7), 688-692.

Wilhelm, J. D. (2001). *Improving comprehension with think-aloud strategies.* New York: Scholastic.

References

Baurmann, J. F., Selfert-Kessell, N., & Jones, L. A. (1992). Effects of think-aloud instruction on elementary students' comprehension monitoring abilities. *Journal of Reading Behavior, 2*, 143-172.

Rinehart, S. D., Stahl, S. A., & Erickson, L. G. (1986). Some effects of summarization training on reading and studying. *Reading Research Quarterly, 21*, 422-438.

Rosenshine, B., Meister, C., & Chapman, S. (1996). Teaching students to generate questions: A review of the intervention studies. *Review of Educational Research, 66*, 181-221.

Zwiers, J. (2004). *Building reading comprehension habits in grades 6-12: A toolkit of classroom activities.* Newark, DE: International Reading Association

NOTE-MAKING

Research Base

Since the 1980s, a strong body of research has indicated the benefits of teaching students to self-regulate and take notes directly from a text (Berkowitz, 1986; Brown, 2005; Rinehart, Stahl, & Erickson, 1986). Note-making means to annotate directly onto the pages of a textbook—or to take notes in an active, rather than passive, way (Burke, 2002; Tomlinson, 1997). Teaching students ways to systematically use note-making when reading content area texts enables them to better understand, and remember, important content material.

Description

Jim Burke (2002) explains a variety of note-making strategies in his book *Tools for Thought*. Many of these strategies are also included on Burke's website—and they are excellent, in addition to being teacher-friendly (www.englishcompanion.com/Tools/notemaking.html).

Examples of Note-making

Debbie Miller's (2002) Wonder Boxes strategy is a simple way to get started with note-making at the 4th-grade level, or with students who have little background with note-making.

Steps

- Throughout the study of questioning and nonfiction, ask the children to place a wonder card, or two, in a basket.
- Two or three days a week, draw one out and search for the answer.
- Another option is to generate wonder questions and have the students choose one, then do research for the answer.

Debbie Miller shows students how to think aloud about certain questions:
- What do I already know about the topic?
- What type of book or other source will help me best?
- Where will I find the information?
- How is the information organized in the source? How will I go about locating what I need?

Wonder Question
What I learned…
Source:

An additional example of note-making is from *Strategies That Work* (Harvey & Goudvis, 2007). These authors suggest using a strategy called Sifting the Topic From the Details.

Steps
- Students note the topic of a reading selection in the first column. To most effectively teach students how to determine the topic, teachers need to explicitly show students the process through a think-aloud and guided practice.
- Next, students will note details about the topic.
- The third column allows students to interact with the text personally and ensures that they have a place to record their thoughts, feelings, and questions.

Three Column Notes

Topic	Detail	Personal Response

Cornell Note-taking is often used at the middle school through high school levels to teach students to take notes from a textbook or a lecture. Figure 11.4 explains the process for teaching students to think critically about a text, while examining important text features of a text reading. Then, students re-examine the material to make connections to the text.

References

Berkowitz, S. J. (1986). Effects of instruction in text organization on sixth-grade students' memory for expository reading. *Reading Research Quarterly, 21*, 161-178.

Brown, R. (2005). Seventh-graders' self-regulatory note-taking from text: Perceptions, preferences, and practices. *Reading Research and Instruction, 44*(4), 1-26.

Burke, J. (2002). *Tools for thought: Graphic organizers for your classroom.* Portsmouth, NH: Heinemann.

Harvey, S., & Goudvis, A. (2007). *Strategies that work* (2nd ed.). Portland, ME: Stenhouse.

Miller, D. (2002). *Reading with meaning: Teaching comprehension in the primary grades.* Portland, ME: Stenhouse.

Rinehart, S. D., Stahl, S. A., & Erickson, L. G. (1986). Some effects of summarization training on reading and studying. *Reading Research Quarterly, 21*, 422-438.

Tomlinson, L. M. (1997). A coding system for notemaking in literature: Preparation for journal writing, class participation, and essay tests. *Journal of Adolescent & Adult Literacy, 40*(6), 468-76.

Directions: Use this Cornell note-taking form when reading a content area text, or when taking notes from a content area lecture.	
Connection Column	**Note-taking Column**
Write down in this column important information, such as • Categories (causes of war, parts of a cell, etc.) • Questions (what caused the Vietnam War? What are the parts of the cell?) • Vocabulary Words • Connections (What connections can you make from material you have already read or studied about the subject?)	Write down notes about important information from the chapter or article as you read, such as: • Words in bold • Word or phrases that are in italics • Any information located in boxes or highlighted • Information from headers or subheadings • Important dates • Try to abbreviate words, use bulleted points, and use symbols to make notes (example: &, +/-)
Leave this section blank, and you can add review notes or possible test questions later as you study your notes.	
Summary In this section, write down a 3- to 4-sentence summary of what you learned from the readings or lecture. Also, list questions that you still need to answer.	

Figure 11.4. Cornell Note-taking System

Adapted from
Burke, J. (2002). *Tools for thought: Graphic organizers for your classroom.* Portsmouth, NH: Heinemann.

Research Base

Harvey and Goudvis (2005) describe in detail the importance of using anchor charts as a way for teachers and students to record thinking about a text, lesson, or strategy. The purpose of the chart is for the students to remember the specific process needed to understand a lesson or strategy. Anchor charts connect past learning and future learning (Harvey & Goudvis, 2005).

Description

For many examples of student-created anchor charts, and ways to implement them in the content areas, please view the following websites:

www.u-46.org/roadmap/dyncat.cfm?catid=431
www.readinglady.com/mosaic/tools/AnchorChartPhotographsfromKellyandGinger/
www.learner.org/channel/workshops/teachreading35/pdf/anchor_charts.pdf
www.edu.gov.on.ca/eng/studentsuccess/lms/files/SocialSkills.pdf

Procedure

One variation of using anchor charts includes the strategy of alphaboxes. Alphaboxes are a way to encourage active engagement while creating an anchor chart (L'Allier & Elish-Piper, 2007).

- Prepare sticky notes before the lesson, similar to an alpha box. Write a letter of the alphabet on each sticky note.
- Have students (either individually or with a partner) jot down on sticky notes the characteristics of a good writer.
- As students place their sticky notes in alphabetical order on chart paper, discuss the many characteristics of good writers.
- Display the anchor chart in the room, so that students can refer to the strategies good writers use when generating ideas, drafting, revising, editing, and publishing their work.

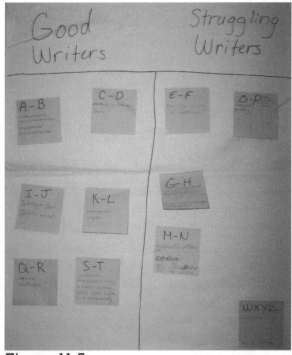

Example

See Figure 11.5. Anchor charts can be developed on almost any topic. The key to

Figure 11.5.
Anchor Chart Example

developing such charts is that they are student-generated, and serve as a reminder of strategies to use to become a better reader or writer.

References

Harvey, S., & Goudvis, A. (2005). *The comprehension toolkit: Language and lessons for active literacy.* Portsmouth, NH: Heinemann.

L'Allier, S. K., & Elish-Piper, L. (2007). "Walking the walk" with teacher education candidates: Strategies for promoting active engagement with assigned readings. *Journal of Adolescent & Adult Literacy, 50*(5), 338-353.

KWL
(WHAT I KNOW, WHAT I WANT TO KNOW, WHAT I LEARNED)

Research Base

KWL (Ogle, 1986) provides a structure for recalling what students know about a topic, what students want to know, and finally listing what students have learned. Since the 1980s, teachers have created many extensions to the basic KWL.

Description

Szabo's (2007) KWHHL is a more recent variation to the KWL. As a middle school reading specialist, Szabo developed a revised KWL to meet the needs of her struggling 8th-grade students. Szabo added two H sections to the traditional KWL chart. The first H section stands for "hard words," which are words that might confuse students as they read, or are words they do not understand. They write them down on the chart. The additional H section refers to "heart words," or words that make students think of other things—good and bad—in their life. They connect to emotions that students have while reading—and to their prior background. Whether teachers choose the traditional KWL as a tool to use, or a recent adaptation of the KWL, students benefit from making personal connections to the texts they are reading.

Procedure for Ogle's KWL

- Draw three columns on the chalkboard, an overhead, a handout, or individual papers.
- Label Column 1 "K," Column 2 "W," Column 3 "L."
- Before reading, students fill in the **K**now column with everything they already know about the topic. This helps generate background knowledge.
- Then, have students predict **W**hat they might learn about the topic, prior to reading a selection. They can make predictions after glancing through chapter headings, titles, or words in bold. This step helps students set their purpose for reading and focuses their attention on important ideas.
- After reading, students fill in the L section of the chart. The L section is a chance for students to demonstrate what they **L**earned from reading a text selection.

Examples

See charts on the next page.

Examples

K What I KNOW	W What I WANT To Know	L What I LEARNED

K What Do You Know?	W What Do You Want To Know?	H What Hard Words Do I Need To Learn?	H What Heart Word or Emotion Has the Reading Allowed Me To Feel?	L What Have You Learned?
This is done before reading the text. Brainstorm by thinking about what you already know about the topic and write it below.	Questions are developed by reader both before and while reading in order to set a purpose for reading.	Hard words are words that confuse you. When we read, we may find words that we do not understand. Write them down.	Heart words tell us what you feel. Sometimes, what we read makes us think of other things that have happened to us—good and bad. Write down the emotional word and the event (reading) that triggered that emotion.	When we read information books, we read to learn. Therefore, we need to think about what we read and what we already know critically.
Positive Ideas/ Thoughts: 1. 2. Negative Ideas/ Thoughts: 1. 2. Neutral Ideas/ Thoughts: 1. 2.	Before Reading: 1. 2. 3. While Reading: 1. 2. 3.	Hard Words: 1. 2. 3. 4. 5.	Heart Words & Why: 1. 2. 3. 4. 5.	New Information Learned: 1. 2. 3. "Stayed the same" "Correct & added to" "Adjusted because flawed"

Szabo, S. (2007). KWHHL: It helps students use multiple strategies. *Focus on Middle School, 19*(3), 1-5.

References

Ogle, D. (1986). K-W-L: A teaching model that develops active reading of expository text. *The Reading Teacher, 39*, 564-570.

Szabo, S. (2007). KWHHL: It helps students use multiple strategies. *Focus on Middle School, 19*(3), 1-5.

THINK-PAIR-SHARE

Research Base

Think-Pair-Share was developed in the early 1980s by Lyman (1981) and his colleagues at the University of Maryland. It refers to introducing a "wait" or "think" time into a cooperative learning structure. This wait time is considered an important feature of improving student responses to questions.

Description

It is a simple strategy, effective from early childhood through graduate school. Think-Pair-Share is a versatile structure that can be easily adapted and used in various contexts, and is also a quick way to assess students' academic language and content understanding. The process involves the teacher posing a question, and then having the students independently think about and answer the question. Then, students meet with a partner to discuss their responses. Once responses are compared, the teacher calls for students to share their responses with the whole class.

Procedure

- THINK: Pose a question or prompt to help students connect their background knowledge to the content you are discussing or reading. The students take about 1-2 minutes to think about the question and their response.
- PAIR: Students either turn to a partner, or meet with an assigned partner (such as with a clock buddy—see variation below), to discuss their response to the question or prompt posed by the teacher.
- SHARE: Once partners have shared their responses, meet back as a whole class for the partners to share their responses with the entire class. Often, the teacher, or a designated scribe, will record the responses on the chalkboard or chart paper.

Think-Pair-Share serves as a format to structure discussions. Accountability is built into the strategy since students must share responses with a partner—and then with the entire class.

One variation to Think-Pair-Share is called Formulate-Share-Listen-Create (Johnson, Johnson, & Smith, 1991). The figure below illustrates how to use this variation.

Formulate-Share-Listen-Create

1. **Formulate** your answer to the question individually.
2. **Share** your answer with your partner.
3. **Listen** carefully to your partner's answer. Distinguish the similarities and differences between the two answers.
4. **Create** a new answer that incorporates the best ideas from you and your partner. Share your answer when called upon.

Clock Buddies

The clock buddies method is a quick way to partner students. The basic idea is that students have their own copy of a clock, with a student's name by each hour of the clock. When the teacher is ready to partner students, she may say, "Find your 4:00 partner." You may have several sets and variations of clocks, depending on how many students are in each class.

Example

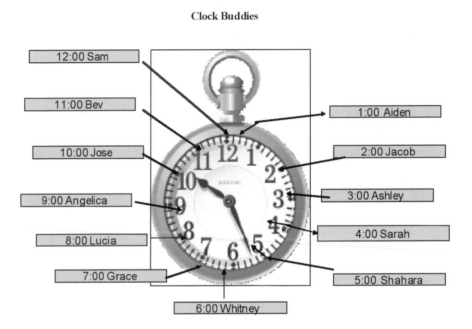

Clock Buddies

References

Johnson, D. W., Johnson, R. T., & Smith, K. A. (1991). *Active learning: Cooperative learning in the college classroom*. Edina, MN: Interaction Book Company.

Lyman, F. T. (1981). The responsive classroom discussion: The inclusion of all students. In A. Anderson (Ed.), *Mainstreaming digest* (pp. 109-113). College Park, MD: University of Maryland Press.

SQ3R

Research Base

Since Robinson (1941) developed his reading comprehension techniques, teachers in the upper elementary through high school levels have asked students to survey, question, read, recite, and review chapters in their content area textbooks (Huber, 2004). Robinson's SQR3 strategy is often termed the "grandfather of study strategies" (Lipson & Wixson, 2003).

Description

The chart below explains the process for using SQR3 in content area teaching.

Survey, Question, Read, Recite, Review (SQ3R)	
1. **S=Survey**	Scan the chapter to determine the structure and organization. • Look at the title. Can you tell what will be included in the chapter, based on the title? • Read the introduction. What main ideas will help you understand the chapter? • Read the words in bold throughout the chapter. Can you tell what the main ideas are from the words in bold? • Read the summary at the end of the chapter. What do you notice about the main ideas from the summary? • Read the questions at the end or beginning of the chapter. What do these questions tell you about the chapter?
2. **Q=Question**	Examine each heading and subheading again. Change each of these headings into a question. Write the questions down, and when you read the chapter, answer the questions.
3. **R1=Read**	Read only that section that corresponds with the heading or subheading. Look for the answers to your questions. As you read, you will evaluate and organize ideas. Do not spend time studying material that does not relate to your questions.
4. **R2=Recite**	Answer your questions—and write out the answers using your own words. We are able to remember our own connections better than ones given to us.
5. **R3=Review**	After repeating steps 2-4 for each section, you will have a list of key phrases that provide an outline for the chapter. To assess whether the strategy worked for you, cover up the key phrases and see if you can recall them. If you cannot, you may need to re-examine, and re-read, a particular section of the chapter.

Additional Resources

Potter, R. L. (1999). Technical reading in the middle school. *Phi Delta Kappa Fastbacks*, Fastback No. 456, 7-56.

Sakta, C. G. (1999). SQRC: A strategy for guiding reading and higher level thinking. *Journal of Adolescent and Adult Literacy, 42*(4), 265-269.

Spor, M., & Schneider, B. (1999). Content reading strategies: What teachers know, use, and want to learn. *Reading Research and Instruction, 38*(3), 221-231.

References

Huber, J. (2004). A closer look at SQ3R. *Reading Improvement, 41*(2),108-112.

Lipson, M. Y., & Wixson, K. K. (2003). *Assessment and instruction of reading and writing disability* (3rd ed.). New York: Longman.

Robinson, F. P. (1941). *Diagnostic and remedial techniques for effective study.* New York: Harper Brothers.

Meet the Authors

Jan Lacina has focused her research and teaching on English language learners (ELLs) and on reading and writing instruction. She teaches undergraduate and graduate literacy courses in both the middle/secondary and early childhood programs at Texas Christian University. She is co-author of the book Helping English Language Learners Succeed in Pre-K-Elementary Schools *(TESOL, 2006), and she has published in numerous journals. Jan also writes the "Technology in the Classroom" column that is published in the journal* Childhood Education. *Prior to teaching at the college level, Jan taught ESL in Texas and Kansas.*

Patricia Watson is an Assistant Professor of Language and Literacy at Texas Tech University. Before completing her doctoral studies at the University of Missouri, Pat taught reading and language arts in middle grade classrooms for 18 years. She enjoys collaborating with practicing and preservice teachers in university/public school partnerships. Her most recent work explores teachers' knowledge, attitudes, and beliefs towards literacy in the content areas.